W. Maziere Brady

Anglo-Roman Papers

I.-The English Palace in Rome : II.-The Eldest Natural Son of Charles II : III....

W. Maziere Brady

Anglo-Roman Papers
I.-The English Palace in Rome : II.-The Eldest Natural Son of Charles II : III....

ISBN/EAN: 9783337019525

Printed in Europe, USA, Canada, Australia, Japan

Cover: Foto ©ninafisch / pixelio.de

More available books at **www.hansebooks.com**

ANGLO-ROMAN PAPERS

ANGLO-ROMAN PAPERS:

I.—The English Palace in Rome
II.—The Eldest Natural Son of Charles II.
III.—Memoirs of Cardinal Erskine, Papal Envoy to the Court of George III.

BY

W. MAZIERE BRADY

Author of "Clerical and Parochial Records of Cork, Cloyne, and Ross," "The English State Church in Ireland," "The M'Gillicuddy Papers," "The Episcopal Succession in England, Scotland, and Ireland, A.D. 1400 to 1875," etc., etc.

ALEXANDER GARDNER
Publisher to Her Majesty the Queen
PAISLEY; AND 26 PATERNOSTER SQUARE, LONDON

1890

PREFACE.

THE following papers require little in way of preface or introduction. The reader need scarcely be reminded that the account of the English Palace is by no means complete, and that no attempt has been made to write at length the histories of its successive owners. The many extracts from the State Papers concerning Lorenzo Campeggi were made by the author some five-and-twenty years ago, when he thought of collecting materials for a life of that great man (a work which remains for an abler hand to accomplish) but they refer chiefly to the Divorce case and Campeggi's two missions to Henry VIII. His missions to Germany, which have been but briefly noticed, are far more important in relation to Luther's revolt against the Church.

Of the eldest natural son of Charles II. nothing need be here said, save that the precise parentage of his mother, Mary Stuart, and the particulars of the death and burial of James Stuart the younger, the grandson of Charles II., are yet to be discovered.

The memoirs of Cardinal Erskine, now first published, give but a sketch of his eventful life, with few comments from the author, who might perhaps have enlarged on many topics, such as the amiable character of the Cardinal, shown by his patience under adversity and by the warm friendships he contracted with many leading men of his day. His personal virtues are also evidenced by the fact that his name is never mentioned in the scandalous and false histories concerning the Roman Court, and that the "Diaries" of the time throw not the slightest slur upon his character.

The Revolution, which in Erskine's time overwhelmed the Papal government, apparently for ever, driving into exile the Pope and Cardinals, and reducing Rome to a French garrison town despotically governed by such Generals as Miollis and Radet, cannot but remind us of the Italian Revolution in our own days, accomplished, similarly, by force of arms, and attended, similarly, by seizure of Rome and the Pontifical States. The more brutal and coarse behaviour of the first Napoleon towards Pius VI. and Pius VII., finds, happily, no parallel in the treatment of Pius IX. by Victor Emmanuel, but in other respects the results of the Italian occupation of Rome were much the same to the Church. The Pope, it is true, was not bodily carried into exile, but was allowed to occupy one of his palaces, the other being broken into by locksmiths to serve as a residence for the victor. The French revolutionists—to adorn Paris—robbed the Vatican of its treasures. The Italians despoiled the Pope as effectually, by annexing the Vatican and its contents as national property. By both revolutions the temporal possessions of the Pontiff were taken from him, but under the later revolution the confiscation of Church property was more complete. The French left the churches in Rome standing, while the Italians threw down many of them, selling the altars by auction, and they not only confiscated the property of all Religious Communities but also seized that of all Charitable Foundations. Italian legislation—personal violence being discarded—bids fair to accomplish, what the

French by brutality effected, the banishment or exile of the Pope.

There is a striking contrast between the policy, a century ago, of Great Britain towards the French Revolution and that of the same country in the present time towards the Italian. George III. and Mr. Pitt, although fully as Protestant as Lord Palmerston, Mr. Gladstone and Lord Salisbury, yet saw no danger to Protestantism and Great Britain in the reception of a Papal envoy at St. James' and the complete restoration of the Pope's temporal power. The later rulers of the British empire fomented the Italian revolution by direct and indirect assistance, regarding the unity of Italy as an event to be worthily accomplished *per fas aut nefas*, and showing no displeasure when the oldest kingdom in Europe was overthrown by brute force.

Yet they might have considered that the Roman States were no more a hindrance to the real unity of Italy than was the Principality of Monaco or the Republic of San Marino, and that revolutions, whether glorified by the genius of a Napoleon, or debased by blasphemy, secret conspiracy and assassination, are dangerous things to foster. The same revolutionists who in Italy clamoured for Rome and got it, now clamour for Trent and Trieste, Savoy and Nice, and are actively stirring up disaffection against British rule in Malta on the false pretext that because the Maltese speak the Italian language—which they do not—the island belongs to Italy!

Rome, October, 1890.

LIST OF AUTHORITIES.

Lettere inedite, by Vincenzo Armanni, printed at Macerata, 1674.
MSS. in the Archivio Borghese, Rome.
    „   „   „   Campeggi, Bologna.
    „   „   „   Colonna, Rome.
    „   „   „   Comunale, Rome.
    „   „   „   dei Gesuiti, Rome.
    „   „   „   di Propaganda Fede, Rome.
    „   „   „   di Stato, Genoa.
    „   „   „   di Stato, Rome.
    „   „   „   Ricci, Rome.
    „   „   „   Segreto Vaticano, Rome.
    „   „   „   Torlonia, Rome.
    „   in possession of Giancarlo Rossi, Rome.
    „   in the English College, Rome.
    „   „   Ghislieri, Rome.
    „   „   National Library, Naples.
    „   „   in the Scots College, Rome.
Register of the Parish of S. Giovanni Carbonara, Naples.
State Papers, Rolls' Office, London.

CONTENTS.

	PAGE
THE ENGLISH PALACE, NOW TORLONIA, IN ROME,	9
THE ELDEST NATURAL SON OF CHARLES II.,	93
MEMOIRS OF CARDINAL ERSKINE, PAPAL ENVOY TO THE COURT OF GEORGE III.,	121
APPENDIX—THE ROCK OF DOZZA,	269
INDEX,	273

CORRECTIONS.

Page 13, 15, 40, *for* Sodorini, *read* Soderini.
,, 16, line 11, ,, Worcestor, ,, Worcester.
,, 17, ,, 9, ,, Winchester, ,, Worcester.
,, 17, ,, 26, ,, Winchester, ,, Worcester.
,, 25, ,, 27, ,, prisoner, ,, poisoner.
,, 29, ,, 11, ,, 1551, ,, 1521.
,, 84, ,, 9, ,, Hutt, ,, Mutte.
,, 154, ,, 18, ,, noveles, ,, novelties.
,, 197, ,, 8, ,, emigre, ,, émigré.

The English Palace, now Torlonia, in Rome.

ON the way to the Vatican, on the right hand of the piazza Scossacavalli, is a large palace, whose massive walls and stone encased windows at once recall the memory of Bramante's masterpieces, while the great entrance gate plainly suggests that it was added or altered by a much inferior architect. The confiding tourist is sometimes told that this palace was given by Henry VIII. to Cardinal Wolsey for his Roman residence. As a matter of fact, Wolsey never saw it. Thirty or forty years ago, all visitors to Rome who were of any consideration from their rank, fortune, or talent, were familiar with this palace as the scene of the magnificent balls, concerts, and theatrical entertainments given by the great bankers, Prince Giovanni and Prince Alexander Torlonia, during the middle part of this century. Of this palace and its successive owners and occupiers, the following pages will treat.

The Torlonia palace in the Borgo, built from designs by the celebrated architect Bramante, is one of the most ancient palaces in Rome. The huge palazzo di Venezia was erected some thirty years earlier, and the Cancelleria was completed about the time when the Torlonia was commenced. But nearly all the other great palaces, such as the Altemps, Altieri, Barberini, Braschi, Borghese, Bonaparte, Caetani, Mattei, Chigi, Falconieri, Farnese, Massimo, Odescalchi, Orsini, Pamfili, Rospigliosi, Sciarra, Spada, etc., have no higher antiquity than the Torlonia. This palace, apart from its age and architecture, has a special interest for Englishmen, inasmuch as it was once the property of Henry VII. and Henry VIII., and was given to the former of these kings for the express purpose of an English national palace, for the use of English kings and English ambassadors in Rome.

During the latter part of the fifteenth century, England sent many orators or envoys to the Papal court. In 1484, under Richard III., John Shirwood, ambassador of England, was consecrated for the See of Durham in the church of S. Onofrio, Rome, on the 26th May, the Feast of S. Augustine, Apostle of England. Shirwood had been present at King Richard's coronation, and the Pope was asked by His Majesty to make Shirwood a cardinal. Bishop Shirwood was first sent to Rome by Edward IV. as a lawyer, to manage civil and ecclesiastical affairs. He wrote verses, and collected books and manuscripts to send to England. In February, 1486, Shirwood, John Dunmowe, [or Dumor, or Dunow] and Hugh Spalding, were made proctors for Henry VII. at Rome. No less than ten orators or ambassadors of Henry VII., on the 8th of May, 1487, at 20 of the clock, entered Rome in procession by the Porta Viridaria, now Angelica, which was called Viridaria in the time of Nicolas IV., and retained that nomenclature until the year 1563. They were Thomas Milling, Bishop of Hereford; John Shirwood, Bishop of Durham; John Dunmowe, Bishop of Limerick; John Weston, Prior of S. John of Jerusalem, *extra muros Londoni;* William, Benedictine Prior of Canterbury; the Deacon of the church of Salisbury; Turcho Pellerius, Knight of S. John of Jerusalem; two lay Knights; and Hugh Spalding, Rector of Coniglon, York. They were all received in audience on the 14th of May, by Pope Innocent VIII.

On the 14th of December, 1492, the Bishop of Durham and John de Gigliis of Luca, (afterwards Bishop of Worcester) appeared in public consistory; and, as orators in name of Henry VII., took the oath of obedience to the new Pope, Alexander VI. (Borgia). On this occasion the Bishop of Durham made an oration "well and elegantly composed, but propter *inexpeditam expressivam*, (hesitation in speech) not over pleasing" to the auditors. The Bishop of Durham died on the 12th of January, 1494, and was carried on the 14th for burial to the church of the English Hospital. The procession included fifty torch-bearers.

In 1496, on the 17th of June, at 22 of the clock, the Ven$^{ble.}$ Robert Sherborne [Bishop of St. David's in 1505, and of Chichester in 1508], Archdeacon of Buckingham and Secretary of Henry VII., came to Rome, and at the instance of the Cardinal Archbishop of Siena, [Todeschini-Piccolomini, afterwards Pius III], Protector of England, was received by all the officials of all the Cardinals, and by the members of the Papal Court, and was escorted to the house of John de Gigliis, who was also an orator. On this occasion there was a dispute for precedence between the ambassadors of England and Spain, which was settled by placing the Englishman, Sherborne, between the Archbishop of Cosenza (Fleury) on the right, and John de Gigliis, on the left. The ambassadors of the King of the Romans, of Spain, Naples, and Venice, followed. On Sunday, July 31st, [same year, 1496], the Pope and Cardinals rode in state to the church of S. Maria in piazza del Popolo, where High Mass was sung by Bartolomeo Fleury, Bishop of Cosenza, in honour of the King of England, who had joined in league with the Pope, the King of the Romans, the King of Spain, and the Dukes of Venice and Milan. The oration was delivered by Hadrian de Corneto, Clerk of the Camera Apostolica. The Bishop of Cosenza was then secretary to the Pope, but, on the 14th of September following, was arrested on the charge of falsification of Briefs, and imprisoned in the castle of S. Angelo; and, in secret consistory of the 11th of October, he was degraded and deprived of all his offices. Seven days later, the Pope made "Adrianum Castellensem de Corneto" his secretary in room of Fleury, and at the same time gave him the Rochet as Protonotary.

This Hadrian, the precise dates of whose birth and death are alike unknown, was born in Corneto about the year 1458, and derived the name of Castellensis, or De Castello, from his mother, the representative of a noble family of Castello di Mont' Alto in the Marches of Ancona. He became secretary to Cardinal Rodrigo (Lenzugli, or Lenzoli] Borgia, afterwards Pope Alexander VI., and held various minor appointments in the Roman Curia. In 1488, he was sent by Pope Innocent VIII. as special envoy to James III., King of Scotland, to make peace between England and Scotland, but he arrived too late, just at the time of the Scotch King's death. He, however, gained much favour with the English monarch Henry VII., and, having resigned, in 1489, his office of Notary of the Camera Apostolica, he took up his residence in England in 1490, as Collector of the rents of the Holy See—an office which he retained during the remainder of the pontificate of Innocent VIII., and during the reigns of the three succeeding pontiffs, namely, Alexander VI., Pius III., and Julius II. Hadrian seems to have resided in England from 1490 to 1492, when he returned to Rome on the death of Innocent, and he lived in England as Collector for some time during the pontificate of Alexander VI.; but during the latter part of his term of office, was permitted to discharge his English duties by deputy. He was Clerk of the Camera in 1494, and also Chamberlain and writer of Apostolical Letters. In 1497, he was Protonotary Partecipante, and in 1498, was sent as Nuncio to Louis XII. of France. He was Treasurer General in 1500. In 1501, he was deputed to carry the pallium to the Archbishop of Canterbury [Henry Dean], and, in February, 1502, was made Bishop of Hereford, which See he held until 1504, when he became Bishop of Bath and Wells.

In the consistory of May 31, 1503, Hadrian was created by his early patron, Alexander VI., a Cardinal, with presbyteral title of S. Grisogonus, and Protector of England.

Cardinal Hadrian was famous for his great learning, and

wrote and spoke Latin with such excellence, that he was reputed a second Cicero. He was an eminent Greek and Hebrew scholar, and commenced a new translation of the Old Testament. He was still more famous for his wealth, and was styled "the rich Cardinal." He obtained most of his money from the English preferments conferred on him by Henry VII., who also employed him as his ambassador at Rome.

Some time before the year 1503, he constructed a magnificent palace, from designs of Bramante, in the Borgo, near to the house and garden of Cardinal Francesco Sodorini, and near also to the villa of another Cardinal, then some time deceased, namely the Cardinal Aleriensis [Ardicinus de la Porta, created 1489, died 1493].

It was in the vineyard or garden of this villa of Cardinal Hadrian, that Pope Alexander VI. caught his mortal illness. The circumstances are variously related. Some accounts are to the effect that the Pope and his son, Duke Valentino, [Cesar Borgia] formed a diabolical plot against the Cardinal's life, in order to possess themselves of his great wealth. They invited themselves to sup with the Cardinal on the evening of the 5th of August, 1503, and sent him a present of poisoned wine. They arrived before the time appointed, and being thirsty, asked for wine to drink. The Coppiere gave them by mistake the poisoned flask. The Pope, the Duke, and the Cardinal all drank of it. The Pope, being aged, was unable to recover from the effects. The Duke, being younger, fared better, having also mixed his portion with water. He took prompt remedies, and was wrapped in the warm body of a slaughtered mule, and recovered, although with much damage to his constitution. The Cardinal, to quench the internal burning heat of his stomach, was put into a large vessel of cold water, and saved his life with the loss of all his skin. Part of this account is vouched by the testimony of Bovio, Bishop of Nocera, who says he heard it from the lips of Cardinal Hadrian himself. But this story, improbable in itself, will not bear the test of research, and can be received only by those who are willing to believe anything wicked, provided it be to the disparagement of the Borgia family. It is not to be credited that the Pope would create Hadrian a Cardinal in May, only to murder him three months afterwards. A much more reasonable version of the affair is given by Giustiniani, who writes that on Saturday, August 12, 1503, the Pope was absent from the meeting of the Segnatura, being ill with fever. At 2 o'clock on the night of the 13th, he says that the Pontiff, after eating, vomited and had fever. The Duke was also in bed with fever. The cause of their maladies was that some eight days previously they went to eat supper in a vineyard of Cardinal Hadrian, remained there till night, and that all were the worse for it—"tutti ne sono risentiti." The first to get ill was the Cardinal, who on Friday (August 11) was at Mass, and after eating got a great paroxysm of fever. On the 14th, the Duke was very bad. On the 18th, Master Scipio, the Medico, told Giustiniani that apoplexy was the origin of the Pope's illness. When it is remembered that the month of August is one of the very worst in Rome for health, and that the neighbourhood of the Vatican is notoriously insalubrious, and that deaths from fever were unusually frequent in that autumn of 1503, no surprise can be felt that fever should have resulted from an imprudent supper, partaken of late in the evening, in a vineyard situated between S. Peter's and the Castle of S. Angelo. The then unfinished palace of Cardinal Hadrian was not, as at present, surrounded by houses and streets, but lay amid vineyards and fields, the arid earth sending up its exhalations to mingle with the poisonous air of the reeking banks of the Tiber.

Within seven months from the death of Alexander VI., his immediate successor, Pope Pius III., being also dead, and Julius II. being the reigning Pontiff, Cardinal Hadrian determined to make a gift to Henry VII. of the palace and garden so unfortunately connected with the last illness of Pope Alexander, who had been Hadrian's first patron and constant friend. The deed by which this princely donation was effected is still extant in the Archivio di Stato in Rome. It bears date in March 150⅔. The Cardinal, in presence of the Notary, Benimbene, acknowledges that he had received, and hopes to receive in future, favours and benefits from the Most Serene King of England, and declares, laying his hands on his breast, after the manner of a prelate's oath, that he freely, spontaneously, and of mere gratuitous good will, gives, transfers, etc., irrevocably and fully, the said palace and garden to King Henry VII., his heirs and successors, and to whomsoever the said King and his successors may wish to cede or transfer them, for the use, however, of the English nation in Rome, or for the use and habitation of the English Ambassadors, or of the King when coming to Rome and residing in the Roman Court. The palace thus given away is described as:—"Certain houses and buildings of the donor, not yet finished, and adorned with magnificent work of marbles and Tiburtine stones, adding not a little to the beauty and splendour of the city, and erected out of the private moneys of the donor, which he obtained by his ecclesiastical preferments." The premises are situate "in the Borgo of the Basilica of Blessed Peter, Prince of the Apostles, in the via Alexandrina, lately constructed and named after Pope Alexander VI., of happy memory. In front of the palace is the said public street, the Via Alexandrina. In the rear is the Via Sistina *prope muros*, leading to the Castle of S. Angelo. The side towards the Apostolic Palace is on the public road, near the house and garden of His Eminence the Cardinal of Volterra [Francesco Soderini]; and on the other side, which is towards the Castle of S. Angelo, is the road which the donor, Cardinal Hadrian, himself granted in order to make his said palace or villa form an island, near to the house and garden of Cardinal Aleriensis, of happy memory."

The Via Alessandrina and the Via Sistina *prope muros*, which are across the Tiber, must not, of course, be confounded with the present Via Alessandrina near the Forum of Trajan, and the Via Sistina near the Pincio.

Cardinal Hadrian was promoted by Henry VII. from the See of Hereford to that of Bath and Wells, in 1504, a short time before his magnificent donation of his palace to the King. Sylvester de Gigliis, Bishop of Worcester, was at that time the English ambassador in Rome, and was entitled to be the first occupant of the new English Palace.

Suddenly, on the 1st of September, 1507, His Eminence Cardinal Hadrian disappeared from Rome. He had some quarrel with the Bishop of Worcestor, ambassador of Henry VII., and had written to the King, complaining of the Bishop, and also animadverting in strong terms upon the conduct of the Pope and Cardinals. The King sent Hadrian's letter to the Pontiff, and sequestrated the Cardinal's English revenues. Cardinal Hadrian, not knowing that his letter to the King had been communicated to His Holiness, went to the Pontiff, and requested his mediation with the King. Ascertaining the awkwardness of his position, and fearing arrest, the Cardinal fled away by night; and afterwards wrote from Spoleto, imploring pardon and permission to return. Julius II., who was the declared foe of Alexander VI., seems to have entertained some animosity against Cardinal Hadrian, whom he, nevertheless, pardoned on this occasion, and accordingly the Cardinal came back and appeared in consistory on the 10th of September.

But Hadrian was not at ease, and distrusted the Pontiff. Again, on the 6th of October, in the same year 1507, he fled by night, and in disguise, to Trani, in Puglia, where he remained until the year 1511, and from 1511 to 1513, he resided at and near Riva, on the banks of Lago di Garda. Here he lived under the protection of the Emperor Maximilian and the Bishop of Trent, and had the parishes of Tione and Tenna under his care, having procured the necessary ecclesiastical licence to hold them. His residence was mostly the

Castle of Tenna, otherwise called the Rock of Riva. On the death of Pope Julius, he returned to Rome and attended the conclave, when Leo X. was elected on the 4th of March, 1513.

For a few years Cardinal Hadrian lived in Rome on good terms with Leo X., who seems to have treated him with much kindness and consideration, and certainly befriended him on many occasions.

In 1514, Henry VIII., urged on by Silvester de Gigliis, Bishop of Winchester, endeavoured to induce the Pope to take the Collectorship in England from Cardinal Hadrian and give it to Andreas Ammonius, the King's Latin secretary. Leo X. after receiving three letters on the subject from Henry VIII., issued a brief, dated 31st of October 1514, (second year of Pontificate), appointing Ammonius to be Collector, but reserving a portion of the fees for Cardinal Hadrian. This arrangement was set aside in consequence of the protest of the Cardinal.

According to a letter written from London on March 3, 1515, by Polydore Vergil, the sub-collector, to Cardinal Hadrian, the Pope had sent a brief to the King on the 8th of January, stating that Hadrian had consented to give up the Collectorship to Ammonius. Another brief of the same date came for the Bishop of Winchester. Vergil says these briefs were either extorted from the Pope or were surreptitious. Vergil uses in this letter the word *mole* for the Bishop of Winchester, to signify his underhand dealings, and calls Ammonius *Harenarius*, and Wolsey *Le mi ;* and depicts Wolsey as a tyrant.

A copy of this letter was made by Ammonius, and has a postscript addressed to Wolsey. The postscript (written doubtless by the Bishop of Worcester) says that the Pope's thanks had been sent to the King and Wolsey, and that the unbecoming words used by Vergil when speaking of the Pope had been noted. The writer says that the Pope had seen similar letters in which King Henry is described as a boy, ruled by others, and signing papers without knowing their contents. It is then stated that the Pope would be glad to have some manifest reason for chastising Cardinal Hadrian, and a request is made that the letters of Hadrian and Polydore Vergil may be intercepted.

It was quite false, however, to represent the Pope as desirous to injure Cardinal Hadrian, and it may well be believed that the name of King Henry VIII. was unwarrantably used in this malicious communication. Indiscreet letters of Vergil were doubtless intercepted, but those of Cardinal Hadrian to Vergil if intercepted, gave no opportunity for injury to him at this time, when he seemed on good terms with the King and Wolsey, and ignorant, to a great extent, of the plot formed against him.

Cardinal Hadrian, on the 26th of March, 1515, signed a deed appointing Andreas Ammonius sub-collector in perpetuity, and on the next day wrote to Wolsey, thanking him for the favour shown to himself and Polydore in the office of collector, and commending their cause to his consideration. The Bishop of Worcester, on the 29th of March, writing to Wolsey, says :— "The Pope had expedited bulls in favour of the appointment of Ammonius to the collectorship, making sure that Hadrian would not oppose it, which he did, affirming that the King never dictated the letters, and that he had heard from a very high councillor in England that the King did not intend he should be turned out of his office. The Pope compromised the matter, appointing Andreas sub-collector, reserving to the Cardinal a pension of 1400 ducats, as the King will learn from Ammonius, by which the Cardinal will suffer no loss. . . . It is the intention of His Holiness that the King should declare Ammonius his sub-collector, and that a deed should be given him by the Cardinal for that purpose."

Polydore Vergil, doubtless for his insolent language respecting the King and Wolsey, was imprisoned, but had powerful friends in Rome. Leo X. on the 30th of August, 1515, wrote to Henry VIII. to say that he had written to the King already in behalf of Polydore Vergil, sub-collector, detained in prison some months at the King's command. The Pope repeats his request for Polydore's liberation and the restoration of his goods. He commends Hadrian, Cardinal of Bath. Julius, Cardinal de Medici, also wrote from Verona on the 3rd of September, to Henry VIII., saying that he would not have written so strongly in behalf of Polydore, who, he is sorry to hear has been thrown into prison, had not Cardinal Hadrian been so ready to comply with the King's wishes in the matter of the collectorship. As Ammonius has obtained possession, he begs that the King will not allow Polydore to be detained any longer.

Cardinal Hadrian promoted the advancement of Wolsey to the purple, and wrote a congratulatory letter to him on the 10th of September, 1515, the day Wolsey became a Cardinal. Leo X. on the 19th of September, wrote to the King in praise of Cardinal Hadrian, who is a great friend to his Majesty. On the 6th of October, Cardinal Wolsey wrote to Hadrian to say that he cannot fail to comply with his request to forgive Polydore Vergil his offences. And on the 8th of November, the Cardinal of Santa Prassede writes to Wolsey, testifying to Cardinal Hadrian's zeal in advancing Wolsey's promotion, which his enemies [the Bishop of Worcester among them] denied. Leo X., in a letter dated the 1st of December, 1515, and written to Henry VIII., again commends Cardinal Hadrian as a constant defender of the Holy See, and well deserving of his Majesty's favour.

The Bishop of Worcester, however, on the 19th of January, 1516, in a letter to Cardinal Wolsey, says that the Pope bids him write that Cardinal Hadrian is always obtaining briefs from him in his own commendation, and in praise of the services which he has rendered in procuring the Cardinalate for Wolsey. These letters—so says the Bishop—are not to be trusted. Whenever the Pope grants such a brief, and the word *nostro* is not found at the foot of it, he is not to pay any attention to it. It is quite as well that Wolsey should know how to repay deceit by deceit. Polydore is deceitful and malicious. The Bishop, on the 20th of April, 1516, told Ammonius that Cardinal Hadrian regards him with the whites of his eyes and always insults him to his face. He also says no man is a greater enemy of England than this "ribaldo" Hadrian. Cardinal Hadrian, on the 11th of May, 1516, writing to Wolsey, speaks of Wolsey's friendship to him, now that he has discovered the falsehood of his maligners.

In 1517 both Hadrian and the Bishop of Worcester fell under the indignation of Henry VIII., on account of their presumed neglect in not forwarding to the English Court certain intelligence respecting Tournay. Hadrian was considered bound to watch the King's interests, and the Bishop was the King's special ambassador and orator at Rome for the King's subjects at Tournay. In the month of February, 1517, De Gigliis received a most bitter letter, touching the revocation, granted by the Pope to the French, respecting the Bishopric of Tournay, and excused himself by professing his entire ignorance of the whole proceeding, however incredible it might seem that the Pope should pass a bull and he should be ignorant of it. Cardinal Hadrian had told De Gigliis nothing of this bull. Leo X., on the 21st of February, 1517, wrote to Wolsey in behalf of Hadrian, who complains of being unjustly accused by Wolsey of not having informed him of the restitution of the Bishop of Tournay. He asserts that he (the Pope) never communicated the affair to the Cardinal Hadrian or any one else.

Hadrian, on the 22nd of March, 1517, Lætare Sunday, celebrated Mass in the chapel of the Palace before the Pope. On the 31st of March, 1517, the Cardinal writes a confidential letter to Henry VIII., excusing himself for not writing more frequently, and saying that yesterday he had a long talk with the Pope, and this day read out in consistory the Papal letters to the Emperor. On the 23rd of April, Hadrian tells Wolsey that he (Hadrian) was appointed by the Pope to be one of a select commission of Cardinals; and in a letter dated the 23rd of May, from London, written by the Venetian ambassador to the Doge, it is mentioned that Cardinal Hadrian is to be the King's Commissioner with the Pope, but without recalling Bishop De Gigliis.

On the same day, May 23, Cardinal Hadrian wrote from Rome to Wolsey, announcing that on Tuesday the 19th, the two Cardinals, De Sauli and Siena, were brought to the Castle of S. Angelo, and accused by the Pope, in presence of the other Cardinals, of attempting to poison him by means of a Surgeon, who was taken at Florence. On the 12th of June, the Bishop of Worcester writes from Rome of the confession of Cardinals Sauli and Siena; and of Cardinal St. George, who acknowledges that he was privy to their designs; of the consistory summoned on the 8th; their profession of their innocence; the Pope's urgency that they should confess whether they knew of any conspiracy against him, (for at that time the perjury of Cardinal Hadrian was unknown); of the solemn denial of Cardinal Volaterra; of the confessions of the two guilty Cardinals which had been taken apart, one confessing that Hadrian was his accomplice, the other, Volaterra; but one was not privy to the other. The consistory urged Hadrian and Volaterra to fall at the Pope's feet and beg his pardon, which they did with tears in their eyes, confessing their guilt. He pardoned them, referring their penalty to the consistory, which was set at 60,000 ducats, and was finally fixed by the Pope at 25,000. . . . Cardinal Hadrian—so says the Bishop of Worcester—has the assurance to request a brief from the Pope to the King, attesting his innocence, but has been refused.

Marco Minio, the Venetian ambassador at Rome, gave a different and more truthful account, when writing to the Doge on the 13th of June:—This morning Hadrian went to the

Palace with the Cardinals S. Crucis and Grimain on money business, "and he, as it were, asked pardon a second time, although, according to report, his transgression was very slight. For being with the Cardinal of Siena, [Cardinal Alfonso] Petrucci and that ribald, Master Giovanni Battista of Vercelli, (the same who was to have poisoned the Pope's fistula) as Hadrian chanced to pass by, Siena said, 'That fellow will get the College out of trouble;' and the Right Reverend Hadrian, for having heard these words and not reporting them, has been in great peril so as to be obliged to expiate his crime in coin."

The Bishop of Worcester was evidently a watchful enemy of Cardinal Hadrian, for he now wrote to Ammonius to tell him he might be quite at his ease about the Collectorship (which Hadrian held) and his 1000 ducats, and that the Pope will find means to cancel his obligations to Hadrian.

Cardinal Hadrian paid the fine of 12,500 scudi in gold, and the night after, namely on the 31st of June, 1517, fled away from Rome. He was traced to Tivoli and Fondi, and lastly to Venice. On the morning of the 7th of July, a safe conduct to allow him to stay at Venice was made out for him at his request by the Signory in full college. This is mentioned in the Diary of Marin Sanuto, who adds: "It is said he will go to Padua, or to England, where he is liked, and has his income."

On the 19th of July, Cardinal Hadrian, apparently unconscious of Wolsey's enmity, wrote from Venice to Wolsey:— He had written, on the 12th of July, of the disturbances at Rome and his own troubles. He has inclosed his letters to the King in this to Wolsey, and begs his intercession with the King to procure his pardon from the Pope, and that he may remain in Venice and devote himself to letters. The Venetians —he adds—are very good friends to the King, and he was recommended to them by Henry VII. and Pope Julius.

The Bishop of Worcester, in a letter to Ammonius, says:— Cardinal Hadrian has reached Venice, disguised as a fool, as he left Rome. He demanded and obtained audience of the college [of Ten] who gave him a safe conduct. No doubt Hadrian has written much to excuse himself. The Pope advises them to beware of him. His privation *in facto* shall be pronounced as soon as he is expelled from where he is. Even now he does not desist from intriguing. But at least Worcester's 1000 ducats are safe, and also, he trusts, the Collectorship, if sufficient influence be used. This must be well thought of, for if he (Hadrian) be deprived of the Collectorship, and not of the Cardinalate, the former may be restored in time, and if Ammonius have only the name, he will be compelled to pay 200 ducats a year to Hadrian.

Sebastiano Giustiniani, Venetian ambassador in London, writes to the Council of Ten, on the 31st of July:—He had sent his son to the Bishop of Winchester [Fox] with the letters and those of Cardinal Hadrian. He apprehends some difficulty in Hadrian's business, as Wolsey has already obtained the See (of Bath). Giustiniani again writes on the 6th of August to the Doge:—He presented to the King the letters from the Signory and Hadrian, which last he "extracted from the packet addressed by his Lordship to the Cardinal of York;" otherwise Wolsey would never have delivered it to his Majesty. The King said he was perfectly acquainted with the business, and had heard from the Pope that he intended to deprive and degrade Hadrian. On his endeavouring to excuse Cardinal Hadrian for absenting himself from Rome, rather than incur danger, the King said:—"I understand this matter better than you Venetians;" and seemed greatly exasperated against him. He thinks this is owing to Wolsey. He would have presented the letter to Wolsey but he "has been ill of this sweating sickness, and would that the perspiration had carried off his wish for these benefices!"

His (Giustiniani's) son has returned from the Bishop of Winchester, who had likewise taken the sweat. He (Fox) said that one of the pontifical briefs greatly exaggerated

Hadrian's crimes, and urged that the See of Bath should be given to Wolsey *in commendam*. But in the second brief the anger of the Pope was much softened, and he seemed to delay the execution of the former one. The second brief, however, is not to be found, and your highness will comprehend by whose means it has been secreted.

On the 15th of August, Giustiniani, in a letter to the Doge, says :—Upon sending his secretary to Cardinal Wolsey, the latter made bitter complaints against the Signory, and especially against the writer. "Your master"—he said to the secretary—"has had the daring to give letters, and to canvass against me, at the request of a rebel (Hadrian) against his Holiness. Nor can I but complain of the Signory for taking such a delinquent under her protection." "Continuing a long while in this state of mental excitement, he again bursts forth to the secretary thus :—'I charge your ambassador and you not to write anything out of this kingdom without my consent, under pain of the indignation of the King and of the heaviest penalties ;' which expressions and all those above mentioned, he repeated several times, becoming more and more exasperated. While thus irritated, he held a cane in his hand, and kept knawing it with his teeth."

The ambassador, Giustiniani, called in person upon Wolsey early in the morning and found him in bed, and waited three hours, but was refused admission on the plea of Wolsey's indisposition. On the 17th of August, Giustiniani again called on Wolsey in the morning, was admitted, and begged to be heard, and detailed to Wolsey the whole of Hadrian's conduct and his arrival at Venice. Wolsey exculpated Giustiniani and turned his anger against the Signory. Giustiniani made the best apology he could, and said that rather than offend him, the Signory would incur the ill-will of the whole college of Cardinals. "Whilst delivering this defence, I could not express to your highness the rabid and insolent language used by him, both against your sublimity and myself, repeating, as he did several times, that he held me not in the slightest account, nor yet the Venetians, who were wont to favour ribalds and rebels, and to persecute the good ; that God and the potentates of the world would avenge such deeds ; and that your highness was always for the rebels of the Church, and opposed to the pontiffs past and present ; and that for this you had done penance, and were accustomed to proceed with deceit and mendacity ; and that the city of Venice would be a seat for conspirators against the Pontiff; on which account he meant to be the State's bitter enemy and mine, though at the same time, by reason of my other good qualities, he regretted my being the minister of such iniquities ; and that your Signory would find also that his Majesty took the thing very much amiss, saying, Go on, and write to the State to proceed in favouring rebels against me, for she will see what victory she will gain."

Giustiniani told Wolsey that he had received letters of the 22nd of July from Venice, stating that the Pope was much mollified towards Hadrian and thanked the Signory for its conduct in that respect. Wolsey declared that he did'nt believe the letter ; because six days ago he had received a brief from the Pope, stating that if the Venetians wrote anything in favour of Hadrian, Wolsey was not to believe them. Giustiniani made no answer to his bitter and insolent language ; but as to his insinuation that Venice had been adverse to the Church, he said it had done more for the Church than any other potentate. At the conclusion of the colloquy, Wolsey said that if Venice persevered in favouring this rebel prisoner, who is said also to have poisoned Pope Alexander, the King and himself would be most hostile to them. The Venetian ambassador desires a soothing answer to be sent, but is quite ready to do his duty stoutly and is not terrified at the punishment of others, and would feel no scruple in retaliating the insolent language to which he has been subjected.

In August and September 1517, Cardinal Hadrian was still at Venice. The Emperor wrote to the Venetians in his behalf.

The King of France was also anxious to intercede for the unfortunate Cardinal. But Henry VIII. was inexorable, and urgently pressed the Pope, through the Bishop of Worcester, to deprive him.

On the 8th of October, 1517, Giustiniani, writing from London to the Doge, says:—I obtained an interview with Cardinal Wolsey with difficulty . . . and communicated to him their (the Council of Ten's) apology respecting Hadrian. He replied:—" I do not doubt but that the Signory did not write with the intention of offending me, and I believe, as you say, that the circumstances were not understood at Venice : still you cannot acquit yourself of having done evil against me, contrary to your debt of gratitude, considering the love I bore you : and in truth I should have expected such an injury from any other person in the world rather than from you. He proceeded thus with such wrath and violence, and so much threatening and bitter language, that I could not repeat one half of it. In fact he hemmed me in on every side, and great need had I for patience to tolerate what he said to me." After a while Giustiniani overcame his arrogance and he said :—" I regretted that a man of your ability and worth should be deceived by a ribald, and for the future I shall be more yours and the Signory's likewise than ever." He also warned Venice to beware of Hadrian, as he communicated with the Emperor and had always acted with him against the Signory. . . . On taking leave he allowed Giustiniani to kiss his hand, contrary to his custom.

From this month of October, 1517, the name of Hadrian seems no longer mentioned by the Venetian ambassador, and Hadrian's foes at Rome became more active. The agents of Wolsey in Rome were incited by bribes to hasten the process for the deprivation of Hadrian, and the Bishop of Worcester was promised a pension by Wolsey as a reward for his services. The Bishop, writing from Rome, on the 10th of December, 1517, to Wolsey, says he has urged the Pope to perform his promises and deprive Hadrian, but found him dilatory as usual. The Pope had issued a bull of citation but would not publish it at present. Some friends of Hadrian had offered in his name to resign Bath and Wells to Wolsey with a pension of 3,000 ducats, if he will prevent the sentence of deprivation. Worcester told the Pope that such terms would be refused, and that justice and not avarice was the motive for pressing for the sentence. Had the King wished, he might have impounded the revenues of the See by reason of a debt that Hadrian owed to Henry VII., but the King will not permit any Bishop in his realm to conspire against the universal Head of the Church.

Leo X. was by no means desirous to ruin Cardinal Hadrian, but was rather inclined to pardon him, and had actually issued a brief for that purpose. But the continued absence of Hadrian left the Pope unable to do more than to delay the process. In February, 1518, he writes to Henry VIII. that he will comply with his wish to proceed against Hadrian, but it must be done consistently with the honour of the Holy See. Two days later, the Vice-Chancellor at Rome reminds the impatient Henry that the law must be strictly observed, to avoid scandal, and that some delay must take place. Sylvester de Gigliis, the Bishop of Worcester, was as much interested—so he wrote—in the business he has on hand against Hadrian, as if his life depended on it, and attributes the delay to the infrequency of letters from the King and Wolsey. In reply to this hint, Wolsey writes to the Bishop, on the 27th of February, saying that he would do nothing more in Hadrian's affair, only that he knew how much the King felt on the subject. He blames the procrastination, and desires the Bishop to tell the Pope that he cannot oblige the King more highly than by depriving that infamous Cardinal, and allowing Wolsey to hold Bath and Wells in conjunction with his present, or any other, archbishopric. He will let the Bishop know, when Hadrian is deprived, what is to be done with Hadrian's palace.

Henry VIII. also tells the Pope :—That his Holiness may

understand how much he has at heart the deprivation of Cardinal Hadrian, he has thought right to ask it again under his own hand. This letter had its effect, and on the 10th of April, 1518, the Bishop of Worcester was quite certain of the deprivation. Henry VIII. had also begged the Emperor not to intercede for Hadrian.

The absence of Cardinal Hadrian from Rome without license from the Pope had been mentioned in the consistory of June the 22nd, 1517, but it was not until the consistory of April 12, 1518, that the formal accusation of contumacy for non-appearance was made by the Procurators Fiscal, and further proceedings ordered. On the 26th of April, 1518, the articles of accusation were admitted, and sworn evidence was taken concerning his flight and absence. In June, the Papal Legate, Campeggi, was stopped at Calais by order of Henry VIII., because of delay in pronouncing sentence on Hadrian, although a provisional sentence of contumacy had been given in the consistory of May 17. At last, on the 5th of July, final sentence of deprivation was passed in consistory, by which Cardinal Hadrian de Castello was stripped of his Cardinalate and all his privileges, bishopric and benefices of every kind.

The last mention of Hadrian's name in the State Papers occurs in a letter of the Cardinal of Gurk [Girolamo Balbo] to Wolsey, dated from Augsburg the 20th of December, 1518, stating that the Pope has appointed payment to be made of a debt of 600 ducats due to the writer from Cardinal Hadrian, deposed, out of the fruits of his benefices confiscated in England. Cardinal De Medici and the Pope will write to Wolsey in that behalf. The writer begs Wolsey's favourable interference in this matter.

Of what became of Cardinal Hadrian after his deprivation, nothing is known with certainty. It is said by some that he went to France and finally to Constantinople, where he lived —so it was reported—under an assumed name until he died. The precise time of his death cannot be ascertained, but it is probable that he died before 1522, the year of the death of Leo X., as, if he had survived that Pontiff, he would most likely have returned to Rome and claimed a seat in the Conclave. Perhaps a search in the Venetian archives would elucidate the mystery of Hadrian's ultimate fate.

It was said of Cardinal Hadrian that his learning brought him honour, his riches envy, and his ambition calamity, and that he had applied to himself a prophecy, said to have been uttered by a witch or magician in the Appenine mountains, to the effect that a Hadrian would be Pope. The prophecy, if ever uttered, was fulfilled by the election, in 1551, to the pontificate, not of Hadrian de Corneto, but of Hadrian VI. of Utrecht.

Among the English ambassadors who may have occupied apartments in the palace given by Cardinal Hadrian, was Christopher Bainbridge, made bishop of London in 1507 and archbishop of York in 1508. He was created Cardinal Priest with title of S. Prassede by Julius II. on the 11th of September, 1508, and in May, 1510, appears as ambassador of Henry VIII. of England, and Custos of the English Hospital. He died—not without suspicion of foul play—in Rome on the 14th of July, 1514, and was buried in the English Hospital. Sylvester de Gigliis, who was Bishop of Worcester from December, 1498, to his death in Rome in April, 1521, seems to have succeeded his uncle John in the ambassadorship, as well as in the bishopric of Worcester, and probably lived for a short time in the English Palace in Rome.

The palace, however, which had been given in 1504-5, to Henry VII. on the express provision that it was to serve as a residence for English Kings and their ambassadors when in Rome, was, in 1519, granted, freely, and without any reservation, by Henry VIII. to Cardinal Lorenzo Campeggi, one of the most notable personages of his day.

The Campeggi family was of Bologna and of considerable antiquity. Records still extant mention one Lorenzo da

Campeggio in the year 1170. His grandson, Benvenuto was Prior of S. Maria dei Galluzzi, a church afterwards demolished to give a site for the Cathedral of S. Petronio. Ugolino, son of Lorenzo da Campeggio, was Captain-General of the Pisani and defeated the combined fleets of the Kings of Hungary and Bohemia, and for this victory was permitted to add to his family arms two anchors of silver. Donato, son of Ugolino, conquered in combat one Vinceslao Lambertazzi, and adjoined a dead man's skull to his armorial bearings. In succession to Donato were Ugolinazzo, Nicolo and Faciolo, all men of repute in Bologna. Faciolo's son, Bartolomeo, was Doctor of Laws and so highly esteemed for his goodness that his houses were spared by the populace when, after the death of Annibale Bentivoglio, the residences of the partizans of the Canetoli were destroyed.

Giovanni Zaccaria, son of Bartolomeo, and brother of Girolamo, Bishop of Parenzo, and Privy Councillor of Charles V., was a famous lawyer, and ambassador to Pope Julius II., and he married Dorotea Tabaldini of Mantua, and died on the 3rd of September 1511, leaving, besides three daughters, five sons, namely, Lorenzo, afterwards Cardinal; Tomaso, Bishop of Parma and Piacenza, and afterwards of Feltre; Marc Antonio, Bishop of Grosseto; Antonio Maria, Senator of Bologna; and Bartolomeo, Count of Pescina and Captain in the army of the Emperor Charles V.

Lorenzo, the future Cardinal, was born in Milan in the year 1474. When nineteen years old he was Professor in the University of Padua, and three years later held a chair in Bologna. He was reputed the most learned Canonist of his times. He married in 1500 Francesca de' Guastavillani, a lady of noble birth, and had five children by her. She died in 1510. Lorenzo Campeggi, being then 36 years old, was induced by Julius II. to embrace the ecclesiastical career, and was made Bishop of Majorca in 1510, and auditor of the Rota in 1511. He was then appointed Nuncio to the Emperor

Maximilian to detach him from the party of the French King Louis XII., and to induce the Emperor to withdraw his favour from the pseudo-council of Pisa, and send envoys to the intended council of the Lateran. Campeggi set out for Vienna on the 11th of August, 1511, but Maximilian refused to see him, or to acknowledge him as Nuncio. After two month's delay, by the assistance of Matthew Lange, Bishop of Gurk, Campeggi succeeded in getting a secret audience with Maximilian in a forest during a hunting party, and made such good use of the interview that the Emperor accepted him as Nuncio, and took him into friendship; eventually, and after much hesitation, consenting to break with Louis and side with the Pope. The Bishop of Gurk was sent to Rome to represent Maximilian, and at the same time Campeggi was recalled from Vienna. The Emperor, on Campeggi's departure, gave him on the 20th of August, 1512, the rank and privileges of Count Palatine, including the right to legitimate persons born out of wedlock, grant the degree of Doctor, and confer the dignity of Knighthood. On the 20th of November, 1512, at the request of the Bishop of Gurk, Campeggi was made Bishop of Feltre; and soon after was made Papal Nuncio to the court of the restored Duke of Milan, Maximilian Maria Sforza, and as such was present at the Duke's installation in Milan on the 29th of December, 1512.

In February 1513, Julius II. died, and De Medici succeeded him as Leo X. By this Pope Campeggi was confirmed as Nuncio to Milan, and was also made administrator of the cities of Parma and Piacenza, then restored to the Pope.

In December 1513, Campeggi was sent on a second embassy to the Emperor Maximilian, to make peace between the Emperor and the King of Hungary, and form a league against the Turk. He was away on this harassing mission for nearly four years, and was the constant companion of the Emperor in many fatiguing journeys and festivities, the result being that he laid the foundation for future gout in his constitution. The

Emperor had a high opinion of Campeggi, and gave him the secular government of Feltre and the right to carry the sword as well as the crozier, and urged the Pope to make him a cardinal. Leo X. acceded to the request, and mentioned before Albert, the Emperor's ambassador, the names of some twenty or thirty intended cardinals. When Campeggi's name was pronounced, Albert said, " Holy Father, this one name is worth fifteen of the others." On the 27th of June, 1517, Campeggi, while absent, was made Cardinal Priest with title of S. Thomas in Parione. On the 30th of October, 1517, the Emperor confirmed the Palatinate rights previously granted to Lorenzo, and extended them to his sons, his brothers, and their successors, and to his uncle Jerome, Bishop of Parenzo. Campeggi, departing, arrived at Bologna on the 29th of November; there received the cardinal's hat, and on December the 29th, left Bologna for Rome, where he hired for residence the palace of Tor Millina from the Mellini family The lease is dated in 1517.

Cardinal Campeggi was appointed on the 3rd of March, 1518, as Legate a Latere to Henry VIII. to form a league against the Turk. No such Legate had been in England for 200 years previously, and Henry was at first disposed to reject this mission, but said that if however he had no other business except that of treating against the Turk, he would admit him. He stipulated that all those faculties which are usually conceded to Legates *de jure* should be suspended, that Cardinal Wolsey should be joined in the Commission as first and senior Legate, and with equal authority, and that but one cross, that of Wolsey, should be carried before them, and also that the deprivation of Cardinal Hadrian de Castello should be formally pronounced. The Pope agreed to these demands. His Holiness addressed a brief,[*] dated the 10th of April, 1518, to the Duke of Norfolk, High Treasurer of England, informing his

---

[*] The original of this brief is extant among the Campeggi archives in Bologna.

Grace of the mission of Campeggi, and desiring him to place full and entire confidence in whatever Campeggi might communicate to him on behalf of the Pope, and requesting the aid and assistance of the Duke towards the furtherance of the Pope's desires.

Cardinal Campeggi soon afterwards set out on his mission to England. On the 19th of May, 1518, he was at Lyons, where he stopped over Easter, sending on his secretary, Florianus Montinus, and on the 28th of May was at La Palisse. He was at Calais on or before the 21st of June, but was ordered to wait there by Henry VIII., who was resolved that Cardinal Hadrian's deprivation should be effected before the Legate entered England. On the 29th of June, Campeggi wrote from Calais to Wolsey, to remonstrate about this delay. When the King at last learned from Rome that Hadrian was deprived, he sent a Knight of the Garter to Campeggi at Calais. On Friday the 23rd of July, 1518, the Legate took ship and landed at Deal near Sandwich, where he was received by the Bishop of Chichester, Lords Abergavenny and Cobham, and a great number of nobles and gentry, who conducted him to Sandwich, where he remained that night. On the next day, they conducted him to Canterbury, where he arrived between 9 and 10 A.M., and after changing his clothes was received by all the clergy, with the mayor and aldermen, who conducted him to the gates of Christchurch, where he was received by the Archbishop of Canterbury, the Bishop of Rochester, the Abbots of S. Augustine and Faversham, and the Priors of Christchurch and S. Gregory, all *in pontificalibus*. After kissing the Holy Crucifix, he was brought up to the high altar, the monks singing *Summæ Trinitati*, etc., and thereupon the Archbishop said prayers over him. After kissing certain relics, he was led to S. Thomas's shrine, with anthem of S. Thomas; which ended, he sang the collect *Deus pro cujus ecclesia*, etc., and then solemnly blessed the people. He was then conducted by the Archbishop and said lords to S. Augustine's Abbey, where he was received by the Abbot and brethren, and led up to the high altar, and thence to his lodging. The Archbishop returned to his palace with most of the lords to dinner.

On Sunday the Legate remained at S. Augustine's, and heard high mass in the choir; after which he had a great dinner, at which the Archbishop and nobles were present. After dinner he went to Christchurch, and saw S. Thomas's shrine and other relics, and then returned to his lodging at S. Augustine's.

Early on Monday (26th of July) morning, when it thundered, lightened, and rained sore, Campeggi departed with the bishops and lords; dined at Sittingbourne, and then went to Boxley Abbey, where he passed the night. On Tuesday, attended by the archbishop and a thousand horse, many in armour and gold chains, he went to the archbishop's palace at Oxford, where the archbishop received him, and there he remained two days, during which time the archbishop made him good and great cheer and divers pleasures and goodly pastimes. On the Thursday (29th of July) after, he went on to Levisham near Greenwich, where he dined with Mr. Wm. Hattecliff, one of the clerks of the green cloth. After dinner, about one o'clock, he proceeded to Blackheath, and was met by the Duke of Norfolk, the Bishop of Ely, and all the ambassadors, with a great number of lords, the Bishop of Durham pronouncing a congratulatory oration on his coming. This done, the company, to the number of 2000 horse, formed in order according to their degrees, and proceeded towards London. The King's tent, of cloth of gold, was set up in a meadow two miles from London, beyond S. Thomas Watergate, wherein the Legate changed his apparel and his mule. The Bishop of Lincoln, the Earl of Surrey, Lord Admiral, Lord D'Arcy and others, joined the pageant here. Campeggi, dressed in pontificals, then went on to London, with his cross borne before him, with "two pillers and two balaxes." The nobles rode before him, and after him his brother, a prothonotary, with Thomas Halsey, an Englishman, who is a bishop in Ireland. The Legate's servants came next, dressed all in red, and after them the Archbishop's servants, clothed in one livery with red hats, (except the chaplains) to the number of 200 horse. From S. George's Church to London Bridge, the way was lined on both sides with the clergy of London, in copes of gold, friars and monks, with gold and silver crosses, singing hymns, and, as the Legate passed, censing him and sprinkling him with holy water. At London Bridge an oration was made to him. At the foot of the bridge were two bishops in pontificals, who received him and presented him with the relics of the Saints to kiss. So loud were the rejoicings, and such salvos of artillery rent the air, as if the heavens themselves would fall. The London crafts began their order in "Gracious Strete," in Cheapside, welcomed by the mayor and aldermen; and a brief Latin oration was made by Mr. Moore. At Paul's Church, the Bishops of Lincoln and London, and all the ministers of Paul's received him, and the Bishop of London made a short oration; after which he was taken up to the high altar; then returned to his mule, and was conveyed to his lodging in Bath's place.

On Tuesday, the 3rd of August, the two Legates, Thomas, Archbishop of York, and Cardinal, first Legate in commission, and the Legate from the Bishop of Rome, were received by the King as follows: first the King, with the Lords Spiritual and Temporal, and other noble men, went from his dining chamber into the hall, and a little below the middle waited till they had entered. He then advanced as far as the spear, and there they embraced. After a little speech the two Legates separated; the Cardinal Wolsey, being chief in commission, on the King's right hand, and a little before him; one bearing his train on the right, a little behind him. The other Legate, Campeggi, in like manner, on the King's left. Their crosses, pillars, and hats were borne before them. The King's sword was borne by the Earl of Surrey, the Admiral, between the Legates. They were followed into the dining chamber by all the Lords Spiritual and Temporal. The room was hung with arras, having a cloth of estate, chair and cushions, for the King, of rich cloth of gold of tissue. The chair stood on a timber stage, about six inches from the ground, covered with cloth of gold; and two chairs of cloth of gold were set for the Legates on the King's right.

Giustiniani, writing to the Doge, says:—He was invited to join the two Legates at Greenwich. "His Majesty went as far as the lower hall to meet them, dressed in his royal insignia, with the greater part of the prelates and barons of the Kingdom; and the Legates saluted him with great marks of respect. He likewise returned the salute, doffing his bonnet with respectful gestures; and being taken between them, he came to the upper hall, where, at the extremity, the throne had been prepared, and two benches, one on the right hand, the other on the left." The two Primates, with the Bishops, stood on the right of the throne. The two Legates sat on two gilt chairs: in the larger, the Legate of York; in the lesser, Campeggi, then the Spanish Ambassador. On the left were the three Dukes and other lords. Wolsey, standing cap in hand, the King standing likewise, made a Latin speech. "To this his Majesty replied, also in Latin, most eloquently and with all gravity, after which they seated themselves." An answer to this was made in the King's name, by one of Wolsey's attendants, stating his Majesty would no wise fail in his duty as a Christian; of which, however, he had no need to be reminded. This ended, the King and the Legates entered a chamber, where they remained an hour.

The Legates went to court on the 8th of August, where Mass was performed, and a banquet given, more sumptuous than had yet been seen. No business was transacted. Little respect (adds Giustiniani) was shown to the See Apostolic.

On the 25th of September, the King gave public audience to the French ambassadors at Greenwich, when Campeggi and

Giustiniani were present. The Bishop of Paris delivered an oration, to which the Bishop of Ely replied. The King then led the French ambassador, attended by Wolsey, into a chamber, Campeggi and others remaining outside.

On the 3rd of October (writes Giustiniani to the Doge), the general peace was proclaimed at St. Paul's. That day, the King, the two Legates, all the ambassadors, the Lords and Bishops, were present at a solemn Mass, celebrated by Wolsey with unusual splendour. After a grave oration by Pace, the King, the Cardinal, and the French ambassadors, proceeded to the high altar, where the peace was read and sworn to in a tone audible only to the parties concerned. Thinks this equivalent to cancelling the clause against the Turks.

The King and the rest then went to dine with the Bishop of London, his Majesty returning afterwards to Durham House in the Strand. "From thence the Cardinal of York was followed by the entire company to his own dwelling, where we sat down to a most sumptuous supper, the like of which, I fancy, was never given either by Cleopatra or Caligula: the whole banqueting hall being so decorated with huge vases of gold and silver, that I fancied myself in the tower of Chosroes, where that monarch caused divine honours to be paid him.

After supper, a mummery, consisting of twelve male and twelve female masquers, made their appearance in the richest and most sumptuous array possible, being all dressed alike. After performing certain dances in their own fashion, they took off their visors. The two leaders were the King and the Queen Dowager of France, and all the others were lords and ladies, who seated themselves apart from the tables, and were served with countless dishes of confections and other delicacies. Having gratified their palates, they then regaled their eyes and hands; large bowls, filled with ducats and dice, being placed on the tables for such as liked to gamble: shortly after which, the supper tables being removed, dancing commenced, and lasted until after midnight."

On the 5th of October, the bridal entertainments for the marriage of the Princess Mary (sister to Henry) and the Dauphin, were celebrated at Greenwich. The decorations were sumptuous. The King stood in front of his throne; on one side was the Queen and the Queen Dowager of France. The Princess was in front of her mother, dressed in cloth of gold, with a cap of black velvet on her head, adorned with many jewels. On the other side were the two Legates. Tunstal made an elegant oration; "which being ended, the most illustrious Princess was taken in arms, and the magnificos, the French ambassadors, asked the consent of the King and Queen on behalf of each of the parties to this marriage contract; and both parties having assented, the Right Reverend Legate, the Cardinal of York, placed on her finger a small ring, *juxta digitum puellæ*, but in which a large diamond was set (supposed to be a present from Wolsey), and my Lord Admiral passed it over the second joint. The bride was then blessed by the two Legates, after a long exordium from the Cardinal of York—every possible ceremony being observed. Mass was then performed by Cardinal Wolsey, in the presence of the King and all the others, the whole of the choir being decorated with cloth of gold, and all the court in such rich array that I never saw the like, either here or elsewhere." All the company then went to dinner, the King "receiving the water for his hands from three Dukes and a Marquis." The two Legates sat on the King's right; on the left were the Lord Admiral and the Bishop of Paris; and the Dukes of Buckingham, Norfolk, and Suffolk, were seated "at the inside of the table. The other two French ambassadors, the Spaniard, one from Denmark," Giustiniani, with others, dined in another chamber. "After dinner, the King and the Cardinal of York, with the French ambassadors, betook themselves into a certain room, to conclude some matters which remained for settlement; and all the rest departed."

Many other entertainments of extraordinary luxury followed,

to which Cardinal Campeggi was invited. The King seemed devoted to amusements. Giustiniani, on the 13th of January, 1519, found his Majesty starting on one of his pleasure excursions. On the 19th, he writes : The King and the Legates are absent, amusing themselves. The business of Campeggi's mission was evidently drawing to a close.

On the 17th of March, 1519, Giustiniani writes to the Doge:— An ambassador from the King Catholic has arrived to ratify the league between the princes of Christendom. Yesterday was appointed for his audience, for which sumptuous preparations were made. A great number of lords and prelates had been convened, "including seventeen bishops not usually in attendance at the great court." As the Pope had sent a fresh commission to the Legates, in confirmation of what had been done, it was arranged that they should come to court as if newly sent by him. Accordingly they were met by the King, the prelates, lords and ambassadors, "with all the ceremonies observed on a first arrival. The prothonotary Campeggi (brother of the Legate) delivered an eloquent oration, lauding the King for his promptitude in the Christian expedition. Then a Spanish ambassador made an oration, thanking the King for naming his Sovereign as a chief confederate, not mentioning the Pope or any other. Pace replied, qualifying the Pope "*tanquam comitem confœderationis ;* " and, to mitigate the arrogance of such an expression, he added, "*comitem et quod maxime optavit hic sacratissimus rex, principem confœderationis.*" The chief author of these proceedings is Wolsey, whose sole aim is to procure incense for his King and himself.

Cardinal Campeggi seems to have given, during this embassy to England, satisfaction both to the Pope and the King. Henry VIII. was very liberal in his gifts. He gave to Campeggi the palace which Cardinal Hadrian, in 150⅔, had presented to Henry VII. It is described—in the patent, which is dated from Westminster, March 12, 1519 (tenth year of the reign of Henry)—as an unfinished house at Rome, near the house of the Canons and Chapter of St. Peter's and the house of Cardinal Francesco Sodorini. Cardinal Wolsey, writing on March 25, 1519, to Sylvester de Gigliis, Bishop of Worcester, the King's ambassador in Rome, states that "out of consideration for the many good qualities of Campeggi, the King has given him a house at Rome;" and the Bishop is "to see that there is no difficulty in investing Campeggi with it."

On the 20th of March, 1519, Cardinal Campeggi celebrated High Mass in state at Greenwich, giving plenary indulgence to all present; after which, near the High Altar, the two Legates, in the name of his Holiness, confirmed the League. A banquet was afterwards given, the two Legates sitting at the same table with the King.

Leo X. wrote on the 13th of April, 1519 (seventh of his Pontificate), to Henry VIII., thanking him for his hospitality to Cardinal Campeggi and his noble present to him. It is stated that Campeggi received from the King 6000 scudi to furnish the palace, besides ten superb horses, and also forty vessels of gold and silver, worth 6000 scudi.*

Henry VIII. wrote from Greenwich on the 18th of August, 1519, to the Pope, to say that he could not but regret that his Holiness had recalled Campeggi, and that he doubted if any other man could have performed his office with such splendour, skill, and assiduity, and served the cause of Christendom with

---

* The gold and silver plate given by Henry VIII. to Cardinal Campeggi remained for many years in possession of his descendants, but having been divided among various members of the family at different periods, cannot now be traced. The Cardinal was also presented by Henry with several pieces of tapestry, which once adorned his palace in the Borgo and his castle of Dozza. These tapestries at present are possessed by the Marchese Girolamo and the Marchese Pietro, sons of the late Marchese Emilio Malvezzi Campeggi, and are preserved at Bologna. These tapestries, sufficient for five rooms, were executed from designs of Luca d' Olanda. A picture, also by Luca d' Olanda, representing the Presepio, now belongs to Marchese Alfonzo, son of the late Marchese Carlo Malvezzi Campeggi, of Bologna.

equal honour to his Holiness. The King has given him the ratification of the five years' truce, and entrusted him with a message to the Pope.

Cardinal Wolsey, writing on the following day to the Bishop of Worcester at Rome, says:—" Campeggi, who is now returning, has acted with great moderation and prudence, and gained the good opinion of all men. . . . The King was not well satisfied with the Pope's neglect in the affairs of Germany, but he (Wolsey) and Campeggi have removed his dissatisfaction."

On the 22nd of August, 1519, Campeggi, on his way to Rome, wrote from Dover to Henry VIII., thanking his Majesty for his kindness and liberal gifts of plate, and stating that Sir Edward Belknapp, who accompanied him from London, had been very attentive to him. He wrote also to Wolsey to the same effect. The details of the cost of embarking the Cardinal were :—Expense of the passage of the Lord Legate and his company by the commandment of Sir Edward Belknapp on the 24th of August: The freight of the *Henry*, £5 ; the *Myghell Bayly*, £3 6s. 8d.; for more mariners for the Legate being in the same ship, 20s.; the *Myghell Yong*, £3 6s. 8d.; the *Barbera Foche*, £3 6s. 8d.; prymmage of the horses and stuff, 20s.; the bridges, 5s.; for the boats carrying the company on board, 8s.; for the porters carrying the company into the boats, 2s. 6d. *Mem.*—My Lord Legate's whole charge of shipping amounted to £17 15s. 6d. "There is a privy seal for three of the ships, directed to the Customer there."

Campeggi left for Calais on the 24th at seven o'clock, and he arrived, after a good passage, about eleven o'clock. He was well received by the magistrates and townsmen, and especially by the Treasurer, at Calais, and started on the morning of the 26th, at seven o'clock, for Flanders.

Campeggi, on September 21, 1519, wrote to Wolsey from Blois :—He had not written to him since his last letter from Calais. He proceeded thence through France to Brussels, and paid his respects to the Lady Margaret and Prince Ferdinand,

and satisfied them of the King's and Wolsey's good feelings towards them. He arrived at the court of France on the 19th. He had an interview with the King the next day. He spoke of the kind treatment he had received in England. The King expressed his great affection to England, and his desire for a firm union. He is well aware of Henry's cordiality from other proofs than the restitution of Tournay, and begged Campeggi to say so. On presenting his letters, he embraced him, and offered him with great delicacy a pension of 8000 francs. Is indebted for this liberality to the King of England, but would accept no benefit except from England. He will proceed on his journey to-morrow.

Another account of this interview with the French King was sent to Wolsey by Boleyn, who wrote from Blois on the 24th of September, 1519, and says:—On Sunday came the Pope's Legate that was late in England, and was brought to the court on Monday by the Cardinal of Bourbon and others. The King received him "in his dining chamber somewhat within the door," embraced him, and led him by the hand "to a beddys syde in the same chamber, and so standing there talked with hym half a quarter of an howre," when he delivered the King a letter from England, which he read; and calling the other Legate, "talked with him, leaning on the bedd, more than half an howre," whilst the Cardinal of Bourbon talked with the other Legate. The Legate speaks very highly of the liberality of England; says that the King willed the other Legate to shew him that he would give him an annual pension of 8000 francs a year, which he refused, as he could not serve two masters, and wished to remain faithful to Henry. He left Blois yesterday morning, when Boleyn accompanied him a mile on his way, and received from him two letters, transmitted herewith—one to Wolsey, the other to the Venetian ambassador in England. Campeggi had no other convoy than his own company of twenty-four horses and five mules.

Campeggi next writes from Lyons on the 3rd of October,

1519, to Wolsey, saying :—" I arrived here on the 1st, intending to cross the Alps in two days." Since he wrote from Blois, nothing worth mentioning has occurred, except that by reason of the rain the roads have been very difficult. It seems that Erasmus supped with Campeggi at Bruges, and liked the sincerity and openness of the Cardinal.

On the 9th of November, 1519, the Bishop of Worcester, writing to Henry VIII. from Rome, says :—" The return of the Legate Campeggi, who has sounded the King's praises everywhere, has greatly augmented the King's reputation at Rome. He extols the balls, music, and tournaments, and the wonderful splendour of the English court, and is an excellent trumpeter."

Campeggi writes to Wolsey on December 4, 1519 :—" He has not written since his last from Blois. Had very bad weather and much rain. Reached Bologna on the 20th of October, and stayed there to recruit until the 14th of November. He started for Rome on the 26th with no better weather, and entered the city *incognito*. Next day, the 28th, was received by all ranks at the city gates, and was conducted from Sta Maria del Popolo to the palace, where he saluted the Pope and Cardinals. Afterwards, the consistory being dismissed, had, with the Bishop of Worcester, an audience of the Pope. He expressed to his Holiness the King's friendship for the Holy See, his desire for the peace of Christendom, and presented his letters, which the Pope returned to Campeggi to read ; then he presented those relating to the treaty ; thirdly, those referring to his own return ; fourthly, those containing his promised promotion to the See of Salisbury. . . . A consistory was held on the 2nd of December, in which the Pope announced the return of Campeggi, commended the King, and ordered his letter to be read. This was done by Dom. Cornarus, Dean of the Deacons, with a loud voice. The rules of the consistory did not allow Campeggi to make an oration, but he seconded the Pope's eulogium by buzzing about the King's praises, *seorsum et levi susurro.*"

On the 20th of February, 1520, Campeggi, in a letter from Rome to Wolsey, says :—He has sent the sapphire ring, which Wolsey gave him on their voyage to Greenwich, to a Moor confined in Hadrian's Mole, who reads the inscription—*In nomine Dei regnavit Rex Solomon super Syon.* The Moor has since turned Christian, and has been baptized by the Pope in St. Peter's. Sends six byreta made according to the measure given him, and two enclosed in a case (in techa).

On the 3rd of March, 1520, Cardinal Campeggi wrote to Wolsey to say that he was in great trouble for means to repair the house given him by the King, which is, he states, in a ruinous condition. He proposes to borrow £1000 for three years, for which he offers a bond to John Cavalcanti [a merchant of Florence] or some other responsible merchant. He hopes, as the King has given him the bishopric of Salisbury, and promises to do more for him, he will not deny him this favour. The See of Salisbury, it may be noted, was not then vacant, and Campeggi did not get possession of it until after the death of Bishop Audley, which occurred on the 24th of August, 1524.

On the 10th of October, 1520, Campeggi tells Wolsey :— "He (the Pope) gave me, without my asking, the office of Signatura Justiciæ, also held by the said Cardinal (a nephew of Julius II., Bishop of Agen, just dead); and though this has no revenue, it is the hinge of the whole court and the right hand of the Pope, and is usually given to a Cardinal of known faith and learning." He was made Papal Secretary on the 8th of November, 1520.

Campeggi wrote from Rome to Henry VIII. on the 10th of February, 1521, to say that he had sent him by Parker a horse which he had procured from a Roman noble by the advice of Gregory Casali. In March of the preceding year, a similar present had been made by Campeggi to the King.

On the 15th of April, 1521, when Sylvester de Gigliis, Bishop of Worcester, was dying, and again on the 15th of May, when

The English Palace in Rome.   45

the Bishop had been a month dead, Campeggi wrote from Rome to Henry VIII., asking to have the See of Worcester until such time as Salisbury should be vacant. The King did not accede to this request, but gave the bishopric to Cardinal de Medici, at the same time satisfying Campeggi that it would be wiser for him to wait.

During the fourteen years between 1505 and 1519, the period during which the palace was the property of English Kings, Cardinal Bainbridge and Bishop Sylvester de Gigliis, as already stated, were entitled to residence in the English Embassy. After 1519, when Campeggi became owner, no further right of residence for English envoys existed. Accordingly, in April, 1521, John Clerk, ambassador of England, when entering Rome, was waited on by the retinues and officials of Cardinals Campeggi and de Medici, but went to the house of de Medici, from whence he dates a letter on the 8th of July same year. But in September, 1522, it is stated that Cardinal Campeggi has lodged another envoy of the King, namely, Mr. Thomas Hannibal, and his servants. This Thomas Hannibal, writing from Rome to Wolsey on the 13th of December, 1522, asserts that he cannot get a house in Rome "that is anything honest" under 150 ducats a year. Again, John Clerk, now Bishop of Bath, when entering Rome on the 3rd of June, 1523, went to reside in the house of Cardinal de Medici.

On the 11th of June, 1523, it is mentioned that Campeggi, alone of the Cardinals, lives in the Pope's palace. And on the 14th of September, 1523, Hannibal and Clerk, writing to Wolsey from Rome, say:—"The Cardinals of the greatest authority here are Medici, SS. Quatuor and Campeggi, who form a triumvirate in the College."

For more than three years, from 1519 to 1524, Cardinal Campeggi resided in his palace in Rome, and during that period took part in two conclaves. Leo X. died December 1, 1521, and was succeeded by Adrian VI., who entered Rome on the 29th of August, 1522, and died on the 24th of September,

1523. Clement VII. (de Medici) was elected Pope on the 18th of October, 1523, and on the 2nd of December, same year, gave to Campeggi the archbishopric of Bologna.

The Duke of Austria at this time entreated the Pope for aid against Luther, whose heresy was daily increasing; and Clement VII., as Wolsey was informed by letters from Rome, dated January 9, 1524, determined to send Campeggi as Legate. On the 17th of January, writing to Henry VIII., the Pope says:—When about to send Campeggi to the Diet at Nuremberg, he heard with pleasure of Henry's resolve to send ambassadors thither, and has ordered his Legate to consult with them. He will not allow Henry's interests to suffer by the absence of Campeggi. On the 20th of January, Campeggi informs Henry VIII. of his appointment as Legate to Germany. It is,—he writes,—a very onerous office, but he trusts to the Pope's authority and Henry's. Asks if he can serve the King in any way in his new capacity, and expects to leave before the end of the month.

Campeggi, when he set out on his mission, took Bologna in his way. He made his public entry, as Archbishop, into Bologna on the 12th of February, 1524, sang Mass in St. Petronius on the 14th, and gave a grand banquet to the nobles. After dinner, the Senate presented him with a silver basin, worth 500 scudi in gold. On the 18th of February, he left Bologna for Germany.

On the 2nd of April, 1524, Campeggi writes to Henry VIII. from Nuremberg, to thank the King for appointing him Protector of the English nation and for commending him to the Pope. Campeggi wishes he were at Rome to perform his duties as Protector, but the Pope's will and the calamities of the times compel him to undertake the present most odious charge. Clement VII., on the 16th of May, 1524, informs Henry VIII. that at the last Diet at Nuremberg, the Pope by Campeggi and the Emperor by the Arch Duke, required that the decrees of the Diet of Worms should be observed.

Clerk, writing to Wolsey from Rome on the 26th of June, 1524, says that he had thanked the Pope for consulting the King as to whether he should send another Legate to England about Turkish affairs ; and said that Wolsey had so much authority, etc., that the King was content with him. The Pope, smiling, turned to Campeggi and said :—"*Nonne hæc prediximus?*" Clerk immediately added, that if any one were sent, no one would be more acceptable than Campeggi ; who thanked the King and Wolsey for their good mind, and said that if they had wished for another Legate, it would have given him pleasure to have gone.

Audley, Bishop of Salisbury, died on the 23rd of August, 1524, and Campeggi for some years had had the King's express promise to give it to him. It was not, however, given to him at once, or without several applications. Clement VII., on the 21st of September, 1524, wrote to Henry VIII. in behalf of Campeggi, for the bishopric which had already been promised him by the King and Wolsey. On the 22nd of September, Gio. Matt. Giberto, Datary, writing to the Florentine ambassadors with Charles V., says :—From Germany, Cardinal Campeggi writes that the affairs of Luther are becoming settled, but the Duke of Saxony and the Free towns are daily growing more obstinate in their perfidy. The Archduke is acting nobly. On the 1st of October, 1524, Campeggi wrote from Vienna to Henry VIII., asking his Majesty to confer the bishopric of Salisbury on him ; and on the 10th of same month wrote to Wolsey, reminding him of his necessities, as he hears the Bishop of Salisbury is dead, and enclosing a letter for the King, to be delivered if Wolsey thinks right.

On the 1st of November, 1524, Henry VIII. wrote to the Pope, requesting him to promote Campeggi to Salisbury ; and on the 11th of November, Wolsey wrote to the Pope to acknowledge the receipt of his two letters recommending Campeggi for Salisbury. "The King," Wolsey adds, "has written to his Holiness for the promotion of Campeggi, although many objected to the appointment of a cardinal and a foreigner."

Clement VII., on the 29th of November, 1524, thanked Wolsey for his letters and for his commendation of Campeggi, who is now in Germany.

On the same day (November 29), Campeggi wrote from Vienna to the King and to Wolsey, thanking them for his promotion. In his letter to Wolsey, he acknowledges that it is their benevolence, and not his deserts, and he feels the difficulty caused by his being a foreigner. By zeal and faithfulness he will prevent Wolsey from repenting his kindness. Wolsey has saved Campeggi's dignity and fortune from destruction. His agents will attend to the business at Rome. Hopes that Wolsey will see to his duties to the King and the Church at Salisbury, and inform him or "Jacobum meum" what else is to be done. He refers Wolsey to Giacomo for an account of his embassy.

Dr. Clerk, Bishop of Bath, writes to Wolsey on the 5th of December, 1524, from Rome, saying he had received, on the 27th of November, Wolsey's letters of the 11th, and one of them is the King's pleasure concerning the see of Salisbury. The Pope is grateful to Wolsey for his exertions in behalf of Campeggi. The appointment is very popular in Rome, and therefore Clerk in his last letters had spoken in Campeggi's favour.

On the 28th of December, 1524, Campeggi wrote to Henry VIII. from Buda. He wrote last from Vienna to thank the King for his liberality. He arrived at Buda on the 18th, and was met by the King of Hungary more than two miles from the city.

The College of Cardinals wrote letters, on the 2nd of January, 1525, both to Henry VIII. and Wolsey, to testify their pleasure at the promotion of Campeggi to the see of Salisbury.

On the 16th of January, 1525, Cardinal Wolsey, writing to Clerk, Bishop of Bath, says—The Lutheran heresy makes it necessary to act wisely. . . Campeggi's journey into Almain has done much good.

Dr. Thomas Benet wrote to Wolsey on the 6th of February, 1525, to say that he had accomplished all things touching the installation of the Bishop of Salisbury, for which the Chapter demands £10, which he has deferred till he knows Wolsey's pleasure. "The bishop's Vicar here in the Cathedral church is destitute, whom your Grace doth name to the Chapter." The value of it is £12 a year. He must be a priest and a singing man, and keep the choir daily.

Campeggi, on the 7th of February, 1525, in a letter to Wolsey, from Buda, states that he hears from Giacomo that the Bishop of London has lately tendered Campeggi's oath of allegiance to the King. Expresses his great obligations to him. Refers him to Giacomo for the news. On the same day Campeggi wrote to Henry VIII. to the same effect.

On the 26th of April, 1525, Campeggi writes to Wolsey from Buda. He is still detained here by Bohemian affairs, which are yet in such a case that they will be altogether finished within the next month. Is troubled by private as well as public cares. Many who have hitherto assisted him with money are pressing for repayment, thinking that he is rich through the instrumentality of the King here. Asks Wolsey to assist him.

Campeggi, on the 21st of July, 1525, wrote to Wolsey from Bologna :—He arrived at Bologna on the 13th of July. Wolsey's letter of May 31 was brought to him there from Buda. It made him forget the trouble of his long journey to hear of Wolsey's health and kindness to him (on which his friend Giacomo enlarged), and of the arrangements for paying the revenues of Salisbury to Giacomo. Would wish to stay here during August to rest himself, his servants, and cattle, and to avoid the heat of the city (Rome); but the state of affairs and the Pope's wishes prevent it. Is the less vexed at this, as he knows that Wolsey and the King will employ him there.

Will not stay longer in Bologna than family matters compel him. In another letter to Wolsey, undated, Campeggi reminds him of his request, that of the two houses occupied by Francis Bombarderio in the Cathedral of Salisbury, the smaller may be taken from him, and the keys sent to the Cardinal.

On the 20th of September, 1525, Henry VIII. and Wolsey, in separate letters, notify to the Pope the recall of the Bishop of Bath (Clerk), whose services are required in England, and whose place will be taken by Jerome Ghinucci, Bishop of Worcester, and Sir Gregory Casale.

Campeggi, on the 24th of October, 1525, writes to Henry VIII. to announce his return to Rome. He arrived on the 18th, tired out with the difficulties and troubles of the embassy to Germany and Hungary. He shudders at the recollection of the dangerous places he has passed through. He can say, without boasting, that he has prevented from falling many places which were tottering, and has raised up others which had fallen. The popular, so-called, Evangelical fervour has driven both the bad and the good to arms, as he predicted. Many have already expiated their crime by blood, but there is great hope that the application of steel and cautery will prevent the cancer from proceeding further. Nothing was a greater hardship to him during his embassy than his absence from the city, and his inability to serve his Majesty. He will devote himself and the See of Salisbury to his service.

A letter of the same date and tenor was addressed to Wolsey.

Cardinal Campeggi wrote, on the 5th of November, 1525, a complimentary letter on the return of Clerk, Bishop of Bath, to England, in whose place arrived the Bishop of Worcester and Sir Gregory Casale. Casale wrote from Rome on the 7th of November to say that Clerk left to-day for England. The Bishop of Worcester had arrived in Rome on the 31st of October.

The year 1526 was one of disaster for Rome and Christendom.

A plague broke out, and although it abated in May, it increased in June.

On the 29th of August, 1526, the King of Hungary was totally defeated by the Turks, and was drowned while attempting to escape.

In a Consistory, summoned on receipt of the sad news, Cardinal Campeggi made a long speech, bewailing the state of Christendom and the helpless condition of the Pope.

Taking advantage of the defenceless condition of Rome, and breaking the agreement lately made with the Pope, the troops of the Colonna, under Hugh Moncada, Viceroy of Naples, surprised Rome on the night of the 18th of September, 1526, and seizing three gates, passed by Ponte Sisto through the Trastevere to St. Peter's. The invaders forced the Pope to take refuge in the castle of St. Angelo, and plundered the Basilica of St. Peter's, the palace of his Holiness, and the houses in the Leonine city. The greater part of the Borgo Nuovo escaped, being protected by the guns of St. Angelo. Ghinucci, Bishop of Worcester, wrote on the 20th and 23rd of September an account of this event to Wolsey, and says that Don Hugo visited the Pope, who gave as hostages his nephews, Cardinal Cibo and de Ridulphis. Don Hugo demanded that the castle and other hostages should be given up, but the Pope refused. On the following day, the 21st, an agreement was made between the Pope and Don Hugo de Moncada, Captain General of the Imperial fleet, and was approved by the College of Cardinals. It was dated Rome, in the castle of St. Angelo; present: the College of Cardinals and Don Hugo, Don Martin of Portugal, the Portuguese ambassador, and the Bishop of Trevesi, Governor of the city. The Pope was still in the castle on the 23rd of September.

Sir Gregory Casale gives the following account:—" Next morning (the 19th September), the Colonnas, with whom his Holiness had truce, at break of day were at the Porta di San Giovanni without the Pope's knowledge, who, having some days before sent out of Rome 1000 foot, whom he had kept as a guard, was obliged to send two Cardinals (one of whom was Campeggi) to pray the Romans to take arms in his defence. No one stirred except some friends ; and the good Colonnas, with 600 horse and 6000 foot, of which there were not 2000 that were not of the rabble *(villani)*, marched through Rome, with only a little resistance at the Porta di San Spirito. They sacked the Pope's palace, the half of the Borgo, and a number of houses, including those of the Cardinal Aracœli and the Venetian ambassador, and robbed vestries, etc. Never was such cruelty and sacrilege. The Pope appealed to several Cardinals in vain, till the writer, leaving his house in danger, came to the castle and urged Signor Alberto (Count de Carpi, the French ambassador,) and the Venetian ambassador not to allow the Pope to suffer so great an indignity. At last, next morning, the Pope held a Consistory, and a truce was arranged."

On the 24th of September, 1526, Campeggi wrote from Rome to Henry VIII., saying :—" The Pope, who is in great trouble, is sending to England the Bishop of Worcester, to inform the King of recent occurrences at which he was present. All his hope in this critical time is in the King. All Christendom is in danger from the Turk, now that the King of Hungary has been defeated and slain."

Campeggi wrote to Wolsey on the 7th of February, 1527, expressing the satisfaction he felt when he first had the happiness of being personally introduced to Wolsey, and thanking him for the care he has taken of his interests, and especially for his late letters when Campeggi had fallen into some disgrace with the King, for which there was no foundation. Has now been able to throw away all trouble, and can sleep safe from fear of destruction. He cannot express the delight with which the Consistory heard from the Pope that the King had sent him an ambassador (Russell), who had arrived from Civita Vecchia with a large sum of money ; and, in order to display his liberality to the Holy See, had received orders from the King to denounce war against the Viceroy and Bourbon if they did not forthwith abandon the siege of different cities of the Church. The Cardinals are unanimous in declaring that Henry was God's blessing to them—the patron of Italian liberty and the real defender of the Faith. He praises the King's book against Luther highly, which, he says, is to be reprinted in many thousands of copies, to show that he can defend Christendom not less by genius and learning than by money and arms.

Evil days, however, for Rome and Campeggi were at hand. On Saturday, May the 4th, 1527, the Duke of Bourbon arrived before the city, and asked the Pope's consent to his passing to Naples, offering to pay for provisions. He received a rough refusal from Signor Rans [Renzo da Ceri], at the instigation of the Pope, who had obtained for the recruiting of his army 300,000 ducats by creating eight new Cardinals. On Sunday, the 5th, Bourbon drew off his troops from Rome behind St. Peter's, pretending to cross the Tiber; but early on Monday, the 6th, while there was a great mist, he prepared to assault the town behind the Campo Santo at Thurion (Torrione, now Cavalleggieri) gate; and the said Sieur (Bourbon) was among the first to mount the walls, where four ensigns were planted. He was there wounded by artillery, (directed by Benvenuto Cellini,) and assisted to descend, and carried into a neighbouring chapel; but when the gate of Thurion was taken, he was conveyed to the church of Campo Santo. Captain Rans, who was on the walls with 4000 men, seeing that they retreated, as many men were killed by the artillery of the assailants, cried out that Bourbon, Orange, and four ensigns were taken, in order to encourage them to return to the wall. They, however, retreated to the Piazza di Santo Spirito; but Rans left them, and went to the castle of St. Angelo, where was the Pope, with five or six Cardinals. Cardinal SS. Quatuor, who was wounded, and Cardinal de Cesis, retired with Rans. The besiegers continued to advance ; and the Romans, seeing that Rans had deserted them, tried to escape, some jumping into the Tiber. The Imperialists killed everyone they met—men, women, and children. This lasted from the morning till 2 P.M., during which time Bourbon was killed. Before his death he confessed, received his Creator, and desired to be carried into Milan, although some think he meant Rome, for he was continually saying "à Rome, à Rome, à Rome." About two in the afternoon, the Imperialists took the gate of S. Pancras, where they encountered some resistance, and then began to pillage, which lasted at least ten or twelve days (or, according to other accounts, three or four days), without there being any resistance, except in three or four houses, which they mined and blew up. Many people had sent their goods, amounting to two millions of gold, to the house of the Portuguese ambassador ; but they were obliged to surrender on promise of their lives. They gave out that as soon as the city was taken, the Prince of Orange took possession of the Pope's palace, in which were lodged Cardinals Campeggi, Cibo, and Rodulpho. Both the Generals tried to stop the pillage, but unsuccessfully, though afterwards the Germans obeyed the Prince, and the Spaniards Captain D'Urbin.

Volumes (wrote Sanga to the Nuncio in England) would be required to describe but one of their misdeeds. They strewed on the ground the sacred body of Christ, took away the cup, and trod under foot the relics of the Saints to spoil their ornaments. No church nor monastery was spared. They violated nuns amid the cries of their mothers, burnt the most magnificent buildings, turned churches into stables, and made use of crucifixes and other images as marks for their harquebusses. It is no longer Rome, but Rome's grave. They dressed the old wooden crucifix, revered by all nations, which stood on one of the seven altars of S. Peter's, in the uniform of a lansknecht. S. Peter and S. Paul, who have lain so many years buried under the altar of S. Peter's, never suffered such indignities, even from those who made them martyrs.

The houses of nobles and Cardinals were sacked, even though the owners were reputed Imperialists. Five Cardinals of the party of the Emperor ransomed their houses at sums varying from 45,000 to 25,000 ducats each, making together 185,000 ducats; and after paying these ransoms, their houses were again plundered. No one was spared. The palace of Campeggi was rifled. The German and Spanish troops, but especially the German, many of whom were Lutherans, behaved with amazing cruelty. Many persons were tortured to compel them to reveal their treasures.

For months Clement VII. was a prisoner in S. Angelo. Negotiations were carried on between the Pope and the deputies of the Prince of Orange. It was proposed that his Holiness should pay 300,000 ducats; the Cardinals[*] with him, twelve in number, including Campeggi, 200,000 ducats; and certain merchants, 100,000 ducats. Also that the Pope and eight Cardinals should go as the Emperor's prisoners to Gaeta, and surrender Ostia, Civita Vecchia, Parma, Placentia, and Lucca; and that Cardinal Colonna, who entered four days after the capture, with 8000 men, should be made Vice-Pope!

These terms were rejected, and the Pope, hoping for aid from without, was inclined to refuse all negotiations. Campeggi, alone of the Cardinals, was for making further proposals; "for," said he, "it is not a simple commander of a fortress who is besieged, but a Prince on whom the common safety and the whole life of the Republic hangs: to whom, if any accident shall happen, to what condition will the Republic be reduced?"

---

[*] These included, besides Campeggi, Accolti, Archbishop of Ravenna; Gaddi, Bishop of Ferrara; Alexander Farnese, afterwards Paul III.; Franciotto Orsini; Cibo, nephew of Leo X.; Nicolo Rodolfi, nephew of Leo X.; Giovanni Salviati, nephew of Leo X.; Marco Cornaro, nephew of the Queen of Cyprus; the Cardinal SS. Quatuor, and Cardinal De Cesis. Jacopo Salviati, father of Cardinal Giovanni, was also in the castle during the seige.

Yielding to these arguments, the Pope agreed with the foe on the 6th of June, and gave himself into their hands, certain Cardinals being hostages, and a sum of money being promised. The German and Spanish troops were to guard the Pope until all the money should be paid, and the other conditions fulfilled. Campeggi was sent into the city as Legate, to rule it and try to keep down the excesses of the soldiers; and at this time he received the church of S. Maria in Trastevere for his title. On the same day, June the 6th, the Pope and Cardinal Farnese wrote letters, by Sir Gregory Casale, to Wolsey, to implore the aid of Henry VIII. And on the 7th of June Cardinal Campeggi writes to Wolsey from S. Angelo, saying :—That he writes by Casale, who had been with them at the siege of S. Angelo a month complete, and had rendered good service. Campeggi has been plundered of all he had, and has been compelled to redeem his life with a large sum of money. He wishes his collector in England to gather his rents and transmit them as soon as possible. Six other Cardinals wrote at same time to Wolsey, to implore assistance.

On the 15th of July, Clement VII. issued a bull from the castle of S. Angelo, referring to the Pope's personal danger from the plague during his imprisonment, some of the officers of his chamber having died of it; and empowering the Cardinals, in the event of his death taking place while in captivity, to meet in Bologna, Perugia, or Ancona, for the election of the future Pope; or, if these cities be under interdict, or in open rebellion against the Church, in Florence, Turin, or Mantua. The election may take place wherever a majority of the Cardinals agree that it shall be held. But if the See fall vacant when the Pope is away from Italy, the election is to take place at Rome, unless that city be in rebellion. In the first case, absent Cardinals are to be waited for, ten days; in the second, a month.

From letters of the 3rd of September, it appears it was intended to remove the Pope to Gaeta, and that the Spaniards had fortified themselves in the castle of S. Angelo, and were using great pains to prevent letters being carried to and from Rome.

On the 2nd of October, Laurentio Rodolfo writes from Rome to Cardinal Rodolfo :—" The Germans have re-entered Rome, and will not leave it unless they are paid 150,000 ducats. They have so terrified the people, that their demands are in part listened to, and when they could not get ready money, they have demanded hostages for security. The Pope is very indignant, and has resolved with his Cardinals neither to give hostages nor money, except in their own persons. Whilst they were deliberating, Alarcon (Governor of the castle) made his appearance, saying that the Germans had sworn to commit some great enormity, unless hostages were given to them immediately. The Pope, much moved, said he would not allow it, and shed so many tears that even his enemies were moved to pity him. Alarcon, with all his efforts, and by shutting the door, could scarcely prevent the Pope from joining us as a hostage. At last he suffered us to go. We were conducted honourably by the Spaniards, undergoing only the ceremonial punishment of being exhibited in the Campo de' Fiori, where the Germans had assembled in great tumult. Alarcon delivered us (the hostages) to the German band, and after we had been shown to the infantry, we were taken to the house of the Picard Massatosti, who treated us with great respect. Fears this gentle treatment will not last. They directed us to urge the Pope to pay the money, that we might the sooner be liberated. We replied that we were not hostages for money, but for observance of the terms made between the Pope and the Emperor, which provided that taxes should be imposed by commissioners on the states of the Church to the sum of 250,000 ducats ; and that the Imperialists were bound, if necessary, to see them levied, which it was impossible to do while the Pope was a prisoner. We are reconciled to perpetual imprisonment, as only death is worse than what we have suffered already."

Further news was brought by a person who was sent by Cardinal Triulzi from the castle of S. Angelo to Lautrec on the 7th of October.

The General of the Franciscan Order came from Spain to Rome, and told the Pope, in the Emperor's name, that he should be liberated on condition of holding a general council for the reformation of the Church. The Emperor demands for security, during the war in Italy, Civita Castellana, Orvieto, Forli, Bologna, and Ancona; a promise from the Pope that he will never oppose him; twelve hostages to be named by the Emperor; 200,000 crowns in two months, for the wages of the army, in addition to the 400,000 crowns granted at the first capitulation.

The Pope answered that he would agree to a council, but Christian princes must first agree with each other about the place where it shall be held. He would not promise about giving up the cities named, as he did not know whether they would be contented, and was sure they did not wish to be under Spanish rule. As to the hostages, he desired the General to name those whom the Emperor wished to have; and he would then give an answer. His Holiness said he was not bound to pay the money demanded, and if he was bound to pay it, he had agreed with the Vice-roy to pay it in two years, within which it was impossible.

A person who left the castle of S. Angelo on the 3rd of November, relates: The Pope had made an agreement with the Imperialists, and they had sent to Don Hugo for a ratification, which was expected in six days. The Pope is to give the lance knights 30,000 ducats, for one payment, and the same sum after they leave the city. He is to give the Spaniards 40,000 ducats, which are to be raised in Rome, and 240,000 ducats a month for four months; and 50,000 to the lance knights for three months. The benefices in the kingdom of

Naples are to be sold for 600,000 ducats, to be divided between the Pope and the Emperor, etc. The Imperialists wished to have carried off the Cardinals Campeggi, Triulzi and Pisa, because they would not agree to this treaty.

Although the Pope was kept prisoner in the most strong and straight place of the Castle, called the Rock, and although no one was allowed to see him without witnesses, yet letters and messages passed from the cardinals and others to their friends outside. Communications from the Castle, issued on the 13th, reached the Venetian ambassador and Sir Gregory Casale, and were written by the Cardinal of Pisa. It seems there was no hope of any agreement with the Imperialists, as the Pope could not procure the money demanded. An escape was now planned for His Holiness.

Benvenuto Cellini, by the Pope's order, had some time previously removed the jewels of the tiaras and stitched them into the dresses of the Pope and his chamberlain. The Pope was disguised as a merchant, and, leaving the Castle, was received by Luigi Gonzaga, called Rodomonte of Mantua, and some soldiers. Count Guido Rangoni had ready fifty swift horses. The Pope escaped on the night of the 7th of December, 1527, and fled away to Orvieto.

But although the Pope had escaped from imprisonment, his troubles were not ended. Henry VIII. had already demanded bulls for divorce, and dispensation to marry Anna Boleyn. To grant the divorce was to further exasperate Charles V., the nephew of Queen Katherine; to refuse it, was to incur the bitter resentment of Henry. Agents of the English King had pressed for a favourable answer from the Pope when a captive, and now that he was free they became still more importunate. Wolsey desired that he himself and an English ecclesiastic should be commissioned by his Holiness to decide the matter without appeal, and various bulls and dispensations were submitted to the Pope, which he refused to sign unless with alterations rendering them useless for the King's purpose. Henry vainly tried to intimidate the Pope by threats that if he refused, the consequence would be the withdrawal of Henry's favour and the loss of England to Catholicism. Clement professed his earnest desire to satisfy the King if possible, and consented to send a Legate to England to hear the cause. Henry was impatient, and on the 27th of December, 1527, wrote asking that Campeggi or Cardinal Trano or Farnese might be sent without delay. "Tell the Pope," he wrote to Sir Gregory Casale, "that haste is of the utmost importance and delays are dangerous. Urge the Cardinal who is appointed to make diligent speed, and tell him he shall be liberally provided for. Let him not excuse himself for want of money." On the 13th of January, 1528, Sir Gregory Casale writes from Orvieto :—The Pope will consent to send whomsoever Casale shall nominate—Campeggi, Cesarini, etc. Campeggi would be the most suitable, but cannot leave Rome immediately, unless Lautrec advances. On the 22nd of February, Casale announces that the Imperialists had quitted Rome on the 17th, and that Campeggi is set at liberty, and that all who belong to the Court are going back to Rome. On the 26th of February, Casale writes to Wolsey from Orvieto :—" Wrote to Campeggi that, when the city is restored to liberty, he can depart and leave some one in his place as Governor of Rome. Asked whether he would go to England, if there were occasion ; to which he answered, that he should be much pleased to revisit the King and yourself." On the 1st of March, Casale again writes from Orvieto, stating that he had spoken to Campeggi, pressing him to go to England. On the 13th of April, 1528, Gardiner and Casale wrote at great length from Orvieto to Wolsey, describing their repeated attempts to worry the Pope into compliance. They say there is no Cardinal here, except Campeggi, fit for this Legation. On the 11th of May, Wolsey urges Campeggi to set out at once, and not to grudge the trouble of the journey. Again, on the 23rd of May, Wolsey tells Campeggi :—Both the King and myself were much pleased at the Pope choosing him as Legate. While eagerly expecting him, received letters from Casale and Gardiner, saying that his journey was delayed by the gout, by his duties as Legate at Rome, and by the difficulty of procuring horses and servants. Presses him to make haste. Gardiner will supply him with money. Advises him to come with few attendants, and let the others follow. He will find horses, mules, money, and all he wants, ready for him in France. Wolsey will cross the sea to conduct him to England. Hopes that his gout is not bad enough to prevent his journey. The Pope will, without delay, appoint a Vice-Legate at Rome. Would not urge haste, but that both the King and Council think it necessary for him to be Wolsey's colleague. Promises him ample recompense. Fears the King may think that the Pope wishes to gratify the Emperor by offending him, and that what has been reported of Campeggi is true. If Campeggi values the King's favour, if he is grateful for benefits, if he thinks Wolsey can ever be of service to him, if he wishes the authority of the Church to be undiminished, he must start on his journey at once, for it cannot be delayed longer without irreparable harm. On the same day, Wolsey wrote to Casale, urging him, if Campeggi is ill, to send any other Cardinal who is fit.

In spite of all these urgent appeals, the commission to Wolsey and Campeggi to examine and decide on the validity of the King's marriage without appeal, was not issued until the 8th of June, 1528, from Viterbo, and that after many altercations with—and promises made to—the Pope.

Letters from Viterbo, of the 13th of June, relate that Campeggi has come hither from Rome to go to England in the cause of the divorce. He stays here, awaiting an answer from Genoa to a request for a galley to carry him to Marseilles; but if it do not come, he will go by land.

Casale writes from Viterbo on the 15th of June, 1528, about the divorce. The Pope seemed to refer the matter to Campeggi and would do nothing without his counsel, so that it was of the utmost importance to prepare him. He is now most anxious to accommodate himself to the King's will. Got him to give up his journey to Bologna, where he would have wasted time. He will travel by post horses, if the gout permits him, by the road we would wish for speed. Having crossed the sea from Corneto to Marseilles, he can make the journey in three days. Has sent Baptista to ask Andrea Doria for two galleys in the name of the Pope and the French ambassador, to conduct the Legate from Corneto. A good deal of tact will be necessary to get them, as he is afraid of more Germans coming to Genoa. Baptista will endeavour to get them *securas et non pestiferas*. Meanwhile, Campeggi will make his will, and arrange to go to Portus Veneris or Leghorn if the galleys are not sent to Corneto. We have got the President of Provence, the French ambassador here, to write that everything may be ready for him at Marseilles. If the galleys cannot be had, he will go by land, and has arranged to procure clothes at Avignon.

Cardinal Campeggi embarked at Corneto on the 25th of July, 1528, for Marseilles, and from thence proceeded by land to Lyons, where Dr. Stephens met him with horses. He was expected to leave Lyons on the 31st of August, and the Bishop of Bath, Dr. Clerk, then in Paris, borrowed of the Pope's Legate to France "a fair well trimmed and furnished mule and four carriage mules; the which, with 20 horses of mine own and four carriage mules also of mine own, and ten horses of the Master of the Rolls," were sent forward to Orleans for the use of Campeggi.

On the 14th of September, 1528, Campeggi arrived at Paris. The Legate, Cardinal Salviati, with a goodly company, met him some three miles outside Paris; and fifteen or sixteen Bishops and Archbishops met him at the gates. Clerk and Tayler offered him money, which he refused, saying he would take nothing except horses and mules for his journey. He had a long audience on the 15th with the King of France, who treated him with much respect, and kept him in conversation more than two hours. Campeggi was visited by the Cardinal of Bourbon, the Duke of Albany, and many noblemen.

On the 16th of September, Campeggi wrote to Wolsey from Paris, acknowledging letters, and stating that he cannot sit on horseback and will require a litter and other conveniences, and must stay in Paris two or three days.

On the same day, he wrote to Giacomo Salviati, the Pope's Secretary:—On the 8th (of September), at Orleans, I received yours of the 21st of August, and, on the 13th, your second letter of the 28th. Since then I have arrived in Paris, and received yours of the 3rd by the hands of the Legate here. I will say nothing of my journey and its perils, or of my infirmity. My negotiation proceeds smoothly. As you recommend, I will endeavour to give no cause for scandal. These [English] ambassadors urge me to depart. The Bishop of Bath returns with me to England, and Dr. Tayler remains here. Master (Sir) Francis Brian, of the King's chamber, is here; he came many days ago to accompany me to England. In order to obtain a litter, and to get some clothes made, I shall not depart hence for two days. As to proceeding prudently, I will follow your instructions and what I know to be the Pope's mind. I promised him that I would exert all my powers to move [the King from his determination]. As to not binding myself, or giving any promise, his Holiness may trust to my fidelity. Neither with all his kingdom, nor with all his treasure, will he [the King] be able to cause me to deviate from my duty. I will be careful, when speaking with him, not to promise any sentence. If you mean to say that I am to do nothing whatever without informing the Pope, I do not see how, in case it should be impossible to shake the King's opinion, the trial can be avoided without scandal. They would think I had come to hoodwink them, and might resent it. You know how much that would involve. But, so far as the sentence itself is concerned, I will observe all your instructions, and they shall never learn my opinion until I am about to give judgment,—that is to say, if the cause should proceed so far.

Campeggi, on the 18th of September, was "seven leagues out of Paris in a horse litter, troubled with the gout all the way." On the 19th (Saturday), he was to be at Clermont, another seven leagues. He was to reach Breteuil on Sunday, Amiens on Monday, Abbeyville on Tuesday, Motrell on Wednesday, Boulogne on Thursday, and Calais on Friday. On the 24th of September, Bishop Clerk writes to Wolsey from Mottreul [Montreuil] :—" My lord Cardinal Campegius, ever since our departing from Paris, hath been very sore troubled with the gout in both hands and also somewhat in his feet, and for all that he hath put himself to as much pain as was possible. Without tarrying or sojourning any day, thanked be God, he has arrived here in Moottrell, still carried in a litter, for he cannot ride, his feet being not able to abide the sqwasse of the stirrup, ne his hands to hold the bridle, as more plainly Sir Francis Bryan will inform your Grace, who hath right well done his part here, I assure your Grace, in assisting diligently and conducting the said Cardinal, as in providing him, from time to time, horses for his carriage," etc.

On Monday, September 28, Campeggi was at Calais, and they intended to cross the channel on the morrow, if the wind was favourable. Campeggi still suffered from gout, and as the horse litter he used when coming from Paris had to be sent back, the Archbishop of Canterbury* had consented to lend

---

* The Archbishop of Canterbury, Dr. Warham, was now an invalid and disinclined for much exertion. He wrote from Otforde to Wolsey on the 21st of September, 1528, to say he had received Wolsey's letters, bidding him to receive the Legate Campegius and accompany him to Rochester. He was at Canterbury lately, intending to stay there most of the winter, but was obliged for his health's sake to remove. He fears that if he went thither now or in October, at which time he is usually troubled with his old disease in his head, he would not escape without extreme danger. In spite of all precautions he feels signs of it, and he fears that after the shaking in his horse litter he should not be able to do anything. Would be right glad to wait on the said Legate, but it would not be meet for him

his own horse litter to Campeggi for the journey between Dover and Canterbury. Campeggi, on the 1st of October, wrote from Canterbury to the King and Wolsey, saying that he had crossed over from Calais on the 29th, and had a prosperous voyage, but was very ill of the gout and much shattered. His brother Antonio takes these letters.

Campeggi was received at Canterbury, on the 30th of September, by Sir Francis Bryan, the Bishop of Chichester, the Archbishop of Canterbury, the Mayor and Aldermen, the Prior of Christchurch, the Abbot of St. Austins, a Suffragan Bishop in pontificals, friars, and others.

On Monday, the 5th of October, Campeggi arrived at Dartford, being provided with a litter sent by Wolsey. He arrived at Dartford at ten in the morning, and rested there that day, "for he can in no wise labour after his dinner." He was sore vexed since leaving Canterbury. Clerk wrote to Wolsey, that the Legate is very ill appointed for wine. That sent was very bad. On the 6th of October, the Cardinal was at Lewisham. In a letter to Salviati, dated 17th of October, 1528, Campeggi says :—When I arrived within four miles of London, I wrote to Di Feltro. On Wednesday, the 7th of October, I reached the suburbs of London, and lodged at the house of the Duke of Suffolk. It was arranged that my entry should be made publicly the next day, and the Cardinal of York was to take part in it. But I was so prostrated by the gout, that I could not travel any further, either in a litter or on horseback. So I remained in the Duke's house all the next day, and in the evening the Cardinal conveyed me to the river, and I proceeded in a barge to the lodging assigned to me—namely, Bath House —without any noise or pomp. I have remained there till this present time, and am confined to bed, my agony being greater

---

to go in a litter while the other rode on horseback. He asks, therefore, to be excused, and desires credence for his steward, whom he sends. Dr. Warham, however, was obliged to attend in person on Campeggi.

than usual, owing to the journey. I do not know when I shall be sufficiently free from pain to be able to visit the King. The following day, Wolsey came to see me. I had believed and hoped that he would not discuss any business with me; but he entered immediately into the cause of my coming. . . . .

The King, being desirous to give me audience, removed to his palace here in London on the river, not far distant from my lodging. Although I could neither ride nor walk, and could not sit without discomfort, I was compelled on the 22nd of October to go for my first audience. I was warmly received and welcomed by his Majesty. The ambassadors and all the prelates and princes of the kingdom were assembled in a large hall. Public audience was given us, and, in the name of us two Legates, my secretary, Floriano, made an appropriate speech. Dr. Fox replied. The King then withdrew with us into another chamber, where I presented the Pope's letter.

Bath Place, where Campeggi was lodged, was the London residence of the Bishop of Bath, Dr. Clerk, who was by no means pleased to be obliged to vacate it for the Cardinal. Dr. Clerk wrote on the 18th of September to Dr. Stephen Gardiner, saying :—If there is no remedy but that the Cardinal must lie in my house, I must take it patiently. It is strange, that as there are other houses better than mine, men cannot be contented with them. I should like to know where I am to lodge. My lord's Grace must give his commandment to the owners, or else my folks will not be admitted. Again he writes on same day to Gardiner :—" I assur you that lewd knave Jamys (Giacomo, Campeggi's chamberlain,) that nevyr ded good, hath so paynted Norwyche Place to the Cardynall, that it seemyth that logyng hym ther ye wold have logyd hym in a pygge stye." He must, therefore, be lodged in Bath Place ; but Duresme Place would doubtless have been better, as it is a goodlier house than Bath Place. If Wolsey cannot spare Durham Place, or otherwise disposes of Bath Place, Gardiner must ask Wolsey for some convenient lodging for Clerk, as it would grieve him to be turned out of his own, unless it were the King's and Wolsey's pleasure. Asks Gardiner to find out Wolsey's wish, and let Clerk's people know. Knows Campeggi would be better lodged at Durham Place, but would not tell him so here, as he would think he did not wish to let him have his house. On the 14th of October, 1528, a warrant was issued to Sir Andrew Windesore, Master of the Great Wardrobe, to deliver for the use of the Legate of Rome 12 feather beds and bolsters, 24 pairs of sheets, 12 pairs of blankets, and 12 counterpoints.

The situation of Campeggi may be imagined from the secret instructions he had received from the Pope through Sanga, that he was "not to proceed to sentence under any pretext, without express commission; but to protract the matter as long as possible, if haply God shall put into the King's heart some holy thought, so that he may not desire from his Holiness a thing which cannot be granted without injustice, peril, and scandal."

On the 23rd of October, after dinner, the King visited Campeggi privately, and the interview lasted four hours. Campeggi exhorted his Majesty not to attempt this matter of divorce, but, in order to confirm and clear his conscience, to establish the succession of the kingdom and to avoid scandals; and said that if he had any scruples, he could have a new dispensation. Campeggi was convinced that the King wanted a divorce and was so certain of the nullity of the marriage with Katherine, that nothing could make him believe the contrary.

On the 26th of October, Campeggi writes to Salviati, the Pope's Secretary, saying: These people warmly insist on the affair being despatched with all celerity; but it is necessary that the Pope should take some resolution, and write what I am to do, in such a manner that I may exhibit it, so as to leave no burden on my shoulders; for I am unable, being here, to defend myself from their constant solicitation. At Christmas all the barons and prelates of the kingdom are to be here for this "expedition," and therefore this movement cannot be suspended without peril. Again I humbly implore that such a reply may be given me that I may be able to breathe freely. You may judge of my condition, when, in addition to bodily indisposition, I find myself in an infinite agitation of mind. For twenty days I have had the gout in one of my knees, so that I am unable to use it without great pain.

Yesterday I wrote thus far. This morning at daybreak, being in bed not a little tormented with the gout, the Cardinal of York came to visit me, and gave me to understand that the King had spoken with the Queen, who had demanded of him foreign councillors, proctors and advocates, and that the King had granted her for councillors the Archbishop of Canterbury, the bishops of Rochester, Bath and London, and others. He will not agree to her having a Spaniard. Then the Cardinal told me the Queen had asked permission of the King to come and confess to me ; which he had granted. Accordingly at 9 o'clock, the second hour of the day, she came privately and was with me for a long space. Although she told me all under the seal of confession, yet she gave me liberty, indeed she besought me, to write to our Lord, the Pope, certain resolutions, etc. Campeggi urged her to enter into religion and to remove all difficulty, but she refused, and her obstinacy in not accepting this sound council did not much please Campeggi.

On the 28th of October, Campeggi wrote in the same strain to Sanga, and said, in the end of his letter : In my last conversation with Wolsey, he repeated many times (in Latin) ; "Most reverend Lord, beware lest, in like manner as the greater part of Germany, owing to the harshness and severity of a certain Cardinal, has become estranged from the Apostolic See and from the Faith, it may be said that another cardinal has given the same occasion to England with the same result." He (Wolsey) often impresses upon me that if this (divorce) is not granted, the authority of the See Apostolic in this kingdom will be annihilated ; and he certainly proves himself very zealous for its preservation—having done and still doing for it very great services—because all his grandeur is connected with it.

On Saturday November 24, 1528, Wolsey and Campeggi visited the Queen, and suggested that she might remove all difficulties by entering into religion, and thus leaving the King free to marry again. By this course she would lose nothing, for the King's affection was already lost to her, and she would secure the peace of Christendom, her own rank as a princess, and the succession to her daughter, in the event of Henry having no male issue by a subsequent marriage. The Queen obstinately refused these offers.

Sir Francis Bryan and Peter Vannes were now (Nov. 28) sent to Rome to induce the Pope to condemn as forged or inefficient the dispensation granted by Pope Julius, and to inquire whether the Pope will dispense with the King to have two wives, making the children of the second marriage legitimate as well as those of the first; whereof some great reasons and precedents, especially of the Old Testament, appear.

These repeated applications to His Holiness failed to change the mind of the Pope, who, while desirous to please the King in all things possible, professed himself unable to do anything contrary to justice and the honour of the Holy See.

At last on the 31st of May, 1529, the Legatine Court was opened in the Parliament chamber, near the Convent of the Friars Preachers, and the Legates summoned the King and Queen to appear before them on the 18th of June, between 9 and 10 am.

On the 16th of June Campeggi informs Salviati that the Queen on the previous day "came to visit me, even to my bedside, owing to my gout, which is accompanied by a slight feverishness, she being very anxious and perplexed about her affairs. The cause of her coming was to tell me that her advocates, who ought to have come from Flanders, had not come, because, it seemed, the Emperor had given them to understand that he did not wish them to do so, as the place is not safe." Consequently the Queen found herself without any one to plead for her; for although she had certain other English councillors assigned her by the King, it was easy to believe that they would in every thing have greater regard to the King's pleasure than to her necessity. She therefore requested my aid and counsel. In reply, I exhorted her to keep a good heart, to rely upon the King's justice, and upon the conscience and learning of those prelates who have been assigned to her for councillors, and to rest sure that nothing inconsistent with justice and reason would be done by us Legates. She did not accede in the least to Campeggi's hints of taking vows.

On Friday, June 18, the Court met a second time, and the Queen appeared in person and protested against the jurisdiction of the Cardinals, who cited the Queen to re-appear before them on Monday the 21st of June, to hear their decision. On the 21st the Queen again protested against the jurisdiction of the Legates, and appealed to the Pope himself. On the refusal of the Cardinals to admit her protest, she left the Court.

On the 17th of July, 1529, the Pope revoked the commission to the Cardinals, and on the 23rd, Cardinal Campeggi adjourned the Cause to Rome. On the 29th of August and on the 1st of September, the Pope wrote to Henry VIII., to Wolsey and Campeggi, advoking the King's cause to Rome.

Campeggi was now anxious to leave England, and on the 14th of September went with Wolsey to see the King and endeavour to take farewell, as he had had his recall. Du Bellay, writing to Montmorency, says he thinks Campeggi will obtain permission and be off as soon as possible. Du Bellay, in a letter to the same, dated September 18, says that Campeggi expected to leave within ten or twelve days, and adds: I think they would like to treat him at his departure rather more graciously than they had intended to do, hoping that there may be some change at Rome, if the Emperor treat the Pope as badly as they expect he will; so that Campeggi might still be of use to them, or at least not do them injury, as he would if ill-treated at his departure.

On the 22nd of September, 1529, Cardinal Campeggi gave license to Wolsey to take timber from the manor of Sonnyng, Berks, for his college at Oxford, and also confirmed Wolsey as his Proctor in the diocese of Salisbury.

Henry VIII., on the 30th of September, 1529, writes to the Pope: On the return to your Holiness of Cardinal Campeggi, we could have wished, not less for your sake than our own, that all things had been so expedited as to have corresponded to our expectations, not rashly conceived but owing to your promises. As it is, we are compelled to regard with grief and wonder the incredible confusion which has arisen. If the Pope can relax divine laws at his pleasure, surely he has as much power over human laws. Complains that he has been often deceived by the Pope's promises, on which there is no dependence to be placed; and that his dignity has not been consulted in the treatment he has received. If the Pope, as his ambassadors write, will perform what he has promised, and keep the cause now advoked to Rome in his own hands, until it can be decided by impartial judges, and in an indifferent place, in a manner satisfactory to the King's scruples, he will forget what is past, and repay kindness by kindness, as Campeggi will explain.

On the 7th of October, 1529, Campeggi writes to Salviati:—I suspect that my letters have been intercepted . . . I was requested by the Cardinal of York to repair to a town of his called the More, where he has a very fine palace. I went there accordingly. On the day following my arrival, which was on the 5th ult., two breves were sent from the King's court to the Cardinal, both of the same date, I think the 19th of July,—the one concerning the federation made with the Emperor, the other concerning the citation. Seeing that both contained credentials for me, and that no other letters appeared, I was somewhat annoyed. All diligence was used to discover them, but there was no order, and they excused themselves, saying that they had not reached their hands. . . . This done, I sent to request an audience of the King, which was deferred a week, owing to the arrival at that time of an ambassador from the Emperor. Meanwhile, the duplicates arrived of your letters of 19 and 23 July, continued to August 1. The originals, which you announce having dispatched with the "capitulation," had never reached me. I repaired, therefore, to the King at the appointed time. . . . Whatever it may be, as his Majesty is of this opinion, and is persuaded by others that the marriage is null by divine law, his mind cannot but be somewhat enraged and disappointed because the affair has not succeeded to his liking. In other things, the King's mind is good. He has told me, with apparent sincerity, that he would never fail to be a most Christian King and a good Defender of the Faith ; and that, though all the world should prove false, he himself would never fail in doing service as a good Christian King. In this conversation I alluded to the Lutheran affairs, and to this Parliament which is about to be holden, and I earnestly pressed upon him the liberty of the Church. He certainly seemed to me very well disposed to exert his power to the utmost. . . . Lastly, he gave me a kind dismissal. On returning home, I was attacked with a pain in the side, together with the gout, which have tortured me ceaselessly for ten days ; in which, however, I have collected my baggage, and I departed on the 5th [of October] from London. To-day I reached Canterbury.

On the 12th of October, the Bishop of Bayonne, writing to Francis I., says in a post-script :—Campeggi is still at Dover, and I have just heard that, on pretence of want of ships, they will not let him pass, without consulting about it, for fear he carries off the treasure of the Cardinal of York.

Chapuys, in a letter to Charles V., describes the outrage on Campeggi thus :—It was feared that Cardinal Wolsey would get his goods out of the country, and therefore a strict watch was kept at the ports; and the watch insisted on opening the coffers of Cardinal Campeggi, notwithstanding his passport, and, on his refusal, broke open the locks. He said they had done him great wrong to suppose that he could be corrupted by the Cardinal, since he had been proof against the innumerable presents offered him by the King.

Cardinal Campeggi, of course, protested against this uncourteous treatment, more fitting for a criminal than an ambassador; and in reply, the King wrote to him the following letter, dated from Windsor, the 22nd of October, 1529:— I have read your latter letters, in which you complain grievously of the disrespect shown to the Pontifical dignity, and the violation of your Legatine authority, because certain porters of ours have examined your baggage; and a rumour has prevailed that you and the Cardinal of York had been guilty of collusion in our cause; and that you would not leave England until this calumny had been cleared up, and satisfaction given for so atrocious a wrong.

I cannot sufficiently wonder—proceeds the King—that your wisdom should exaggerate such minute offences, and take such dire offence, as though it were in my power to anticipate the temerity of the mob, or the excessive officiousness of others in discharge of their duty. As to your Legateship, no wrong has been done by me or mine, seeing that your authority only extended so far as to the termination of my cause, and when that was revoked by Papal inhibition, it had expired; and neither I nor my subjects acknowledge that you have any other authority. I wonder that you are so ignorant of the laws of this kingdom that you were not afraid to make use of the title of Legate when it became defunct, seeing that you are a bishop here, and so bound by the most solemn obligation to observe and respect my royal dignity, jurisdiction, prerogative, etc.

As to the business of the porters, long before your return into Italy they had received orders to allow no one to pass on any legal suspicion, even with our letters patent, without diligent examination of their baggage. As we had no intention that this should prove an annoyance to you, nor hinder your journey, or cause you any loss, we request that you will take this in good part; and we regret that greater caution and prudence was not shown by the officers in discharge of their duty. As it was done in fulfilment of their oath, we trust you will not consider them deserving of punishment. You will do us wrong if you think the worse for this fact.

As to the other part of your complaint, touching the rumour which has arisen, it would be hopeless for you to stay here in the expectation of removing it by any process. A wise man will pay no attention to ordinary rumours. You may infer from it that my subjects are not very well pleased that my cause has come to no better conclusion. I shall have reason to doubt your faith and the integrity of your friendship when your words and professions so little agree.

Campeggi did not cross the sea till the 26th of October, owing to the various hindrances which met him between London and Dover. But before he crossed, he had learned that Cardinal Wolsey had been deprived of the Seal and of the management of all affairs, and of a great part of his servants; and that an inquiry was being made respecting his money and other possessions, with very evident signs of his tending ruin. Campeggi thought that Wolsey had done nothing in the past, so far as ecclesiastical matters are concerned, to merit such disgrace.

On the 4th of November, 1529, Campeggi arrived at Paris, and had audience of the French King on the 8th, and on the day following set out for Italy.

In January, 1530, Campeggi, the Pope, and the Emperor were all at Bologna, where the Emperor's coronation took place on the 24th of February. On the 21st of March, Croke reported that the King's friends were like to lose many by the solicitation of Campeggi, who procures for the Queen against the King all the friends he can. On the 27th of March, the Bishop of Tarbes wrote to Francis I., announcing the departure of the Emperor from Bologna, and saying :—The Pope will leave on Monday next for Rome. Campeggi is going with the Emperor as Legate. He shows great desire to do you service, and would be a good means of intimating to the Emperor anything you would not wish should appear to come from you.

The Diet at Augsburg commenced on the 19th of June, 1530: Cardinal Campeggi, as Papal Legate, took part in it, and wrote from thence to Henry VIII. on the 28th of June, saying :—Certain Princes of Germany, who favour Luther, produced their propositions, feeble, and to say the truth, not fit to be listened to. Were it not for the obstinacy of the heretics, he would be in good hope of bringing them back to the way of Christ. The piety of the Emperor and Ferdinand is a great encouragement. The proceedings of Henry, though so far away, had much contributed ; and the reports of his burning the books of heretics, which have much added to his renown, and strengthened others.

Clement VII., in order to further mark his sense of the value of Campeggi's services, issued on the 3rd of May, 1530, a brief for investing him with the Lordship of Dozza, or Doccia, a feudal estate with a castle built on the rock, formerly belonging to Imola, and bringing to its possessor the title of Count. In the Rock is a chamber once adorned with tapestry, which was given to Lorenzo Campeggi by Henry VIII. (See Appendix.)

Cardinal Campeggi, about the year 1531, seems to have been deprived by Henry VIII. of the English Protectorate, for Augustine de Augustinis, Campeggi's physician, writing on the 3rd of June, 1531, to the Duke of Norfolk, says :—After Campeggi had recovered from his gout, he had a long interview with the Emperor. He told me that his mind was entirely set upon justice. He said this, after he had been deprived of the Protectorate, at which he is very much grieved, and thinks it was done at the suggestion of the Casalis. A successor to him in this office was not immediately appointed, for on the 20th of March, 1532, Cardinal de Trani was seeking the nomination, and the King was inclined to get either Cardinal de Monte or de Trani as Protector, if Cardinal Farnese would not accept the post. The matter was still undecided on April 29, 1532.

On the 24th of December, 1532, Augustine, writing to Cromwell, says :—The Pope, on the 19th day after he had left the city (Rome), came to this town, Bologna. He was mounted on a Turkish horse and wore a red cloak. The Emperor arrived on Friday, the 13th, and was met at seven miles distance by the Cardinals, who waited two hours for his arrival. The Emperor, when received by the Pope, knelt down to kiss his toe, which the Pope would not permit. When the Emperor entered the church and saw Campeggi in the throng, he turned some steps out of the way to embrace him, and asked after his health.

On the same day, Nicholas Hawkins, writing to Henry VIII. from Bologna, says :—" The Emperor hath given Campegius a bishopric, and at his coming now to Bologna, came to him sitting among the Cardinals, and did him great honour and reverence," etc.

In 1533, March 6, Campeggi writes from Bologna to Henry VIII. to thank him for his letter assuring him of the King's favour. He hopes nothing will ever deprive him of the conscience of having served Henry with faith and zeal.

In June of this year (1533), Dr. Benet, writing from Rome on the 13th, says :—" The Consistory being held this day. . . Cardinal de Monte took the King's part, and shewed himself rather your protector than otherwise, where[as] Campegius, your Protector, did it not so earnestly."

And in June, or July, 1533, the King writes to Boner :— " And where[as], as ye write in your said letters, [of June 19, but not found,] ye be secretly informed of the unkind and ingrate dealing and proceeding of Cardinal Campeggius against us, who, of good congruence, and in manner, as the case standeth, of duty, ought not, of all others, to be our adversary, as well for that he hath been of long time in visage, countenance, and demonstration, our friend, and hath been promoted and beneficed by us, as specially for that he is our Protector, whereby he endureth, as it were, our own person for the defence of us and our realm, in all matters to be there treated touching the same."

On the 25th of March, 1534, sentence was pronounced in the King's divorce case, establishing the validity of the marriage with Katherine. Henry VIII., enraged at his failure to gain over the Roman Court, vented his anger upon Campeggi and those whom he supposed to have been backward in supporting his cause. Cardinal Wolsey had been long ago punished for presumed remissness, and was dead. Cardinals Campeggi and Ghinucci held English bishoprics, and were so far in his power. Campeggi was deprived of Salisbury on the 21st of March, 1534, according to Hardy's Le Neve, where it says the deprivation was effected by Act of Parliament. Other accounts give the date as March 11, 1535. Cardinal Ghinucci was deprived of the Worcester bishopric about the same time, his successor, Hugh Latimer, having been consecrated for that See in September, 1535.

The connection of Campeggi with Salisbury appears briefly as follows :—The Papal Bulls were dated December 2, 1524, and he got Restitution of Temporalities on January 11, 1525. According to the Sarum Register of " Laurentii de Campegio," there were but four institutions to benefices in 1524, and none were in the Bishop's gift. Thomas Benet was Vicar-General. In 1530, Campeggi made appointments to two livings, the second of them being that of West Kyngton, which he gave to Hugo Latymer. In 1531, the Bishop disposed of five livings, all to Englishmen. In 1533, he gave four benefices, all to Englishmen, excepting one, the Prebend of Highworth, which was given to Guido Jenetto.

In 1534 begins the Register of " Thomas Benet, LL.D.,

Vicar in Spiritualities, by commission of Henry VIII." The Register of Nicholas Shaxton begins in 1535.

Cardinal Campeggi made an effort, in 1536, to regain the favour of Henry VIII. On the 5th of June, 1536, he wrote from Rome to the Duke of Suffolk, to say that he had sent his brother, Mark Antony, [Bishop of Grosseto] to England, on his affairs, and wishes the kind favour of the Duke in his brother's behalf. The instructions given on this occasion to his brother were probably intercepted by the King's agents, as the originals are now preserved in the British Museum, and a Latin copy of them is extant in the State Paper Office in London. Mark Antony was to ask a safe conduct to England, and to request an interview with Henry or his councillors. He was to try whether it would be of any use for Lorenzo Campeggi to supplicate the King to restore to him the revenues of Salisbury, and make his brother agent and proctor to receive them, or at least to retain the revenues in the hands of officials and responsible receivers. Mark Antony was to remind Henry of the Council to be held the next year at Mantua, at which it would be useful to the King to have Campeggi again as Protector. Campeggi's friends were the Dukes of Norfolk and Suffolk, the Bishops of Bath, Durham and Winchester, and Polidore Vergil. If Mark Antony wanted a man to go first to England to get the safe conduct, and engage lodgings, Lorenzo recommended for this purpose "Gerardus Buoncourt, Canon of S. Paul in Liege, formerly my Master of the Stables, and now resident in Leige," who knows the English language.

It is needless to state that this attempt to conciliate Henry, and regain the bishopric of Salisbury, was unavailing.

Paul III., in a bull dated October 8, 1537, convoked a general council to meet at Vicenza, on May 1, 1538, nominating three Legates, Cardinals Campeggi, Simonetti, and Aleandro, to preside at the opening ; but no bishops attended, and the council was suspended.

Two years later the career of Lorenzo Campeggi drew to its

close. He had long suffered from gout and rheumatism, and in July, 1539, was attacked with dysentry. The last will and testament of Cardinal Lorenzo Campeggi, Bishop of Palestrina, bears date the 19th of July, Saturday, 1539, and was signed in palazzo Trastyberino, testator's usual residence. He left his eldest son, Count Rodolfo, General of the Venetian forces, his heir, [who died in 1545 without male heirs] and mentioned his sons, Alexander, Bishop of Bologna, and Giambattista, Bishop of Majorca. He also mentioned two daughters and a niece Paula, daughter of his brother Antonio Maria Campeggi, and wife to John Philip Malvezzi. He charged his brother, Thomas, Bishop of Feltre, and his son Alexander, Archbishop of Bologna, to bury him in the church of S. Maria in Trastevere,*

---

* In the outer vestibule of S. Maria in Trastevere, on a sarcophagus, with, on the top, a pediment for a bust, is the following inscription :—

D. O. M.
LAUREN ET ALEX
CAMPEGGIOR. BONONIEN.
S. R. E.
CARDINALIUM
OSSA.

LAURENTIO CAMPEGGIO. EP. CARD. TIT. BASIL. HUJUS QUI MATURA ÆTATE SACRIS INITIATUS ATQUE IN COLL. PATRUM PURPURATOR. OB MERITA ADSCITUS LEGATIONIBUS GERMANICA ET ANGLICA ALIISQUE PUBLICIS MUNERIBUS EGREGIE FUNCTUS DECESSIT VIII KAL. AUG A. MDXXXIX ANNOS NATUS LXVII. ITEMQUE ALEXANDRO F. EJUS PRESB. CARD. TIT. S. LUCLE AD SEPTEM SOLIA QUEM PRUDENTIA RERUM GERENDAR. DOCTRINA FAMA RELIGIONIS PROPAGANDÆ STUDIO FLORENTEM MORS INTERCEPIT XI KAL. ACT. MDLIV ÆT SUÆ XLVII.

Underneath in smaller letters :—

HORUM COMMUNE SEPULCRUM CUM PAVIMENTUM BASIL. RESTITUERETUR FORTUITO REPERTUM EX CONLAT. MARCH. ÆMILII ET CAROLI MALVEZZI CAMPEGG. BONON. HEREDUM PRÆFECTI NOVOV. OPER. LOCO ILLUSTRI STATUENDUM ET EXORNANDUM CURARUNT A. MDCCCLXVIII.

The remains of Cardinal Lorenzo were never removed to Bologna. The Cardinal's eldest son, Count Rodolfo, who died in 1545, was buried in the Church of S. Proculo in Bologna.

and to remove his body afterwards to Bologna, to the Church of S. Procolo. He named in his will some six or seven nieces or grand-daughters. He died on the 25th of July, 1539, and was buried in the Church of S. Maria in Trastevere, of which he had been the titular Cardinal. Two days before Campeggi's death, the Pope gave the administration of Salisbury to Cardinal Contarini.

Lorenzo had one uncle, two brothers, and two sons, bishops, and one of these sons became a Cardinal. Thus five of the Campeggi family were mitred, and four of them were at the Council of Trent.

The palace in the Borgo became the property of the male children of Cardinal Lorenzo; and Cardinal Alexander, his son, dying in 1554, bequeathed his portion of it, with the furniture and plate, to his cousin John, Archbishop of Bologna, who died in 1563, leaving his brothers Vincenzo, Baldassare, and Annibale, his residuary legatees. Giambattista, Bishop of Majorca, another son of Cardinal Lorenzo, sold his portion on 22nd January, 1555, to John, Archbishop of Bologna, for 2,500 scudi.

On the 9th of June, 1561, Counts Vincenzo and Lorenzo Campeggi leased the Palace in the Borgo to Cardinal Tolomeo Galli.

In February, 1607, the Campeggi family determined to sell the Palace in the Borgo, and Battista Volta was chosen as Proctor for Count Rodolfo, Count Antonio and Count Lorenzo Campeggi. Count Rodolfo by deeds dated March 8, and 29, 1608, purchased one third part of the palace for 2,117 scudi, from Count Girolamo, the last descendant of Count Vincenzo, and thus had two parts. The remaining third belonged to Counts Antonio and Lorenzo, sons of Count Annibale Campeggi. Rodolfo was son of Count Baldassare. And Counts Vincenzo, Baldassare and Annibale were all sons of Antonio Maria Campeggi, Senator of Bologna, and brother to Cardinal Lorenzo, whose son Rodolfo had no male issue.

The sale of the palace was effected by instruments dated the 3rd and 13th of July, 1609, to the then tenant under lease, John Baptist Borghese, for the sum of 12,000 scudi. Paul V., a Borghese, was then Pope, and ratified the purchase, which was declared to have been made for Cardinal Scipione Borghese, nephew to John Baptist.

Six and twenty years later, by instrument date March 12, 1635, Marc Antonio Borghese, Prince of Sulmona, sold the palace in the Borgo for 17,000 scudi, to the Marchese Antonio Campeggi.

But in 1650 the Campeggi family finally parted with their interest in the palace once possessed by Henry VII., for by deed of sale, dated 19th April, 1650, the Marchese Tommaso Campeggi transferred it, for the sum of 15,000 scudi, to Cardinal Girolamo Colonna. The palace, at the time of this sale, was let to the venerable the "Arciconfraternita della Morte."

Girolamo Colonna was created Cardinal by Urban VIII., in 1627, was archbishop of Bologna from 1632 to 1645, arch priest of S. John Lateran from 1645 to 1661, and in the latter year became Bishop of Frascati. In 1650, the year of Jubilee, he purchased the palace in the Borgo which he occupied occasionally, having a residence elsewhere, in addition to the episcopal palace in Frascati. He lived in the Borgo in time of Easter, Holy Week, "Cavalcate," and other functions, and often gave receptions there to his friends and relatives. The Cardinal's apartments on the first and ground floors were sumptuously furnished. Don Antonio Colonna also lived in this palace, in the first floor when the Cardinal was absent, and in the second floor when his Eminence came to reside. The Cardinal died in 1666.

The Constable of Naples, Don Lorenzo Onofrio Colonna, succeeded as the Cardinal's heir to the possession of the palace, and by instrument dated the 2nd of December, 1669, let it to the Queen Maria Cristina of Sweden. The rent was 500 scudi annually, and the lease was for three years, with condition that unless notice to the contrary were given, the lease should be continued for another term of three years, and so on, with similar clause of renewal. The Queen, however, after some time moved to the Riario palace in Trasterere, now called the Corsini, where she died, in the year 1689.

On the demise of Don Lorenzo, his successor, the Constable Don Filippo II., let the palace to Cardinal Radziejowski [created 1686, died 1705] for the annual rent of 700 scudi. The same Don Filippo, on the 4th of April, 1693, obtained license from Pope Innocent XII., to sell or mortage certain properties of the Colonna family, including this palace. And by instrument dated February 26, 1699, the Reverenda Camera Apostolica, or the Pope himself, purchased it from Don Filippo, for 14,000 scudi, and on the 18th of June, same year, gave it to the Ecclesiastical College or Hospital of the Cento Preti, which was subsequently transferred to Ponte Sisto by Clement XI. The "Cento Preti" was established for receiving poor priests suffering from infirmities and maladies.

The palace which had been found too small for the numerous sick inmates, was sold on the 17th of October, 1720, by Cardinal Imperiali, "Protettore degli Infirmarii e del Collegio Ecclesiastico," to Conte Pietro Giraud (son of Giovanni Giraud, of Lyons in France, deceased), for the sum of 14,000 scudi, and for ninety-six years was known as the Palazzo Giraud.

Conte Pietro Giraud died in 1746, and in his will, dated 20th November, 1743, and opened on the 2nd of July, 1746, makes mention (besides a brother and five children deceased) of his sons Alessio, Stefano, Bernardino, and Ferdinando, and a daughter, Maria Plauditta, who had been married on the 5th of February, 1742, to the Marchese Tiberio Astalli. The will has an inventory attached, of the Count's property, in which is mentioned—"Il Palazzo in Borgo nuovo, sulla Piazzo di S. Giacomo, Scossacavalli, isolato."

Bernardino, one of the younger sons of Count Pietro, was

born in Rome, in the family palace, on the 14th of July, 1721, was created Cardinal on the 19th of April, 1773, and died on the 3rd of May, 1782. The Cardinal's will, made September 8, 1781, and opened June, 1782, makes mention of the furniture of the palace in the Borgo, and of his brothers Counts Alessio and Ferdinando.

In 1816, the Counts Pietro, Giovanni, Giuseppe and Francesco Giraud, sold their palace to the Fabbrica of S. Pietro, for a Studio di Musaici. The price was only 8,000 scudi, as it was in want of substantial repairs. The date of this sale was February 20, 1816. At that time Don Tommaso Boschi was Economo, and Cardinal Braschi was Prefect, of the Reverenda Fabbrica di S. Pietro.

The Mosaic Manufactory was soon removed to the Vatican, as the palace in the Borgo was found unsuitable, owing to its bad state of repair. The Reverenda Fabbrica of St. Peter's then sold the palace with its furniture to Prince Giovanni Torlonia, for the sum of 8,200 scudi. The deed of sale bears date March 29, 1820, and the Economo of the Fabbrica was Monsignor Pietro Maccaiani. The price now given appears small, but Prince Torlonia expended in repairs of the palace, and on buildings in its rear, the sum of 200,000 scudi in the year of its purchase.

The origin of the Torlonia family is recent. Two Frenchmen, the brothers Marino and Giovanni Torlony, whose parents were dead, left Angerolles, in the department of Puy-de-Dome, in 1780, for Paris. There they commenced business on a small scale, and being honest and frugal, had moderate success. In 1789 they became contractors or sub-contractors for supplying the wants of the French Army on its way to Italy, and they accompanied the Regiment of General Miollis, and arrived in Rome in 1792. Marino Torlonia died a few days after arrival, and Giovanni was left alone to continue his struggle for advancement.

Giovanni was on intimate terms with Ugo Basville, the

French Consul in Rome, who in anticipation of death by violence, gave into Torlonia's secret keeping a large sum of money, the property of the French Government. Basville was killed, as he expected, in a riot which he himself provoked by driving in the Corso and displaying revolutionary emblems before a hostile crowd. He tried at first to escape and took refuge in the house of one Hutt, a banker, who lived in the Palombara palace in via dell' Impresa near Montecitorio. Basville was followed to this house, and after a short resistance was killed. The date of this tragical occurrence, which involved Rome and the Papacy in many calamities, was the 14th of January, 1793.

Basville's money was well employed by Torlonia, and was subsequently returned with interest to the French Government.

So rapid was the advancement of Giovanni Torlonia in wealth and honour, that he is found in 1796 contributing, as a Marchese, eighty horsemen towards the formation of the Guarda Civica or Nazionale, while the Colonna furnished a regiment; the Marchese Camillo Massimo, 56 horsemen, Prince Giustiniani, 37; Prince Barberini, 37; Prince Chigi, 26; Duke Sforza Cesarini, 56; Conte Giraud, 30; and Conte Corridori, 120 footmen. During the occupation of Rome by the French revolutionists, Giovanni Torlonia bought the church of S. Romualdo (now demolished) to save it from profanation, and he restored it in 1814 to the then Abbot, Mauro Cappellari, afterwards Pope Gregory XVI.

In 1809 Giovanni was formally enrolled among the Roman Patricians, and in 1813 he purchased from Prince Pallavicini the estate of Civitella-Cesi; and in 1814 was created by Pius VII., Prince of Civitella-Cesi. He was also Duke of Poli and Bracciano. Dying in 1829, he left issue by his wife, Anna Maria Sculthcis, two sons and two daughters. Of the daughters, one, Maria Luigia, by her husband, Prince Domenico Orsini, was mother of Filippo Orsini, the present Prince Assistant at the Pontifical Throne. The other daughter, Maria Teresa, married Conte Mariscotti, whose family palace is now occupied by the Banca Romana.

Prince Giovanni's elder son, Marino [born 1796, died 1865], Duke of Poli and of Bracciano, married, in 1821, Anna, daughter and reputed heiress of Duke Sforza Cesarini, and had by her Giulio, Duke of Poli, father, by his wife Teresa Chigi, of Leopoldo, Duke of Poli, formerly Syndic of Rome, who married in 1886 Eleonora, daughter of Prince di Belmonte. The second son of Duke Marino and Anna Sforza Cesarini was Giovanni, who married Francesca Ruspoli.

Prince Giovanni's second son, Alessandro, Prince of Civitella-Cesi, was born June 1, 1800, and died February 7, 1888. He married in 1840, Teresa, daughter of Prince Colonna, and by her had issue two daughters: Giovannina, who died in 1875, and Anna Maria Conesti, who married in 1872 Don Giulio Borghese, third son of the late Prince Borghese. On this marriage, Don Giulio assumed the name of Torlonia, and this change of name was confirmed by Royal decree in 1875.

The palace in the Borgo was used by Prince Giovanni Torlonia and his son, Prince Alessandro, for many years, not as a residence, but as a place for giving entertainments. A large room on the first floor was magnificently fitted up to serve, as occasion offered, for a ball room, a theatre, or concert room. For these monster gatherings, held once a month during the season, as many as 1300 cards of invitation were sometimes issued. The guests included, besides the Cardinals, Ambassadors, and members of the Papal Court, the principal Roman nobles, Royal and distinguished persons visiting Rome, and strangers of every country. The lists of the persons invited, and details of the expenses incurred, are still preserved in the Torlonia archives.

Among these lists occur the names, for 1827, of Sir Archibald and Lady Campbell, Lady Westmoreland, George Rennie and his wife, the Duke and Duchess of Hamilton, Don Jerome Napoleon Bonaparte, and Captain and Mrs. Arthur Blackwood.

In January, 1839, at a ball given for the Grand Duke of Russia, the Duke and Duchess of Sutherland and the Duke of Devonshire were present. The cost of that entertainment was 7000 francs, the wine bill including 94 bottles, 40 being champagne. In Advent of the same year, three concerts were given, at a cost of about 10,000 francs. In May, 1846, the performers at a theatrical entertainment were paid over 4000 francs. Among those invited were Lords Cadogan, Compton, Walpole, Northesk, Headford, Fingall, Tullamore ; Ladies Clifford, Bury, Montague, Duff Gordon, Charleville, Susannah Cunninghame, Stuart, Malcolm ; and Lord and Lady Brabazon, the Bertie Matthews family, Scully, More O'Ferrall, the Welds, Ruxtons, Petre, Hon. Mr. Cust, Col. Caldwell, and Mr. Bodenham ; besides the Duchess de Cadore, Count Nesselrode, Lamartine, the Prince de Holstein, etc. In March, 1851, Lady Georgina Grey, Lord Grey de Wilton, Lord Charles Bruce, Lord Dunglass, Sir Adam Hay and Mrs. Sherlock and family ; four *Americani distincti*, namely, Messrs. Stone, Post, Forbes and Howe ; Lord and Lady Manners, Lady Caroline Barrington, Lord Gormanston, Lady Vane, Lord Rendlesham, Lord and Lady Blantyre, Sir John and Lady Packington, Lord and Lady Campden, Lady Bateson, Sir James and Lady Carnegie, and over one thousand other persons, were invited to a ball which cost 7,300 francs. The candles were 1383 in number, and 96 bottles of champagne were used.

On the 18th of February, 1852, the "annual Monster Ball," as the *Globe* called it, was given. The invitations were 1500. Among the guests were Major and Lady Spencer, Lady Dufferin, Lord Gifford, Sir Coutts Lindsay, Lord and Lady Middleton and three daughters, Lord and Lady Overstone and Miss Strutt, a trio marked :—*molto distinto ;* Viscount and Viscountess Fielding, Raikes Currie, Smith Barry, Madame, Miss and Mr. Sherlock [cogniti] ; Mr. Wheble, *Cattolico distinto ;* Miss Oddy, Madame Eustace *e famiglia già cognita ;*

Earl of Walpole, Miss Campbell, sister of Lady Leven; Mr. Howard Galton, *antico amico della casa;* Messrs. Lockwood and Cartwright, *cogniti;* Mr. and Mrs. Winton Corry, and their brother Mr. Fortescue, who were recommended by the Prussian Minister.

On the 20th of February 1854, at another Festa in Borga, were present nine Cardinals, including Cardinals Antonelli and Wiseman. The cost of these various entertainments, which were very numerous, was about 5,000 francs each on an average, for the refreshments alone, exclusive of the decorations. The wine bills, it is notable, were very moderate, but did not include any wines which were not in bottles. The invitation cards were generally for eight o'clock p.m., at which hour the Cardinals and the ecclesiastics arrived. They remained until 9.30 or 10 p.m., and always left before the dancing commenced. A special supper room was always reserved for the Prince and a few of his most distinguished guests. These sumptuous entertainments were continued until the Princess Torlonia became afflicted with mental derangement.

In 1853 Prince Torlonia commenced his great work, the drainage of Lake Fucino, which he successfully accomplished after the expenditure of millions of francs. On its completion, King Victor Emmanuel presented him with a gold medal specially coined to commemorate the event.

Among the works of art and possessions of Prince Alessandro may be noticed the museum and gallery in the Lungara; the high altar of the church of the Gesù; the Torlonia chapel in S. John Lateran; the palace in piazza Venezia; the villa Nomentana; and the villa Albani. He restored the Apollo and the Argentina theatres. His charity was almost boundless, and he founded and endowed the Torlonia Conservatory at S. Onofrio, for eighty female orphans, and an infant asylum, for three hundred children, to be fed, clothed, and educated, at his sole cost. By his will, he ordained that his charity institutions should be maintained under the administration of his daughter and her husband, but that they should be closed and suppressed in case of any interference of the authorities, political or ecclesiastical.

The Duke di Saldanha, Portuguese Ambassador, occupied the palace in the Borgo from the 1st of November, 1862, to the end of December, 1864, paying 2400 scudi, or 12,900 francs. He remained in the palace five months longer, to the end of May, 1865, and paid 3000 scudi, or 16,125 francs.

In 1869, the year of the Vatican Council, Prince Alexander Torlonia generously gave the palace in the Borgo to Pope Pius IX., for the use and accommodation of bishops coming to Rome to attend the Council. Among the ecclesiastics who, on that occasion, were given apartments in the palace were the Archbishop of Gaeta, the Bishop of Imola, the Cardinal archbishop of Ravenna, and the Patriarch of Antioch.

After the entry of the Italian troops into Rome in the month of September, 1870, and the seizure of the Pontifical territory by Victor Emmanuel, the sittings of the Vatican Council were suspended, and have not been yet resumed. Pius IX. no longer required palaces in which to give accommodation to bishops, and accordingly restored the palace in the Borgo to its owner.

And as Prince Alexander Torlonia did not want the palace, either for his own residence or for entertainments, he let the principal floor for a time to a Russian nobleman; and afterwards in 1879 to Mr. J. C. Heywood, its present occupant. The upper storey of the palace was let to His Eminence Cardinal Parocchi, and afterwards to Cardinal Laurenzi.

Mr. Heywood, an American gentleman of highly cultivated literary taste, and author of several Dramatic Poems, "Sforza," "Herodias," "Antonius," etc., has converted the large ball room into a library. His well chosen collection of books and manuscripts includes many precious first editions, and ranks as one of the most valuable private libraries in Rome. This library contains about 14,000 volumes, of which over one hundred are

Aldine editions, either "firsts" or *editiones principes*, some in original bindings and all in good condition. There is a Boccaccio of 1478, another of 1492, with woodcuts, and another of 1527 (the genuine edition); the Aldine Horace, in size 164 millimetres; and the Virgil, a "first": Mr. Quaritch paid £145 for his copy: the rarest Elzevir "*Le Patissier Francois*," of 1685, beautifully bound. Noteworthy are:—An Italian Romance of Chivalry, with caricatures by Leonardo da Vinci on the margins; a fine copy of the Rabelais of 1741 (Amsterdam) 3 vols. in large paper, a copy of which sold a few years ago in Paris for 6,500 francs; a volume of woodcuts published in 1549, representing the martyrdom of the Apostles and showing S. Matthias with his head in a perfect guillotine; a very early and fine copy of Froissart's Chronicles; some very early and rare books relating to the discovery of America; *Josephus*, seven books of the Jewish War, printed by Pannaartz in the Massimo palace; a *Silvius Italicus*, by George Laver, Rome 1471; the "Virgil of 1476," which is complete and contains the *Epitaphia Virgilii* which are wanting in Lord Spencer's copy; a Nuremberg Bible, folio, with printed initials, 1477 (Coburger) in antique binding; the Nuremberg Chronicle, 1493, folio; a *Pontificalis Liber*, 1485, folio, editio princeps, printed in red and black Gothic characters, with music, and with eighteen exquisitely painted initials in gold and colours; *Pliny's Natural History*, Jenson, Venice, 1476, folio, Landino's translation into Italian, with thirty-seven large initials in gold and colours; *Liber de Arte distillandi de Simplicibus*, Strasburg, 1500, folio, with 297 coloured woodcuts; *Acta Sanctorum*, (Bollandists), including the original editions of October 1786, Brussels, and October 1794, Tongerloæ; the Lucca edition of Baronius (Annals), large paper; Muratori's *Rerum Italicarum Scriptores*; Montfaucon's *Antiquitates*, fifteen vols, first edition, large paper, folios; Ptolemy's *Geography*, 1508, folio, containing the first map indicating America; Perrault's *Fairy Tales*, with vignettes, 1697; Homer's *Iliad* and *Hymn to Ceres*, 4 volumes folio, Parma, 1808, printed by order of Napoleon I., presentation copy from the Empress to Prince St. Angelo of Naples; the famous Virgil, published by order of the Duchess of Devonshire, Annibale Caro's translations, Rome, 1819, two volumes folio, on vellum paper, with fifty-five full-page engravings: only 150 copies were printed, at the cost to the Duchess of £37,000: Mr. Heywood's copy was the one given by the Duchess to Cardinal della Somaglia and bears her Grace's autograph presentation, and it has two portraits of Caro, one before, the other after, lettering, and also a proof portrait of the Duchess.

Mr. Heywood possesses also several MSS. of value. He purchased one collection of thirty-six MSS. which had been offered to Mr. Astor, the then American Minister in Rome for 30,000 francs. Several of these MSS. are palimpsests: thirty-two are on parchment, and the dates of all but two of them range from the tenth to the fifteenth century. The bindings are antique, and seven bear the arms of Pope Pius VI. One of these *codices* is an Herodotus with richly illuminated large initial letters, and with marginal notes by Paul IV. (Carafa, Pope, 1555-1559): another codex is a *Psalterium*, the music written in very small dots with illuminated tails, and without a single line of music staff, the date of which, according to De Rossi, may be of the 8th, and certainly can not be later than the tenth century. There is also an *Office for Easter* with grotesque illuminations; and there are several *Books of Hours*, one of which is of the fourteenth century and has fifteen large paintings and illuminated initials, the margins being bordered with exquisite work in gold and colours. A collection of autograph letters of Paul IV. (chiefly addressed to his sister) were given by Mr. Heywood to Leo XIII., on the occasion of his jubilee.

A very rare book now in Mr. Heywood's possession merits notice. It is a copy of the works of Flavius Josephus " De Greco in Latinum traductus per Venerabilem presbyterum

Ruffinum Aquilejensem," etc. "Impressum in inclita civitate Venetiarum per Magistrum Raynaldum de Novimagio Alemannum anno salutis 1481 ultimo die Martii." It is a volume in folio with twenty-eight initial letters in gold and colours containing miniature figures of persons, animals, fruits, flowers and arabesques. This edition was unknown to Brunet and also to Graesse. Haym mentions it but asserts that he had never seen a copy. It is undoubtedly exceedingly rare, and there is a strong probability that this well-preserved and very handsome copy is the only one in existence.

It remains for the writer to express his thanks to the Princes Colonna, Borghese, and Torlonia, and to Marchese Alfonso Malvezzi-Campeggi, for their kindness in permitting him to make extracts from their family archives.

A very brief abstract of the foregoing paper was read by the writer at a meeting of the "British and American Archæological Society of Rome" on the 16th of April, 1889.

The Eldest Natural Son of Charles II.*

CHARLES II., although he had no legitimate issue, left many natural children, some of whom he ennobled. A few of them left descendants who still hold a place in the British Peerage. His amours began when he was sixteen or seventeen years old. One of the first of these was with Lucy Waters or Walters or Barlow, by whom he had a son who was created Duke of Monmouth. Charles, during his exile, had children by Catherine Peg and Elizabeth Killegrew, and his "seventeenth mistress abroad" was Eleanor, daughter of Robert Needham, Viscount Kilmorey, and widow of Peter Warburton. She became, in 1644, the second wife of John, the first Lord Byron, and died in 1663.

Barbara Villiers, daughter of Viscount Grandison, and wife to Roger Palmer, bore to Charles, three sons, who were created respectively Dukes of Southampton, Grafton and Northumberland, and a daughter, the Countess of Lichfield. Barbara herself was made Duchess of Cleveland, and her complaisant husband was made Earl of Castlemaine.

Frances, daughter of Walter Stuart, son of Lord Blantyre, was reputed to be another mistress of Charles II., and married, in 1667, the 5th Duke of Richmond.

Louise Querouaille, maid to the Duchess of Orleans, was invited, after the death of her mistress, to England by Charles, and was created, in 1673, Duchess of Portsmouth, and her son

---

* This article, now enlarged and altered, was printed in the *Scottish Review* for April, 1885, under the title of "Stuart Pretenders."

Charles, born 1672, was made Duke of Richmond in 1675, and was naturalized in France, in 1685, as Duke of Aubigny. Louis XIV., at the request of Charles II., conferred on Louise the dukedom of Aubigny, to descend after her death to any of his natural sons whom Charles might nominate, and to the male descendants of such natural son, to the intent that Aubigny might always continue in the possession of the House of Stuart. The title is still held by the Dukes of Richmond.

By Moll or Mary Davies, herself a natural daughter of Colonel Howard, Charles had two daughters, one of whom was Mary, Countess of Derwentwater. By Lady Shannon he had Charlotte, Countess of Yarborough.

By the famous Nell Gwin, Charles had two sons, of whom the eldest, Charles Beauclerc, born in 1670, was created Duke of St. Albans, and was ancestor of the present Duke of that title.

It must be conceded that Charles II. was not ashamed to acknowledge his children, and was liberal in the bestowal of money and titles upon them and their mothers. He gave among them some eight or ten dukedoms, to say nothing of lesser honours.

The above-mentioned ladies were not, however, the only recipients of the favour of the King, and, strange to say, one of the earliest of the amours of Charles has remained to this day wholly unnoticed by English writers, although that amour resulted in the birth of a son, who was older than the Duke of Monmouth, and who was the father of a Prince Stuart, whose existence has never been mentioned by any writer until the present time.

The late Baron de Reumont, formerly Prussian Ambassador at Florence, and author of a *History of the City of Rome*, published, in 1882, in the *Historiches Jarbuch der Goerres Gesellschaft*, a very brief article on 'A Stuart Pretender in the Seventeenth Century.' A learned Jesuit, Father Boero, now dead, wrote a history of the *Conversion of Charles II., King of*

England, to the Catholic Church, which appeared in 1863, in the *Civiltà Cattolica* (Fifth Series, vols. VI. and VII.) and in the course of this history gave an account of the eldest of all the natural sons of that monarch, and published translations of some autograph letters of King Charles, addressed to the then General of the Jesuits, Father Oliva, residing at S. Andrea del Quirinale in Rome. He also gave extracts from the entrance books of the Jesuit Novitiate, proving that a natural son of Charles II. had been admitted a novice into the order of Jesuits. The last will and testament of this son of Charles II. was published in *l' Italia Reale*, a Naples newspaper (1881, No. 13), by Don Scipione Volpicella, first librarian in the National Library, Naples. And also, the parish priest of S. Sofia in St. Giovanni Carbonara, Naples, lately discovered a certificate, partly illegible, of the marriage, on the 19th of February, 1669, of Signor Giacomo Enrico Boveri . . . . and Signora Teresa Corona. The Jesuit Father who wrote the articles in the *Civiltà Cattolica* seems to have been unaware that James Stuart, alias De la Cloche du Bourg de Jersey, *alias* Henri de Rohan, *alias* Boveri, had ever left the Jesuits or committed matrimony, for he concludes his account by expressing his belief that James Stuart went to Flanders to complete his novitiate and died a Jesuit. Both the Jesuit writer and the Baron de Reumont were likewise unaware that many particulars concerning this son of Charles II. were published so far back as the year 1674 by Vincenzo Armanni of Gubbio in the third volume of his *Lettere*, printed at Macerata by Guiseppe Piccini. Armanni gives an account of the courtship and marriage of this Prince James Stuart, and also furnishes a full copy of his last will and testament, but is silent respecting any issue of the marriage of James Stuart with Teresa Corona. Documents exist, however, in the archives of the Propaganda at Rome, which prove that a son was born of the Corona marriage, celebrated at Naples in 1669, and in the following pages the career of that son will be traced, and from the Armanni *Lettere* and the *Civiltà Cattolica* will be given a somewhat fuller notice than has hitherto been published in English of the father.

It is known that in September, 1646, Prince Charles, by licence of King Charles I., went to Jersey. Some accounts say that he went to Jersey from Holland. While in Jersey he became father of his first illegitimate son, by a lady whom the writer in the *Civiltà Cattolica* describes as a *principalissima dama*, and who, Armanni says, was of the Royal Stuart blood. Charles II., writing to the General of the Jesuits, says he was but sixteen or seventeen years old when this affair happened, more through youthful folly than from malice, and describes the mother of his son as a "young lady of a family the most distinguished in the realm." The son, in his will, describes her as "Donna Maria Stuardo della familia delli Baroni di S. Marzo." In 1646 (as Sir Bernard Burke kindly informed the writer), Charles Stuart, sixth Duke of Lennox in Scotland, and third Duke of Richmond in England, was fourth Earl of March. It may be presumed that the Mary Stuart mentioned in the will was a member of the family of which this Earl of March was the head.

The son, James Stuart, was sent, immediately after his birth, to France and Holland, to be brought up secretly. He was provided, when of a sufficient age, with good teachers, and was instructed in literature and science. Unfortunately, according to the Jesuit account, he fell into the hands of heretics and was educated in the sect of the Calvinists. His father was very fond of him, but for grave reasons refrained from publicly acknowledging him as his son. In the year 1665, the King had this son with him in London, and intended to keep him near him for some time longer; but the young man, who was studiously inclined and disliked the idleness of the Court, demanded permission to leave England. This permission was granted, and the son, previous to his departure, received from the King the following curious document, written on parchment, and still preserved among the Jesuit archives :—

"Charles, by the grace of God, King of England, France, Scotland, and Ireland—We confess and acknowledge as our natural son M. James Stuart, who by our order and command has lived in France and other countries under a feigned name up to the year 1665, when we took him under our care. After the said year, he being in London, we of our express will and for just reasons have commanded him still to live under another name, that of De la Cloche* du Bourg de Jersey, and, for important reasons affecting the peace of the realm which we have always promoted, we prohibit him from speaking of this until after our death. Then it shall be permitted him to present to Parliament this our declaration, which with entire good will and justice we consign to him at his request, written in his own language (French) to remove every excuse for his showing it to any other person to be interpreted. Given at Whitehall, 27 September, 1665. Written and subscribed by our hand, sealed with our ordinary seal for letters without any alteration. (Signed) CHARLES."

James Stuart, *alias* De la Cloche, went from London to Holland to pursue his studies, and was provided by his father with sufficient means for his livelihood. Fearing, however, that his father's death might leave him in pecuniary embarrassment, he wrote, in 1667, to the King, and received the following reply :—

"Charles, by the grace of God, King of England, France, Scotland, and Ireland.—M. James Stuart, whom we have already acknowledged for our natural son, and who lives under the name of De la Cloche, has represented to us that he, should he survive our death, might be in want of sustenance if not recognised by our Parliament, and by reason of other difficulties which he might meet in this matter. Therefore we, yielding to his request, have deemed it just to assign and leave him a charge on our realm, if it may so please the successor to our crown and our Parliament, to the amount of £500 sterling per annum; which sum he shall not be permitted to enjoy save on the terms of his residing in London in the religion of his fathers, and observing the English Liturgy.—At Whitehall, 7 February, 1667. Written and sealed by our own hand, CHARLES."

The language of the last part of the document conveys a suspicion that the young James Stuart, who had been reared a Presbyterian or Calvinist, was becoming unsettled in his

---

* There is still a family of this name in Jersey.

religious belief. And so it happened ; for, a few months later, James Stuart is found in Germany, at Hamburg, where the Jesuits had at that time an establishment, and were most successful in making conversions. On the 29th of July, 1667, he made his abjuration and was reconciled to the Roman Church, and on this occasion confided the secret of his birth to the Queen of Sweden,* who wrote to King Charles for confirmation of the statement of the son. On this occasion the Queen of Sweden gave the young convert a certificate, written in Latin, to the following effect :—

"James Stuart being incognito under the feigned name of De la Cloche du Bourg, born in the island of Jersey, the natural son of Charles II., King of England, and as such secretly acknowledged to us by his Britannic Majesty, abandoning the sect of Calvin in which he was born and hitherto lived, was joined to the Holy Roman Church in Hamburg on the 29th of July, 1667. In confirmation of which we have thought good to give attestation under our hand, although contrary to custom, in order that he, under these extraordinary circumstances, may open his mind, to his director only, in confession, and seek counsel for the salvation of his soul. (Signed) CHRISTINA ALEXANDRA."

James Stuart, not being contented with being a Catholic, determined to become a religious, and for this purpose left Hamburg and proceeded to Rome. The certificate given him by the Queen of Sweden was presented under the seal of confession to one of the Jesuit Superiors, and enabled him to get a dispensation from the impediment of illegitimacy, and he was admitted into the novitiate of the Jesuits at S. Andrea del Quirinale. A book, entitled *Ingressus Novitiorum ab anno 1631 ad 1675*, gives the date of his entrance and a list of his clothes, countersigned " Giacomo della Cloche manu propria." It runs thus :—

---

* The archives of the Marchese Ricci in Rome contain a report of the insults offered by the mob in Hamburg to the Queen of Sweden, when she celebrated the creation of the new Pope, Clement IX., in 1667, by illuminating her palace and a display of fireworks, etc. Several of the rioters were killed. Her Majesty showed much courage on the occasion.

"James de la Cloche, of the island of Jersey, under the King of England, aged 24, came to S. Andrea, April 11, 1668. He had with him a hat, a mantlet, and priest's dress of silk, a doublet and breeches of black stuff, a waistcoat of yellow leather, a leather mask, coloured sword sash, a pair of white silk stockings, two shirts and an over-shirt, a pair of under-breeches and stockings of linen, three handkerchiefs and a cap of white cotton, two pairs of small shoes, three collars, three pair of cuffs, a pair of gloves, a hair brush, a pair of shoes, and two pairs of thread collar buttons."

King Charles II., when apprised of the step his son had taken, wrote to the General of the Jesuits to express his satisfaction, and requested that his son might be allowed to visit London. The King wrote in French, not in Latin, and was especially anxious that no Englishman should be called in as interpreter, and that all should be kept as secret as possible. In midst of the cares of royalty he had prayed God that he might find one single person to whom to confide the interests of his salvation without affording the Court a shadow of suspicion that he was a Catholic. Although a multitude of priests were near him, some in the service of the Queens in the palaces of St. James and Somerset House, and some scattered about London, he feared to be seen conversing with any of them, even if disguised, for detection would soon follow. He considers it providential to have a son a Catholic, whom he prefers, however inexperienced, to any other person, as he will be always competent to administer to him secretly the sacraments of confession and communion, which he desires to receive as soon as possible.

"Our son," he continues, "is a young cavalier whom you have admitted into your society in Rome under the name of De la Cloche di Jersey, and who was born when we were not much more than sixteen or seventeen years old, of a young lady, one of the most distinguished in our realms, more through our youthful frailty than deliberate wickedness. He is dear to us on account of his excellent disposition, learning and docility. Many grave reasons of State prevent our public recognition of him at present, but we hope in a few years that these reasons may disappear. We gave him, in 1665, our letters to testify his birth, to be of service to him in the event of our death."

The secret of his parentage is, says His Majesty, known in

London to the Queens only. The General is not to send any reply except through his son; for a letter sent from Rome, in answer to one addressed to the late Pope, occasioned such trouble that, in order to quiet suspicions of the King being in treaty with the Pontiff, his majesty was forced to permit many things to be done to the prejudice of many Irish Catholics. The Queen of Sweden herself is not to be trusted in this business. She is a woman, and that is enough to make him fear that she cannot keep the secret. The General is not to let her know that he is acquainted with the true parentage of De la Cloche. If the Queen enquires about him the General is to say he is gone as a missionary to Jersey or some other part of the kingdom. Charles may perhaps write to the Pope by a secret envoy to get his beloved son ordained a priest without publication of his true name, etc. But the ordination is not to be in Rome. The son might go to Paris and visit the King of France, or if it please him better, the Duchess of Orleans. Either of those personages would manage a private and secret ordination. If he should come to London the Queen or the Queen-mother can easily provide a bishop to ordain him in secret. The king desires much to see his son, not to dissuade him from becoming a Jesuit priest, but to embrace him. His son, while in England, may live with the Jesuits and follow their rule, but not in London, but in some city not far off, and he may afterwards return to Rome and to the Jesuits there. This letter, dated August 3rd, 1668, contained another directed ' For our most honourable son, the Prince Stuart, living among the Reverend Fathers of Jesus under the name of Signor de la Cloche—at Rome.' In this letter the King mentions the transmission of money for his son's maintenance to the Queen of Sweden, and says that the two Queens in London are most impatient to see him, as they had been told the fact of his conversion to the Roman religion.

"We will not," writes Charles, "put the least impediment in your way. Nevertheless, measure well your own strength and consider your constitution, which seems to us rather weak and delicate. One can be a good Catholic without being a Religious. And you must remember that we have had the intention of recognising you publicly in a few years. You must, moreover, consider that for our part you may pretend to equal, and perhaps more ample titles than the Duke of Monmouth, who is as young as you are. If liberty of conscience and the Catholic religion should be restored in this realm, you might have some hopes of the crown, for we assure you that if God permits us and our most honoured brother, the Duke of York, to die without children, the kingdom falls to you, and the Parliament cannot legally oppose it, excepting that you should be excluded from the succession as being a Catholic, liberty of conscience not being established, or, as at present, by the limitation of the choice of a King to Protestant princes.

"If, on mature deliberation, you prefer to serve God in the institute of the Jesuits who have received you, we will not oppose the divine will, which we have already too much irritated by our sins.

"We desire to show our benevolence towards the Jesuits who have received you, and we will aid them in some suitable manner, being assured whatever we give will be employed to the service of God. Besides, we do not wish that a person of your birth should remain with them without leaving something as a memorial of his condition."

This letter was dated from Whitehall, August 4, 1668, and terminated with the words:—"I am your affectionate father, Charles, King of England, France, Scotland, and Ireland."

On the 29th of August, 1668, the King wrote two other letters to the General, in the first of which he urges the immediate departure of his son, and suggests a plan for keeping the Queen of Sweden in ignorance of his son's visit to London. The messenger who brought these letters was not to appear in the house of the Father General, nor to stay more than one day in Rome, lest he should be observed and recognised by some Englishman. Of all the temporal ills which could befall his Majesty, the proof of his being a Catholic would be the worst, for it would infallibly cause his death and occasion many tumults in the realm. Therefore the General is not to feel surprise at the precautions to be taken to ensure secrecy in the affair of his son's visit. He now wishes his son not to visit the King of France and the Duchess of Orleans until he has first seen his father, nor to write to the Queen of Sweden, who is in

Italy.* The son, when he arrives in London, is to take an opportunity of presenting himself to the Queen when at Mass at St. James's, or when visiting the Queen-mother. He is to present a sealed letter to the Queen as if it were a petition, and in this letter to state briefly his name. The Queen has orders to introduce him to the King, in a prudent manner, so as not to excite suspicion. The second letter, written a few moments after the first was sealed, informs the General that the Queens wished a little delay and further precautions for secrecy. They had heard that no Jesuit was ever permitted to go abroad without a companion of the same order. The King approves of the rule in general, but begs that an exception may be made in the case of his son, whom he has charged on his filial obedience to travel alone. All his plans would be ruined if a priest or an Italian accompanied his son to England. Private instructions were given to trusty agents at all the chief ports of the Kingdom to expect a foreign prince, of such and such stature and lineaments, and facilitate his journey. The young prince does not love company nor conversation of companions nor the Court. When in England in 1665 he got tired of his residence there before a year was out. And when he enters our palace, he will have no one to talk to, save us and the Queens, nor will he write letters to any one save to the Father General. Let him go to Genoa, where the Jesuits have a house, and in Genoa let him seek out an English ship. But let no Jesuit visit the ship or speak to the captain. Let him leave his religious dress in the Jesuit house in Genoa, and he can resume it on his return to Rome. On his voyage and on his

---

* From the Colonna archives we are enabled, by the courtesy of Prince Giovanni Colonna, to state that the Queen of Sweden, on the 2nd of December, 1669, contracted to rent from the owners, the Colonna family, the ancient palace of the English Embassy, now the Torlonia Palace, in the Borgo, for a term of three years, at the annual rent of 500 scudi. Her Majesty contemplated a lengthened stay in Rome, as the contract contained a clause providing for further renewals of the lease for additional periods of three years on the expiration of the first and each succeeding term.

arrival in England, he is to call himself Henri de Rohan, the name of a certain Calvinist French prince, who is an intimate friend of the King. So anxious is the King in this affair, that he takes note secretly and circumspectly of all departures and arrivals of vessels at the various ports, and of the arrivals of all strangers.

"This," says His Majesty, "we do on colour of zeal for the Kingdom and on pretext of maintaining the Protestant religion, to which we feign to be more than ever attached, although before God who sees the heart we abhor it as most false and pernicious. We now desire our son not to travel *via* France. We ask you, Father General, to spread a report that he is gone to Jersey or Hanton to see his pretended mother, who wishes to become a Catholic. So far from preventing our son from following his vocation as a Catholic or a Jesuit, we and the Queen will press it upon him more urgently than any spiritual director whom he could have. No doubt, when time and circumstances shall permit our writing to acquaint His Holiness of the obedience which we owe to him as Vicar of Christ, we hope that he will entertain for us such benevolence as not to refuse our son the cardinal's hat. If it should be inconvenient for him to reside in England as a Cardinal, we can send him to reside in Rome, as we intend, with all the royal magnificence due to his rank. If he wishes, nevertheless, to be a simple Jesuit, we shall not force the purple on him against his will. We have consulted our physician as to the effects of sea-sickness on persons of weak constitution, and have been informed that sea-sickness never killed any one, but on the contrary was beneficial to some. Our son may manage that the ship in which he sails, shall, if he becomes ill, stop at different ports on the way. He might, of course, come direct to London, but for important reasons we wish him to land at some other port, and to travel to London by carriage."

The General of the Jesuits, to whom the King of England wrote so frankly and familiarly, placed no obstacle in the way of the departure of the novice, who was not yet a priest, and had not even completed one of the two years of the novitiate, nor made the necessary studies in theology. James Stuart, abandoning for the time the *alias* of De la Cloche, adopted that of Henri de Rohan, and about the middle of October, 1668, left Rome, carrying with him the following brief answer from the General to the King:—

"Sacra Maestà—Dal latore di questa, che e gentilhuomo Francese (De Rohan), intenderà Vostra Maestà la fedele esecuzione da me data alle tre sue lettere, e la mia inesplicabile osservanza alla sua reale persona. Con la stessa prontezza e fede esequirò quanto Vostra Maestà si degnerà d' impormi ; e procurerò di essere, qual Ella mi presuppone e qual mi obliga ad essere : E profondissimamente a V. M. m' inchino.—Livorno, 14 Ottobre, 1668."

The journey of "Henri de Rohan" to London, which was most probably *via* Leghorn not Genoa, must have been prosperous and his stay in England exceeding short, for on the 18th of November, 1668, King Charles sends a letter to the General of the Jesuits by the hands of Signor " De la Cloche, Jesuit, at Rome." In this letter the King informs the General that his son " had earnestly expressed a desire to return to Rome as our Ambassador to your most Reverend Paternity, to which request he gave consent on the condition that he should return to London immediately after speaking to your Paternity and obtaining the things we request, and which our very dear and honoured son will explain to you *viva voce;* and also reconducting to us as he passes through France, the Reverend Father whom he left there." The King, obeying the request of his son, promises a handsome donation towards paying off debts due on S. Andrea del Quirinale and for the purposes of additional buildings or improvements. The young Jesuit brought with him from London a bill for £800 at six months date in favour of the Father General, Signor Gian Paolo Oliva," signed by King Charles on the 18th of November, 1668, and intended for payment of the maintenance and travelling charges of "our most dear and honoured son a Jesuit living under the name of De la Cloche."

The writer of the Stuart articles in the *Civiltà Cattolica* declared that he could find no further traces in the Jesuit records of James Stuart or De la Cloche. He supposed, and probably correctly, that he went again on a journey to London, but he was wrong in supposing that James Stuart ever returned to S. Andrea del Quirinale to complete his novitiate. The learned Father was also in error when he states that no writer, English or foreign, had ever known anything concerning this son of Charles II.

Vincenzo Armanni of Gubbio wrote much about the conversion of England, and had been himself in that country. He was blind for twenty years before his death, but carried on a voluminous correspondence. He knew something of the parentage of James Stuart, but nothing of his connection with the Jesuits. This is not to be wondered at, inasmuch as the Father General of the Jesuits and James Stuart himself observed the strictest secrecy concerning the novice who passed under the name of De la Cloche.

Armanni, in his letter to "Francesco Maria Doria [son] of Brancaleone," relates that Prince James went to Naples, to benefit his health, in company with a Frenchman, a Cavalier of the Order of S. John of Jerusalem. The real condition of the Prince was not then known to any one in Naples. The Cavalier continued his journey and went on to Malta, and before departing from Naples recommended the Prince to the good offices of the Abbate di S. Aniello, one of the Canons regular of S. Salvatore, a church which no longer exists, but was formerly in the Castello dell' Uovo, anciently called Isola di San Salvatore. The Prince chose for his spiritual director one of the Canons of this church, who was also parish priest of the place, and this parish priest was the informant of Armanni.

Two ladies, mother and daughter, were in the habit every Friday of attending the church of S. Salvatore; and after confession and communion they were in the habit of kneeling before a miraculous crucifix and praying to God for the happy settlement in life of the daughter. The parish priest saw them one Friday, just when he was anxious to find a suitable lodging for Prince Stuart, and he at once proposed to the mother to allow the prince to become an inmate of their house. They were of *mezzana* condition, poor but respectable, and the family consisted of Francesco Corona, his wife Annuccia d' Amicij, their sons Gaetano and Giovanni Battista Nicola, and their daughters Teresa and Chiara. The prince was soon struck with the beauty and modesty of Teresa, but was himself a guarded admirer, and gave her no hint of his intentions until one day when he met her issuing from her mother's chamber, and abruptly asked her to accept him as a husband:—*Mi volete voi per marito?* The young lady blushed deeply, and said that if God had intended him for her husband He would have made her his equal in rank. She then went back to her mother's room, and afterwards studiously avoided the company of the prince.

The ardour of the lover was not quenched by this reserved conduct of the lady. He laid the case before the parish priest, his confessor, who strongly disapproved of the attachment, and advised the prince to proceed no further with the courtship. But James Stuart was dissatisfied, and for some time ceased his usual religious devotions, and altogether neglected his first confessor. At last he chose another spiritual director, to whom he revealed not only his passion for Teresa Corona, but also the secret of his birth, showing to him also the letters written by the Queen of Sweden and the Father General of the Jesuits. Under the encouragement of this new director the young lady's scruples were removed, and she consented to be his wife. The prince was anxious to make it appear that his intended father-in-law was not altogether a pauper, and accordingly he gave a sum of money to Signor Francesco Corona to serve as a dowry for Teresa. Signor Corona could not deny himself the pleasure of exhibiting this money before his friends, and he indiscreetly boasted before his neighbours concerning his rich son-in-law. This foolish behaviour caused a report to be spread in Naples that the wealthy Englishman lodging with Signor Corona was an adventurer of whom no one knew anything, and who was probably a coiner of false money. The rumour reached the ears of the Viceroy, who ordered the arrest of the mysterious stranger. The certificates and papers attesting the parentage of James Stuart were then produced, and the excitement in Naples was increased. Crowds flocked to see the English prince and the future princess. The Viceroy ordered that the prince should be lodged in the Castle of S. Elmo, and treated with every consideration due to a prisoner of rank. The princess was sent to a Convent where she received courteous and respectful usage. The prince wrote a letter to the Viceroy imploring release, and begging that the utmost secrecy might be observed in the matter. He also wrote to the Father General of the Jesuits, beseeching him to interpose his good offices with the Viceroy, and to obtain permission for him to go to England *via* Leghorn and Marseilles. The Viceroy had, however, already written to London, and waited for a reply. Immediately on the arrival of the answer from London, the prince was set at liberty and left Naples. It may be supposed he went to England. After a few months he returned to Naples with an assignment of 50,000 scudi, and he intended to remove at once to Venice, and to take with him his wife, her parents, her sister and brothers. But these intentions were never carried out, for the prince was seized with a violent fever and died. He showed much piety during his illness, and when the Viaticum was brought he insisted, although in a very weak condition, upon getting out of bed in order to receive the sacred particle on his knees. His last will and testament, dictated to a notary, is a curious document. Armanni printed it *in extenso*. The testator describes himself as " D. Giacomo Stuardo, Figliuolo naturale di Carlo II., procreato con la Signora D. Maria Stuardo della familia delli Baroni di S. Marzo." He wishes to be buried in the church of the Monastery of S. Francesco di Paola, outside the Porta Capuana, and *sopra terra come è di dovere*, and precisely at the wall of the Chapel of the Misericordia. The Fathers of the convent are to erect a suitable marble monument, with an inscription, and he leaves for this purpose 400 scudi to the Fathers, as well as 600 ducats for a weekly Mass, in perpetuity, to be said for the repose of his soul. The cost of his funeral, which was to be private, was to be defrayed by his father-in-law, according to instructions confided to his spiritual father, the Rev. Father Antonio di Gaglicano, at that time " Correttore " of the convent.

He then makes provision for his heirs, be they son or sons, daughter or daughters, his wife being then pregnant by the marriage which had been celebrated on the 19th of February, 1669, in the parish church of S. Sofia, after *exploratione de voluntà e altri atti solenni* in the cathedral church. " And, therefore," proceeds the testator, " I devotedly supplicate and represent to his Britannic Majesty that he will remit and assign," to my child or children, male or female, one or more as may be, " to be born of the said Teresa Corona, my wife, the ordinary principality, either of Wales or Monmouth, or other province customary to be given to the natural sons of the Crown," of the value of 100,000 scudi. And he supplicates his Majesty with all devotion to regard the will of the Supreme Judge Immortal, who in his universal judgment will rigorously repay all the acts of injustice done to poor innocents.

Furthermore, he prays his Majesty to restore and assign to his heirs 80,000 scudi of income, the property of D. Maria Stuardo, his mother, of her proper fortune, and belonging to him, her son and her rightful heir. He appoints Louis XIV. of France to be the guardian of his child or children. He recommends to the favourable notice of his Majesty all the Corona family, namely, Signor Francesco Corona, a gentleman of Sora ; his consort, Signora Annuccia d' Amicij (father and mother of Teresa); their son Gaetano, their daughter Chiara, another son Giovanni Battista Nicola, and a nephew, a Chierico, called D. Ciccio Arduino. To Corona and his wife and their three children here named he bequeaths 50,000 scudi each, to be paid once by his Britannic Majesty over and above the 180,000 scudi to be paid annually to his heirs. To Fr. Antonio da Gagliano he leaves 10,000 scudi ; and 5,000 to Fr. Feliciano di Hivago, of the same convent, which sums are to be applied according to his secret instructions.

He earnestly prays the King of France to urge the King of

England to carry out all the provisions of this will, and in order to secure the punctual payment of the legacies, which amount to 291,000 scudi, he assigns and gives his lands, called the Marquisate of Juvignis* [Juvigné or Juvigny?], worth 300,000 scudi.

He expressly orders and commands his wife Teresa to remain always a widow, and expresses his certain belief that she will so remain.

He then earnestly prays his father-in-law to go barefooted, after confession and communion in the cathedral, and to pray with his face to the ground before the Blessed Sacrament, for forgiveness of the testator's sins, and to do the same afterwards before the chapel of S. Aspremo, "where I espoused his daughter," and he is to do the same in the church of S. Francesco di Paula before the chapel of the Saint, and also before the chapel where his body shall lie. Each prayer is to be fervent and *di tutto cuore*, and of at least a quarter of an hour in duration. After the payment of the legacies, his sister-in-law Chiara is to be placed in a convent of noble ladies, with a dowry of 5,000 scudi. The interest of the rest of her fortune is to be paid to her personally. Should the notary allow any particulars of the will to be divulged before the testator's death, it is to be torn in pieces by his father confessor. The notary is to be paid 50 ducats by Signor Francesco Corona.

This will, which is without date, was made in 1669, and in that year the unfortunate prince died, aged about twenty-two years. According to his father's account, he was born in 1647, but according to the statement in the entrance books of the Jesuits he was twenty-four years old in 1668, and therefore was born in 1644. The account given by the king is more likely to be the true one. He was, however, the eldest son of all the

---

* Juvignis is probably a mistake for Aubigny, the dukedom which belonged to the Dukes of Richmond and Lennox of the older creation, which, after their death, was given by Louis XIV. to the Duchess of Portsmouth, and to which her descendants, the Dukes of Richmond, succeeded.

natural sons of Charles II., who always professed love and affection for him, and once even held out to him hopes of the inheritance of the English crown. That inconsistent monarch seems to have been afraid to acknowledge his son on account of his being a Catholic, except to the Queen and a few other persons who were pledged to secrecy. It is extremely unlikely that His Majesty gave any approval to the Corona marriage, or took much trouble about the posthumous issue of that marriage. Of course he never dreamed of carrying out all the provisions of the will, and he probably contented himself with sending a sum of money sufficient to provide for the modest wants of his son's widow, and perhaps enough to place her and her family in a position of comparative affluence. Whatever pecuniary arrangements were made on this occasion by Charles II., were made doubtless on the terms that secrecy should be observed in the matter, and that the widow should not be encouraged to claim the rank of an English princess for herself, or the principality of Wales for her son. The Stuart prince was doubtless buried in the church of Francesco di Paola, outside Porta Capuana, according to the directions of his will, but that church and the convent which adjoined it, and the registers and monuments, were totally destroyed in 1806, the epoch of the French military occupation of Naples, in order to form the grand piazza in front of the Royal Palace, and therefore it is impossible to search there for records of his burial, or for traces of the monument erected, if such were ever erected, to the memory of the defunct prince.

The foregoing account of Prince James Stuart has been mainly derived from the documents published in 1674 by Vincenzo Armanni, and from those published in the *Civilta Cattolica*. Armanni and the *Civilta* are both, as has been already noted, silent on the subject of any issue of the marriage celebrated between the prince and the Signorina Teresa Corona.

Documents, however, are still preserved in Naples and in the archives of the Propaganda in Rome, which prove that a posthumous son, the issue of that marriage, was born in Naples in 1669, in the month of December, and was baptised in that same year in the parish church of S. Sofia, by the name of James. Of this son's career from his birth to the year 1711, no particulars have been discovered. But in the year 1711, that son, who was then forty-two years of age, went from Naples, his native country, to Rome, and there gave himself out as Prince James Stuart, grandson to King Charles II., and a prince of the royal family of Stuart. He was at once arrested as a vagabond and impostor by the Pope Clement XI., and the most rigorous inquiries were instituted to ascertain the truth or falsehood of his pretensions. These enquiries resulted in establishing, to the perfect satisfaction of the Pontiff, the identity of the prince, and the truth of his claims to the rank of a grandson of Charles II. As the insult and imprisonment had been public, the Pope wished to make public reparation, and accordingly Prince James Stuart was admitted to a special audience, and permitted to kiss the Pope's foot. This ceremony took place with much formality in the presence of Cardinal Ottoboni, then Grand Chancellor of the Holy Roman Church; Cardinal Paolucci, Secretary of State; and Cardinals Della Tremeglia, Accioli, and Sacropanti. The prince was received with royal honours. The documents concerning this affair were deposited in the office of the Camera Apostolica, sealed with three seals, and entitled "Causa magna Stuarda." Search has been made in the Vatican Secret Archives for these documents, but without success.

After this Pontifical recognition, all Rome and all the ecclesiastical authorities were convinced of the rank and condition of the Prince James Stuart, who remained some time in Rome, no doubt enjoying the hospitalities of the princes and Cardinals.

From Rome the Prince went to Vienna, where he was received with great favour by the Emperor Charles VI. and the

Empress Eleonora Amalia, and where he remained for some years.

He then made a tour of many of the sovereign courts of Germany, being well received by the several princes and by all the sacred Roman empire as a Stuart prince. He was escorted in state from one court to the other, and was assigned attendants and equipages of horses, and obtained all the marks of respect usually accorded to royal personages. An account of the honours paid to him was printed in Cologne, with date of Feb. 6, 1724. The Elector of Bavaria treated him with especial regard.

Having terminated his journeys round great part of Germany, the Prince next visited Venice, and was recognised by the Republic, and was received with all suitable honours. This visit to Venice probably occurred in 1726, for in that year the ecclesiastical authorities in Venice seem to have sent to Naples for information concerning the Prince, and to have received in reply a formal document or certificate dated from Naples, March 30, 1726, signed by "Franciscus Card. Pignatellus," Archbishop of Naples, and addressed to all and singular whom it may concern, and notably to the Patriarch of Venice. This document was printed in Venice for the ecclesiastical authorities, and bears, in attestation of its merits, the signatures of the officials of the ecclesiastical court of Venice. The following extract from it puts the marriage of James Stuart the elder with Teresa Corona, and the birth of a posthumous son, beyond doubt :—

"ex processu . . fabricato super identitate personæ D. Jacobi Stuardo, filii posthumi D. Jacobi Enrici de Boveri Roano Stuardo filii naturalis Caroli II., Regis Angliæ, clare constat de matrimonio contracto inter secundò dictum D. Jacobum Henricum de Boveri Roano Stuardo Anglicanum et D. Theresiam Corona Neapolitanam in hac nostra Metropolitana ecclesia Neapolitana die 19 Feb. an. 1669 (sexagesimi noni); necnon predictum D. Jacobum Stuardo posthumum ortum fuisse in haemet civitate Neapolis, in constantia jam dicti matrimonii, eodem an. 1669, ac Baptizatum in parochiali ecclesia S. Sofiiæ hujus civitatis."

The date of the birth of the posthumous son, and the month

(September, 1669,) in which the father died, appear from the following extract obtained by the present writer from the registry of the parish church of S. Sofia in S. Giovanni a Carbonara—Libro XIII. de' Battezzati, folio 254 :—

"1669 il giorno dieci del mese di Dicembre si è amministrato il sagramento del Battesimo ad un fanciullo nato nel medesimo giorno dal fu D. Giacomo de Boveri Bosano [Roano] Stoardo (il quale mori quattro mesi prima di nascere il figlio) e dalla Sig^a D. Teresa Corona legitimi conjugi domiciliati in questa Parrocchia, al quale fu imposto il nome di Giacomo. La Levatrice fu Giuditta de Paula."

It must be observed that in these documents the son of Charles II. is described as bearing the names of James and Henry de Boveri, probably an *alias*, and De Rohan (Roano), another *alias*, but not as De la Cloche du Bourg de Jersey; while the marriage is said to have been solemnized in the Cathedral, whereas the Prince in his will assigns the marriage to the church of S. Sofia, and the betrothal or espousal to the Cathedral.

Prince James Stuart, the younger, remained in Venice for many years, probably until the year 1734, and then changed his residence to Genoa. The Archbishop of Genoa, Monsignor Nicolo Maria de Franchi, a Dominican, received a letter, dated 11th of May, 1734, from the Archbishop of Naples, recommending the Prince to his notice, and enclosing proofs of his identity. In consequence of this letter, the Archbishop of Genoa was very kind to Prince James, who appears at this time to have been in reduced circumstances. On the 30th of December, 1740, "P. Gio Batta (Giovanni Battista) Filippi, Custode della Metropolitana di S. Lorenzo," certifies that "the Prince has been many years resident in the parish of S. Lorenzo and is now in extreme necessity, and is obliged to inhabit a small room unprovided with necessaries." On the 25th of May, 1741, the Prince writes for pecuniary aid to the Congregation of the Propaganda Fide in Rome, giving details of his arrest in Rome in 1711, and of his visits to various Courts. He sends his baptismal certificate and his letters of naturalisation to this archi-episcopal court. He appeals for aid on the ground of his poverty, and of his constant efforts in behalf of the interests of the Catholic Church in England. He has always continued a Catholic. He does not, however, give any particulars of the great services he professes to have rendered to religion. He now (1741) lives in Genoa in a private manner, but preserves his credit and esteem as a true descendant of the Royal House of Stuart. He had received much assistance from the Most Illustrious and Most Reverend the Master of Misericordia. Don Felix Corneco, the Envoy Extraordinary of the Most Catholic King, had also shown him exceeding kindness, visiting him in his palace, inviting him in public form to his house and table, and giving him money for his appanage and more convenient sustenance. The Genoese Government, when it was rumoured that the Prince was disposed to leave Genoa, decreed him a sum of money to defray the costs of his journey. The Prince encloses documents in proof of his identity, and refers the curious who desire further information to the historical letter published by Vicenzo Armanni, mentioning the page and volume in which the account of his father appears. The Prince, now aged seventy-two years, wrote again to Cardinal Pietra, then the Prefect of Propaganda, on the 15th of February, and also on the 21st of July, 1741, imploring aid, but seems to have had no direct reply. These letters were written by an amanuensis, but bear the autograph signature, in straggling and feeble handwriting, of "Principe Giacomo Stuardo." After the date of July 21, 1741, these letters cease. Cardinal Pietra or the Pope may have sent the aged Prince some pecuniary relief through other channels than that of Propaganda. The legitimate head of the Stuarts was at that time residing in Rome under the title of James III., and may have been the instrument of succouring the needs of his illegitimate kinsman. It may be conjectured that the Prince James Stuart died in Genoa in the year 1741 or later, and it may be presumed that he died unmarried and childless, as in none of his many letters and documents is there the least allusion to wife or issue.

Nothing has been found in the Archives at Genoa which directly concerns this James Stuart. In 1881 and 1885 the Archivist Commendatore Cornelio Desimoni caused the parochial books of S. Lorenzo to be searched for traces of him but in vain. The Registers of the *Magistrato di Misericordia* were also examined. In the Archivio di Stato were examined all the papers of the Signoria, the Senate and Magistrates, and even the treasury accounts to see whether any sums were recorded as paid to Prince Stuart. Nothing whatever has yet been discovered excepting the original in print of the following :—

SERENISSIMO
JACOBO TERTIO
VATICINIUM
JACOBUS TERTIUS ANGLIAE REX.
ANAGRAMMA PURISSIMUM LITTERALE
EXUL ES, AT VICTORIA REGNABIS.
DISTICHON.
EXUL TERRESTRI REGNO COELESTIS AMORE
JACOBUS VINCENS UTRAQUE SCEPTRA GERIT.

Jo Maria Abbas Curti

This paper may have been printed by the charge or in the interest of Prince James. It did not however meet with the approbation of the authorities, for it appears from a note added to it, that the Abbas Curti, the publisher of the paper, was called for and reprimanded for his imprudence. This paper is to be found in the Sala Senato (fil. 4ᵗᵒ) under date of 28th of August 1741.

The writer in the *Civilta Cattolica*, not having before him the accounts published by Armanni, was convinced that James Stuart, the elder, or De la Cloche, completed his novitiate, and he even supposes him to have been present at the death bed of

King Charles, his father, in the year 1685. The Jesuit writer seems to base his argument upon the fact that the original testimonials given by the King to his son still exist among the Jesuit archives. Had the son left the Jesuits he would, so is the contention, have taken away with him the document proving his birth and entitling him to pecuniary support. But De la Cloche, alias De Rohan, had these papers with him in Naples, showed them when he was arrested as an adventurer, and probably they passed, on his death in 1669, to the Jesuit Fathers in Rome. At the time of his arrest he had written to the Father General to help him in his difficulties. It is quite certain from documents extant among the Jesuit archives that Charles II. was a liberal benefactor to S. Andrea del Quirinale. It appears from the King's letter to the Father General, dated November, 10, 1667, that the pecuniary aid then promised was to be paid in a year from that time, and the promise must have been fulfilled after the marriage of the son in February, 1669. It is not unlikely that the delicate health of the Prince was the cause of his leaving the novitiate. His marriage was sudden and a surprise, and undoubtedly a foolish step. But King Charles was a good-natured father, and probably made some provision for his son and grandson through means of the King of France or the Queen of Sweden. Prince James Stuart, the younger, appears not to have been in pressing want until his old age, and during his visits to the German and Italian Courts must have had other resources than the charity of princes.

Some remarks are perhaps required in anticipation of the objections which may be taken to the truth of the foregoing account. The two Stuarts may be deemed by some to have been impostors who traded on forged certificates and letters. What facts, it may be asked, can be adduced in favour of the documents regarding the elder Stuart? There is, first of all, the traditional belief that Charles II. gave a large sum of money to the Church and Convent of S. Andrea del Quirinale in Rome, in recognition of the reception of an illegitimate son into the Order of Jesuits. The documents written by Charles and by the Queen of Sweden are extant among the Jesuit archives, and are regarded as genuine. The Jesuit Father (Boero) who published them *in extenso* in the *Civiltà Cattolica*, was a very learned writer, and not likely to be deceived. The Novitiate entrance book can hardly be a forgery. The elder Stuart, if a spy or impostor, could readily have been detected by reference to the Jesuits at Hamburg, or to the Queen of Sweden, who was undoubtedly in Rome at the time. She states that she had been in communication with Charles II. about the son. If it be said that her certificate was revealed to the Jesuits under the seal of confession, and that, therefore, no reference could have been made to her, it may be rejoined that the letters of the King contain express reference to the Queen, and thus opened the way for free communication with her Majesty. The marriage certificate of James Stuart with Teresa Corona is still to be found in the parish register of S. Sofia in Naples, and his last will and testament lies in the National Library in the same city. The will and all the details of the marriage were published in 1674, within five years of the occurrences, by Armanni, who derived his information from the parish priest who introduced Prince Stuart to his future wife. Neither the priest nor Armanni had any unworthy objects to serve by communicating or publishing these accounts. The elder Stuart, so far as appears, got no money from the Queen of Sweden, the Jesuits, or the Coronas. In 1674, the elder Stuart was dead, and Armanni knew and wrote nothing about the posthumous son. It is easy to understand why the Jesuits in 1669 were silent concerning the marriage or the issue. They were ashamed of their novice, who found he had no true vocation for the religious state, and left them to re-enter the world; but they were grateful for the sums bestowed on them by Charles II. Their silence led afterwards to a general belief, still unshaken, among members of the

Order, that the son of Charles II. always remained a Jesuit until his death. Armanni knew nothing of the precise connection of James Stuart with the Jesuits. If we suppose the elder Stuart to have been an impostor, we must believe that the Jesuits participated in the imposture by giving credence to forged letters from King Charles and the Queen of Sweden; and the letter of Oliva, the Father General of the Order, must be suspected as a forgery. The King's gift of money must likewise have been a myth.

It may be said that the letters of Charles II. and the will of his son betray the hand of an impostor. A Catholic father would be horrified at the notion of confessing to his own son. But Charles II., at the date of his letters, was not a Catholic, although he professed to be one in heart. He wrote loosely and with levity, and it is not surprising that he manifests as little knowledge of Catholic doctrine as of the true principles of morality. That his son should betray ignorance of English customs and modes of government can excite no wonder, as he was brought up in foreign parts. But the general tone of the King's correspondence gives a picture of the manners of the English Court in 1668 which agrees in the main with what is recorded by Papal agents in their confidential reports on the state of England made in 1669 and 1670 to the Holy See. Parts of these reports were published in Vol. III. of *Episcopal Succession in England, Scotland, and Ireland*, pp. 108-117. The King, both in his letters and in the Papal reports, appears the same miserable dissembler—a Catholic to his wife and Father Howard, and speaking to Catholic agents as a Catholic prince ought, but, at the same time, fearful of betraying in public his Catholic sentiments, and ready to sacrifice the interests of his Irish and English Catholic subjects to keep himself on the throne. And his directions for the secret reception of his son in 1668 correspond remarkably with the details of the secret reception, in 1670, of Airoldi, the Papal envoy.

The elder Stuart, if an impostor, profited little by his imposture. He gained a penniless bride of humble rank, and died with deception on his lips. His will, if he were an impostor, was a blasphemous, as well as a foolish composition. If his wife and members of the Corona family knew him to be an impostor, could they have concocted the will, and, if so, to what possible use or purpose? Could they have deceived the parish priest? It is certain the will was not concocted by the younger Stuart, who was five years old when the will was printed by Armanni.

The case of James Stuart the younger is different from that of the elder. Proofs, indeed, are not wanting to identify the James Stuart who came to Rome in 1711 with the James Stuart baptised in Naples in 1669. We might ascertain better the nature of these proofs if we could see the documents which were in 1711 deposited in the *Camera Apostolica* with the title of *Causa magna Stuarda*. Search has been made, hitherto in vain, for these papers, both in the Vatican Library and in the Secret Archives of the Vatican. But the proofs adduced in 1711 were sufficient to satisfy Pope Clement XI. They doubtless included documents from the Archbishop of Naples, which would account for the education and career of the Prince between 1669 and 1711. During the years between 1711 and 1741, the movements of Prince James Stuart seem to have been well known and to have been without concealment. Until his latter years, he seems to have had no pressing pecuniary difficulties. If he were an impostor, no discovery of his imposture appears to have been made, although there was ample time and full opportunity to discover it. His last appeals to the Propaganda are made with confidence, and with bold reference to the proofs of his parentage, and at a time, be it remembered, when the legitimate head of his house, under the title of James III., was actually residing in Rome, and ready to denounce an impostor, especially an impostor who sued for money.

Memoirs of Cardinal Erskine.

THE materials for these Memoirs of Cardinal Erskine are in great part drawn from a manuscript life of His Eminence, written by his secretary, the Reverend Michel Angelo Del Medico, who seems to have received from Erskine all the Cardinal's papers, consisting of numerous letters and documents, and sundry loose notes upon persons and things, some of them written in the English language, but most of them in Italian; and besides these was a diary kept by Erskine, with regularity, save for a very few breaks, from the 12th of December, 1801, to the 11th of April, 1803. This original Diary and nearly all the original papers quoted by Del Medico, are no longer to be found in the Ghislieri College in Rome, to which Del Medico bequeathed all his library and papers, besides a sum of money. In fact no original Erskine papers now remain there, save the Cardinal's Will, the inventory of his furniture at Paris, and the receipt of his servants for their wages, etc.

Many, however, of the original Erskine documents which Del Medico quoted, and some which he did not quote and may never have seen, passed into the possession of the late Giuseppe Angelini, Vice-Gerent of Rome, archbishop in partibus, Canon of S. Peter's, etc., etc. Monsignor Angelini inherited a taste for collecting autographs, and bought a quantity of Erskine papers, and generously gave a portion of them to the Rector of the English College in Rome, and placed the rest among his autographs. At the death of the Vice-Gerent, the entire "Angelini Collection" containing many thousands of valuable autographs, passed, by purchase, to the well known Cavaliere Giancarlo Rossi, now residing in the Odescalchi Palace in Rome. Free access to these original manuscripts was kindly given to the writer by Cavalier Rossi and by Archbishop Henry O'Callaghan and Monsignor Giles, the late and the present Rector of the English College.

The writer obtained access to Del Medico's life of Erskine by favour of Duke Salviati, the present Patron of the Ghislieri College, and was enabled by the Rector of the College, Monsignor Galimberti, to make copious extracts from it. The first twelve pages of this manuscript, which contains on the whole 600 pages, are taken up with a copy of the Erskine genealogy, legally drawn by officials and magistrates of Edinburgh, and bearing the date of May 26, 1769. It was signed at Edinburgh.

The genealogy of the Erskines, Earls of Kellie and Earls of Mar, in Scotland, needs no repetition in these pages. It has in late years been prominently brought into notice by controversies about the right of succession to the Mar Peerage. But in the Papal archives are two dispensations for intermarriage between persons related in the fourth degree, both dated from Avignon and concerning the Erskine family. The first is dated March 3, 1355, and is a dispensation granted by Pope Innocent VI., for removing the impediments to the marriage of the Noble Robert Erskine and the Noble Donna Cristiana de Keth [Keith]. This was granted with consent of the King of Scotland, who was a blood relation of the lady.

The second dispensation was granted by Pope Urban VI., on 29th of November, 1393, for removing impediments to the marriage of the Noble Thomas de Erskine with the Noble Donna Maria de Douglass. These dispensations may tend to fix the dates of these marriages.

In regard to the parentage of Cardinal Erskine, his father was Colin, seventh son of Sir Alexander Erskine of Cambo, Baronet, by the Lady Anne Erskine, daughter of the third

Earl of Kellie. This Colin, an adherent of the Stuarts, went into voluntary exile, and came to Rome, and married Agatha Gigli, who was of the noble family of Gigli of Anagni, which family was one of those called the *Seven Stars* of Anagni. By her, who died on the 28th of September, 1786, aged 75 years, and was buried in the Scotch College in Rome, he had but two children, Charles, born in Rome on the 13th of February, 1739, and Clementina, wife to the Advocate Pio Ferrari.

A portrait of Colin Erskine, which is now in the possession of Monsignor Campbell, rector of the Scots College in Rome, has beneath it the words :—COLINUS ARESKINUS SCOTO-BRITANNUS ALEXANDRI ARESKINI EQUITIS AURATI FAECIALIUM ANTISTITIS VULGO DICTI LEONIS ARMORUM REGIS FILIUS, OBIIT ROMAE 18 JANUARII 1740 ÆTAT. SUÆ 35.

Charles, who, when very young, lost his father, was taken under the care of the Cardinal Duke of York, who placed him, when only nine years old, in the Scots College in Rome. He entered the College on the 27th of May, 1748, and received the sacrament of confirmation from Monsignor De Rossi, Vice-Gerente of Rome, on the 13th of April, 1749. But when called on to decide whether he would take the customary oath against becoming a Religious, he refused, and consequently he left the College on the 4th of November, 1753, being then about fourteen years old.

He now determined upon the study of Law, and steadily acquired knowledge, taking occasional holidays at Caprarola, in the house of his maternal cousin, Canon Domenico Salvatori.

His career as a lawyer, which he completed by serving in the studio of Sala, was very brilliant, and he was soon ranked among the most successful advocates. He took his degree as Doctor in Laws with much eclât in the Roman *Arciginnasio*, on the 21st of November, 1770; obtained success in some celebrated lawsuits, and attracted the favourable notice of the then reigning Pontiff, Pius VI. His Holiness, on the 13th of February, 1776, gave him an annual charge of 200 scudi on the bishopric of Ferrara, and Prince Sigismond Chigi, in 1780, made him his Auditor. Erskine was now in the height of his fame as a leading advocate in Rome. His eloquence and his talent for administration brought him plenty of clients and plenty of money.

Pius VI., however, wished to bind Erskine more nearly to the service of the Holy See, and consequently, in May, 1782, on the death of Cardinal Giraud, he made him his *Pro-uditore*, and at same time made him *Promotore della Fede*, a domestic prelate, Canon of St. Peter's and a Concistorial Advocate. On the 1st of June, 1782, he was made Dean of the College of Concistorial Advocates. These favours, great as they were, caused Erskine to lose his freedom in a great measure, as well as the opportunity for increasing his fame as an advocate, and the further public practice of a profession in which he delighted. Henceforth his eloquence and his exquisite Latinity were to be confined to secret congregations. Notwithstanding his regret at thus losing his favourite practice, he went with the other persons, who at the same time had received promotions, to meet Pius VI. on his way to return to Rome, and offered his thanks, on the 12th of June, 1782, to His Holiness, in Città Castellana.

On the 28th of May, 1783, Monsignor Erskine received the Minor Orders in St. Peters from the Cardinal of York, and the orders of Subdeacon on the 28th of August following, from the same Cardinal. He had been made a *Votante* of the *Segnatura di Grazia* in July of same year. But Erskine's work as a Vatican prelate and in the Roman congregations may be here omitted, as he was in a few years to enter on a different sphere of action.

The French Revolution soon displayed all the ferocity of a pitiless persecution of nobles and clergy, and gave horrible examples of its savagery in the dreadful massacres in Paris, which took place on the second and third days of September, 1792, and were followed by similar enormities in the provinces of France. Emigration gave the only hope of escape, and England offered the surest refuge. Many nobles, and many bishops and ecclesiastics of every grade, fled to Great Britain, which for the priests, however, was not in all respects, owing to the then stringent laws against Catholics, an entirely satisfactory place of abode. The British Government, indeed, and the British people, were prompt, as on all similar occasions, to offer compassionate welcome to the Catholic priests. And even the fish vendors, when the Catholics landed in poverty and misery, showed their sympathy by giving them fish for nothing.

Pius VI. observed, and wished to utilize, this generous feeling displayed by the English towards the refugees, and conceived the idea of sending an envoy to the British Court for the purpose of obtaining some legalized liberty for the French Catholic clergy residing in England. Monsignor Erskine was the most suitable person for such a mission, yet it was feared he would not be received as an envoy, because the laws of England were against it ; and as a private person he could make no treaty, and gain no access to the British Ministers. Besides, there was risk that such a mission might prove useless, or worse, by this intervention of Rome, a thing abhorred by Protestants, and by which the condition of the refugees might be rendered still more painful.

Yet the Pope had some reasons for expecting a favourable issue to his endeavours. He had had kindly intercourse with some members of the Royal Family of England. In the end of of the year 1775, William Henry, Duke of Gloucester, and brother to George III., was in Rome with his wife, and was so well received by Pius VI. that he remained a year and a half in an apartment which he took on lease in the Ripetta, in a palace next the Church of S. Rocco, opposite to the unsightly bridge recently built over the Tiber to replace the old ferryboat. In Rome was born, on the 15th of January, 1776, the Duke's only son, William Frederick, second Duke of Gloucester, and a

Field-marshal. Also in November, 1791, the sixth son of George III., Augustus Frederick, Duke of Sussex, came to Rome, where he resided some years for the winter and spring seasons, and where he contracted a marriage, celebrated by a Protestant minister on the 4th of April, 1793, with Lady Augusta de Ameland, daughter of the fourth Earl of Dunmore, a Scotch peer. The Duke of Sussex went frequently to visit Pius VI., with whom he was on most friendly terms. And once the Duke was seen following on horseback the cortege of the Pope, who was then returning to Rome from the Marches. Of all this was not George III. well informed, and was not His Majesty likely to make a suitable return, by shewing equal urbanity to a Papal Envoy, provided the necessary regards were observed towards the English Government and people?

Pius VI. also was well aware that the actual dispositions at that time existing between England and France were such as strongly aided his purpose. Notwithstanding, he determined to leave nothing to hazard, and resolved that propositions on the subject should be made to the English Government indirectly, through the means of Mr. Jenkins, an Englishman then living in Rome as British Consul or Agent. The answers to these overtures were favourable, but it was stipulated that the mission should not pretend to have a public character.

Monsignor Erskine was now selected by the Pope as the person to whom the English mission should be entrusted. Erskine, indeed, was not only the best, but perhaps the only man suitable for the expedition. Although born in Rome, he was the son of a Scotchman, possessed British nationality, and, according to English laws, was entitled to enter England without permission or passport. Moreover, his journey might be set down to his natural desire to visit and make nearer acquaintance with his paternal and noble relatives, and this presumption would serve to conceal, at least before the eyes of the public, the principal motive of his mission. His personal qualities were altogether in his favour. And his rare talents, his already proved experience in affairs, his knowledge of the laws and customs of Great Britain, not to mention his facility of speaking the English language, with which he was most familiar, marked him out as specially adapted for the service. His position as Envoy was in the highest degree delicate, and altogether novel and without precedent. He could count very little on the instructions given him by Cardinal De Zelada, Papal Secretary of State, for these were necessarily limited to the general view of obtaining protection from Great Britain for the clerical refugees from France, and alleviating, as far as possible, the condition of English Catholics. It was enjoined on him to act with prudence, and thus he was left to rely chiefly on himself, being held personally responsible for all his conduct.

Among the Secret or Private Archives of the Vatican, now so liberally opened to historical students by the wisdom of Leo XIII., is a letter curiously illustrating the feeling current a hundred years ago respecting the subject of diplomatic relations between England and Rome. It was written in Italian, by one Joseph Denham, to the Secretary of State, Cardinal De Zelada, and was dated from Onano, a village near Viterbo, on the 3rd of September, 1793. In English it is as follows:—

"Eminence,—When I was in the world I had the honour of being known to your lordship and of enjoying your patronage; but it is now seven years since I have seen you, and two full years that I have lived in this miserable place, separated from human commerce and little informed of what is passing in the world. Therefore, if what I am about to say has no foundation, your lordship will attribute it only to my ignorance of the facts.

"I have supposed that the Pope has destined Monsignor Erskine as Apostolic Envoy to the Court of London, upon which subject the devotion I profess to his Holiness urges me to inform your Eminence that, as well as my memory serves me of the laws of England, there exists an Act of Parliament inhibiting the King from receiving any Minister of the Pontiff. I would not wish the honour and dignity of the Holy Father to be compromised, for, if my idea be correct, deplorable consequences might ensue.

"I have thought, however, of a *mezzo termine* by means of which the intent might be obtained without the least violation of the Anglican laws. I premise that the affair must be regarded as one merely secular and without introducing a word about religion.

"I would wish, then, that the credentials of the Envoy should be sent in the name of the Senate and people of Rome, setting forth that, for certain interests of theirs, it was necessary to despatch an Envoy to treat concerning them with his Brittannic Majesty, and that for this purpose such or such a person was nominated with all necessary and opportune faculties, etc. The patent of said credentials would be subscribed by the Senators of Rome, with the seal of the Capitol affixed.

"The significance of this would be fully comprehended by the King and his Ministers, and the Envoy would be well received, without giving umbrage either to the laws, or to the populace, who might otherwise be capable of committing excesses, such as happened in 1780, on the occasion of the new laws in favour of the Catholics.

"If my supposition be correct, and if my idea finds favour with your Eminence, make use of it as you please, otherwise let it remain buried. I am always most thankful for the favours received from your Eminence in past years; and, being full of true gratitude and veneration, I salute the sacred purple.

"Your Eminence's most humble, devoted, and obliging servant,

"JOSEPH DENHAM."

The Pope, no doubt, duly considered the advice of Mr. Denham, but declined to follow it. He arranged for this mission in another way, and before the end of autumn all was prepared. Monsignor Erskine, having taken leave of the Pope with all due formalities, began his journey to England on the morning of Friday, the 4th of October, 1793. He, however, went out of his way on the very beginning of his travels, and proceeded to Caprarola, where he passed the night of Friday, and took farewell of his nearest relatives on the mother's side, the Salvatori, with whom he used to spend his vacations as a boy and his leisure time as a man. On the following morning, that of the 5th of October, he resumed his journey by way of Tuscany, passing through Sienna, Florence, Bologna, Modena, Parma, Mantua, Verona, and thence to Trent and Botzen, so as to enter Germany by the gates of the Tyrol. Then he went on by Augsburg and Stuttgart to the Rhine, and then to Aix-la-chapelle, and by Brussels to Ostend, where he took ship for England. He landed at Margate in the little island of Thanet, and crossing to the mainland, arrived at last in London on the 13th of November, forty days from his departure from Rome.

Monsignor Erskine himself stated that the Police and Custom house officials, on his entrance upon British territory, seemed to have been previously advised of the arrival of a diplomatic personage, for they displayed to him a courtesy far exceeding what was due to a mere fellow countryman. And the postillions, divining from this special treatment, the quality of the traveller, took care, on each change of the post horses, to announce, with emphasis, to the postillions who succeeded them, *the Ambassador of the Pope!* This was done the whole way up to London, and Erskine could not perceive that the news was received in any sinister manner, but the rather with an increased desire to serve him. The Papal Government was duly informed of this auspicious beginning, and being satisfied with this reception, published, in the first days of January, in the *Diario di Roma*, the arrival in London of Monsignor Erskine, Promotor of the Faith, and also his departure from London for Edinburgh. This last item of news was to conform to the conduct to be observed by Erskine, as if his primary object was that of visiting his relations.

But it was not precisely to Edinburgh that Monsignor Erskine went on leaving London, but to St. Andrews, which was further north by a day's journey, and in the county of Fife. Here dwelt Lord Kellie, the head of the family, who received him with all demonstrations of affection, and with sincere expressions of his satisfaction in embracing a cousin as yet only known to him by name. It was with much pleasure that Erskine in later years recollected his visits to these cousins on this and other occasions. They were three in number, including Lord Kellie, and all of them were married but without male issue, and they saw with regret that in their families the dignity of a Peer of Scotland could not be continued. They told their Roman cousin to consider that he was to succeed after them to the legal inheritance of all the titled possessions of the family and to the Scotch Earldom, which he must inherit if he survived them, without, however, a seat in Parliament, as he was a Catholic. They went further and proposed to him, that, as they no longer had any hope of male issue, and as he was the only person who could remedy the mischief, he should marry and beget heirs. Monsignor, in reply, scouted the project as wholly incapable of execution, seeing that he was already a sub-deacon and could not take a wife. They insisted that he, if he chose to ask a dispensation, would easily get it, because in this way the succession of the Erskine family and the dignity of a Scotch peerage would be established in a Catholic branch. Monsignor Erskine expressed surprise at hearing the religious motives which his Protestant cousins adduced to prevail on him to abandon the ecclesiastic state. But they must have felt still more astonishment in perceiving that the love of riches and rank had no effect on his mind towards inducing him to such a step, even though the Pope, in the case of a mere sub-deacon and in view of making one of the primary families of Scotland a Catholic one, should give his consent.

London, in a very short time, became the habitual residence of Monsignor Erskine, for there, where the seat of the British government was fixed, he was to fulfil the duties of his mission. He doubtless, besides his Roman credentials, had letters of introduction from Lord Kellie to friends in the great capital. And it was not long before he was admitted to Court, to the State receptions customary to be held by the King on appointed days. On these occasions were assembled in a large saloon in St. James' Palace, the Diplomatic corps and a goodly number of nobles, British and Foreign, all arranged in a great semi-circle. The chief places were occupied, according to their respective ranks, by members of the Diplomatic body, which enjoys, moreover, another distinction in London, namely that of having access to the Royal palace by a courtyard separated from the crowd of all the other carriages of the lords and gentlemen presenting themselves for admission to the same Receptions. Monsignor Erskine well knew that he could not pretend to any distinction for himself as a representative of the Pope, but he proposed to himself to sustain by prudence his own proper character, by availing himself of all circumstances which might offer a favourable opportunity. Accordingly, on the first occasion of a Reception, he presented himself at the entrance of the palace, and there giving his name, heard the order given to his coachman to pass into the courtyard of the Diplomatic body. By this he was enabled to perceive plainly that the English Government, without attributing a special character to him as Papal Envoy, acknowledged him in general as a representative of a Foreign Sovereign.

He had next to decide upon the precise place he was to occupy among the Ambassadors, Ministers, and other Diplomatic personages, who were accustomed to take their places, one after the other, in order according to the etiquette prescribed among themselves ; and in this matter Erskine had to avoid opposition on the part of those, who would not readily yield him precedency, and at the same time to avoid the least exhibition of ostentation in a Court, which up to that time had been hostile to the Holy See, but which in this conjuncture of affairs, assumed, so to speak, an attitude of condescension and courtesy. He therefore chose to take his place as the last of the Diplomatic body, which he did with such tact, as to leave it in doubt whether he was last of that body, or the first among the nobles admitted to the Reception. This discreet behaviour of Erskine was extremely gratifying to the Government, which was not in the least desirous of compromising itself in the face of a Protestant nation. The King himself, George III., showed to Erskine his satisfaction with his conduct, by stopping longer, as he went round, to speak with him, than he stopped with the others, on all occasions when Erskine presented himself. This preference, as might be expected, excited wonder among many who were present, and among some of them raised envy.

Erskine himself, when Cardinal, used to relate what the subjects of his conversations with George III. were. At the first Reception, after various other questions, His Majesty asked him what was his office in the Roman Court. Monsignor Erskine had to explain the duties of the Promotor of the Faith, and this he did with brevity and precision, and concluded by saying that in Rome he was vulgarly styled *The Devil's Advocate*, at which the King burst into a fit of laughter. On another occasion George III. asked Erskine what he thought of London. He promptly answered :—" In London I find a city without limits, a population without number, and riches which overflow into the public streets." His Majesty was highly pleased, and declared that he had never heard a more beautiful nor more expressive definition of London. In fine, George III. found continual matter for conversation with Erskine, to whom he put many and often varied demands, concerning Roman affairs, sacred and profane. The King knew well that Erskine was able to satisfy his curiosity, by reason of his full knowledge of the things asked about, and of his singular facility in conversation.

Many persons, on learning of this frequent attendance of Monsignor Erskine at state receptions, along with ambassadors, ministers and high officials, will be desirous to know in what uniform or dress, he presented himself at Court before the King. Of course he could not wear the dress of a prelate of the Roman Court, a dress with which he never could have got admission to the Court of George III., without exposing himself to insult or to worse. His dress, accordingly, must be that which is usually termed the dress of etiquette, to be worn on occasions of attending the royal receptions. So Erskine chose to put on the black court-dress of a secular, and to wear the sword which generally gives to that dress an imposing and formal appearance. Erskine relied much on the colour, because he only wore the same dress, and so could not be confounded with other persons who might wear black on certain occasions, but not always, in the King's presence. It so happened that Erskine presented himself at Court in this black dress, on the anniversary of the King's birthday. The Master of Ceremonies, on seeing him, told him that no black dresses were admissible on that day, and that on account of his dress, and for that reason solely, he was obliged to refuse him entrance to the royal reception. Monsignor Erskine replied resolutely that his dress was that of his representative character, and not a dress of mourning. The Master of Ceremonies then begged him to wait a little, and passed into the King's apartment, from whence he issued in a few moments to tell Erskine he might enter, and at the same time he excused himself for having put difficulties in the way of his introduction. Thus it happened on that state reception, when black dresses are strictly prohibited, that Erskine was permitted to wear an entirely black costume in deference to his quality as a Roman ecclesiastic, a quality then and in this way publicly acknowledged, not without amazement on the part of the numerous nobles who were present. From this incident it may be seen how prudently Erskine acted in his choice of his court dress, a matter which to some might seem of very trivial moment, but which to him, at that court and in those times, was one deserving his special consideration. Subsequently, on many occasions, inside Catholic churches and chapels, Erskine did not hesitate to show himself as a prelate of the Roman Church, and within them to celebrate ecclesiastical functions, such as never had been attempted or even named in all England, since the epoch of the Anglican schism and heresy.

Monsignor Erskine did not fail to keep De Zelada, the Cardinal Secretary of State, fully informed of all his doings in London; and he maintained also a very brisk correspondence with Cardinal Filippo Campanelli, the Pro-Datary, who was highly esteemed by the Pontiff. That Pius VI. was fully satisfied with Erskine's proceedings, and pleased with his manner of acting, and with the results obtained from the very beginning of his mission, was manifestly proved by the anxiety of the Pope to advance Erskine to a higher position in the Roman prelacy.

Erskine had hardly completed three months of his residence in England, when the Pope, in secret consistory of the 21st of February, 1794, made him his *Uditore*, in room of Aurelio Roverella, promoted to the cardinalate. This high office had been held by Cardinal Giraud as *Pro-Auditore* until his death, and after that by Campanelli and Roverella successively, until they became cardinals. It was arranged that the Abbate Donato as *Vice-Uditore* should discharge the duties of the office in the absence of Erskine. With singular goodness the Pope ordered that the revenues of the auditorship, from time to time as they accrued, should be funded and placed in deposit in order that Erskine, who had other revenues for his support in England, might, on his return to Rome, find an accumulation of money very convenient to meet the expenses of his elevation to the purple. This shows the kindness and forethought of Pius VI., who intended to create Erskine a cardinal. But alas! the unfortunate irruption of the French troops into the Papal States, caused Erskine to lose all the money thus deposited in his favour. Erskine, on the 28th of February, 1794, wrote to thank the Pope and the Secretary of State for his promotion.

The fury of the Revolution was now no longer confined within the limits of France. War was kindled with Piedmont, Austria, Spain and England, and the peace of Europe was threatened. The Great Powers began to seriously occupy themselves with the affairs of France, in order to provide for public tranquillity and security. Rumours prevailed about the month of May, 1795, that the Powers allied against France had it in contemplation to assemble a Congress of Plenipotentiaries to establish the means of an accommodation and a general peace. This intelligence was of high importance, and the Pope determined to take timely measures to have a Papal representative in that Congress, to sustain the rights of the Holy See in the preservation of the Catholic religion, now oppressed by France, and in defence of the Papal States, assailed by the invasion of Avignon and Venaissin. The Pope chose Erskine to be his representative in the expected Congress, and a dispatch to that effect was sent to him on the 6th of June, 1795.

This dispatch states that in view of the assembly of a Congress, Erskine was to be, in anticipation, furnished with provisional credentials as Papal Representative, to obviate all possible delays in transmission or loss of letters, etc. These credentials were to be kept secret until occasion arose for their production. But Erskine, if he thought it advantageous, might, but with due caution, confide the secret of these credentials to the Ministers of Great Britain, or of any other of the Allied Powers. The chief object of the Pope and the one nearest his heart, was the safety and protection of the Catholic religion and its complete restoration in France. His second object concerned the temporal interests of the Holy See, the restitution of Avignon and Venaissin, reparation for the injuries inflicted on the Pontiff, his ministers, etc., during the first years of the Revolution, and compensation for the losses incurred by the Papal Treasury. The letters of credence, addressed to Monsignor Erskine by Cardinal De Zelada, Secretary of State, were as follows :—

"Most Illustrious and Most Reverend Sir,

"In the event of the realization, hereafter, of the reports which are now spread abroad of the probability of the convocation of a Congress, in which will take part the Plenipotentiary of His Majesty the Emperor and representatives of the other Powers allied in the actual war against France, in order to deliberate upon an accommodation and a general Peace, His Holiness the Pope, for the purpose of avoiding prejudicial delay, has determined from this very moment to authorize your Lordship and to charge you—as by these presents He does authorize and charge you—to present yourself, in His Pontifical name and in quality of His Representative, to the Congress and to the aforesaid Plenipotentiaries, to set forth and guarantee the just claims and the incontestable rights of the Holy See, upon the several subjects which can affect the interests, as well spiritual as temporal, of the same, in the said matter of an accommodation and general peace with France, the said Plenipotentiaries of the allied Powers being therefore entreated to recognize your Lordship, provisionally, as such, and as provided, for that purpose, with the Pontifical confidence and authorization, until such time as there shall be opportunity to receive from the Papal Court, powers more in conformity with the customs of Courts and of similar Congresses, together with ulterior and opportune instructions for the full discharge of this your commission.

"This will suffice to serve your Lordship for rule and

guidance according to opportunities, and with sentiments of the most distinguished esteem I cordially kiss your hands. I remain your Lordship's faithful servant, F. X. Card. de Zelada. Rome 6. June 1795."

In consequence of disagreements among the allied Powers, the Congress did not take place, yet the instructions and credentials, which duly reached Monsignor Erskine, were not wholly useless. For as he was now furnished with credentials, which put him in a position to present himself as an Envoy Extraordinary of the Holy See in a general Congress of the Powers allied against France, his diplomatic character at the Court of Great Britain acquired a much higher consideration. For it cannot be supposed that the commission entrusted to Erskine by the Pope remained unknown to the Ministers of the British Government. And Monsignor Erskine himself must have communicated the secret, in accordance with the suggestions given to him to do so whenever the opportunity offered to further, by so doing, the cause of the Pontiff. And although no Congress of the kind expected was held, yet Monsignor Erskine was enabled to provide that in all the English treaties with France the interests of the Holy See should be effectually served.

A society of antiquaries in London, having compiled a volume of *Roman Military Antiquities*, presented, with a courtesy then rather uncommon in a Protestant association, a copy to the Pope, through the instrumentality of Erskine, who sent it on 12th of June, 1795, to Rome, by the Italian courier, Pio Rotondi, together with letters from himself. Pius VI. was surprised and pleased on its arrival, and desired Monsignor to thank the antiquaries in his name, and to say that although he could not himself read English, he was quite certain the book was admirably composed. The Pope then proceeded to express to Erskine his sense of the loss of Cardinal Campanelli, who had died on 17th of February, 1795. Campanelli was a devoted friend and trusted adviser of the Pontiff, and also a constant correspondent of Monsignor Erskine, who had written to him at least eighty letters from London in the course of fifteen months.

The Pope, after deploring Campanelli's loss as irreparable, expressed his astonishment at the treaty of peace between Spain and France, which had been signed at Basle on the 22nd of July, 1795. The conduct of the Minister of Spain was by no means pleasing, for he gave festive entertainments in Rome to the French officers, who were then exacting exorbitant contributions from the Papal States, and were about to spoil the city of those monuments which were the delight of Pius VI.

Meanwhile the life led by Erskine in London, was a busy one. He communicated with the Vicars Apostolic of England and Scotland and with the Irish bishops, and gave to them advice and instructions. He had frequent and friendly interviews with the minister, Mr. Pitt, and pleaded for the interests of the Holy See and for British Catholics and the French refugees. Among these Frenchmen were some Trappists who lived in the country, supporting themselves on land given them by a rich Englishman. They professed their Rule, and wore their habit, inside and around their house, with a liberty and tranquillity up to that time unknown in England. And when Erskine visited them, they met him with a procession headed by the Cross. A community of Nuns had escaped from the Low Countries to England, with all their valuables, and the Austrian Government had meanly applied to the British Minister for restitution of all the precious objects which the poor nuns had carried off. On Erskine's representations, the Austrian demand was quietly set aside by Mr. Pitt.

Erskine met in society many Anglican bishops and clergymen, and almost invariably their conversations ended in controversy, carried on, however, with good humour. He used to quote against them their own Church Catechism. On one occasion, a bishop said to him that "in his judgment the

Roman Church went too far in the pomp of her external worship, while the English went to the contrary extreme, but between the two he preferred the Roman mode, for it acted efficaciously on the popular class."

It is unnecessary here to enter into details of the French occupation of Rome and the brutal violence practised on the person of Pius VI., who rashly consented to the treaty of Tolentino, made under compulsion on the 19th of February, 1797. Previously to that time the Pope had been violently stripped of the greater part of his dominions, and was virtually prisoner, soon to become one in dread reality, and he was as helpless before Bonaparte, as his successor, Pius IX., was before Victor Emmanuel.

The events of the sad years, 1796 and 1797, threw additional labour upon the shoulders of Erskine. As Great Britain had more open intercourse with foreign parts, London became a centre of correspondence between Erskine and the Papal Nuncios in Madrid, Lisbon, Vienna, the Rhine and Holland. He wrote frequent despatches to Monsignors Casoni, Pacca, Ruffo, Della Genga and Brancadoro. His Vienna despatches were sent sometimes through the hands of Marchese de Circelli, Neapolitan Minister at London, and sometimes through Mr. Canning, then Under Secretary of State; and very often in these roundabout ways he contrived to send letters to Rome and the Pope, as also to the Papal Secretary of State, Cardinal Giuseppe Doria.

Erskine had given a large parcel and letters for the Pope and Doria into the hands of Pio Rotondi, the courier, who was sent to Tuscany by Cavalier Angiolini, the then diplomatic agent in England of the Grand Duke. Pio left London not before the 30th of December, 1797, and taking a longer route than usual, in order to avoid armies on the march, did not reach Tuscany until the end of February, 1798, when he found the Pope in Sienna, where had lived since the 25th of that month.

Pius VI., on the 16th of March, 1798, wrote from Sienna to thank Erskine for the parcel, which was a present to the Pope of a service of table linen and an assortment of razors, which latter articles were very welcome to His Holiness. The Pope's letter, after mention of the razors, proceeds as follows :—

"We have said that We received your kind present in this place of *exile*, because the French force compelled Us to decamp from Rome, declaring that the Civil Government belonged to the people. The first step which the French took at the opening of the Revolution was to burn Us, in effigy, publicly in Paris. Next they possessed themselves of Avignon and Venaissin, and then they seized the three provinces of Bologna, Ferrara and the Romagna, and, piece by piece, they took all the rest; so that of all our Sovereignty nothing remains to Us save the memory. The war, for them so fortunate, is a war against Religion, for they perpetrated a thousand sacriligious outrages against the Church,—as the late Bishop of Spires wrote to Us—against the priests and friars, confiscating their property. And this was the system which they have always pursued, and still continue to pursue in Rome. They found out a pretended excuse in the circumstance that General Duphôt was killed by Our civic troops; but his death was in consequence of his own attempt to force their quarters and disperse them. They resisted, as was their duty, and in the confusion shots were fired, and a bullet happened to kill the General. This is the undeniable truth, as results from the Process instituted by order of Our Secretary of State. But they have determined to colour all their iniquities by this pretext, in order to carry into execution the plan they had concerted beforehand, which was to impose intolerable contributions, to quarter their soldiers by compulsion, stimulating poor families, who could scarcely feed themselves, to give entertainment to officers, soldiers, and horses. Several prelates were arrested in Castel S. Angelo and sent to the convent of the Convertite, in the Corso, as hostages for six or seven Cardinals who are to be banished—they say—to Sicily, and have already been sent to Civita Vecchia. If maltreatment had been offered to the French, there might be excuse for them, but in reality every attention and consideration was shewn them.

"Before entering Rome they gave assurances in writing that the form of Government would not be changed; but at their very first ingress, they insisted that the keys of the city gates and of Castel S. Angelo should be consigned to them. Before Our enforced departure, they posted guards within the innermost rooms of Our apartment, put seals on Our presses, and carried away every thing there was of any value. They despoiled the Vatican of its most precious monuments, such as statues, pictures and codexes; and they did the same in many private houses, notwithstanding their declaration that all property would be safe.

"We Ourselves determined not to leave—whatever might be the cost—Our Residence, taking into consideration Our age, over eighty years, our state of convalescence after a malady of the duration of two years and a half, which took away the use of our feet. But it was not possible for Us to obtain the favour of remaining, as they threatened to make Us leave the Palace by force, so that we were obliged to drink the bitter cup, and to go out from Our States, and retire, as they ordered, to the dominions of Tuscany. Could greater barbarity be shown? On leaving the palace, which was before day, We found at foot of the grand staircase, an escort of seventy Dragoons and two Commissaries. The Commissaries accompanied Us all the way here to Sienna, though the Guards on horseback were dismissed at the end of the first stage.

"Now although We quite understand that in London you cannot bring to the front religious motives, yet such motives, when they involve questions of Sovereignty and the rights of nations, must make a strong impression. And for the same reason We, being personally known to the Emperor of Russia, have written a Brief to him, imploring his aid under the present most bitter circumstances, and We doubt not that he, albeit a Schismatic, will take to heart Our unfortunate situation. And therefore your Lordship must employ means to secure that in the Congress, which must be held for peace, either in Rastadt or elsewhere, restitution shall be made to Us of the States which were violently taken from Us, beginning with Avignon and Venaissin. It is a thing certain, and not disputed, that what is gained in an unjust war must be restored and cannot pass into the dominion of the unjust possessor. A war more unjust than that of the French against the Holy See, cannot be imagined, wherefore We have the most just of titles to claim back all that has been taken from Us. He who shall be destined to act for Us in the quality of Our Commissary for Great Britain, must make himself Our Advocate, and put forward the afore-mentioned reasons of the spoil and sackage committed against Us without the smallest cause of complaint. We leave this business to you, to whom are not wanting activity and eloquence.

"On the evening of the seventh of this month, seven cardinals were carried to Città Vecchia for transportation to Sicily, or, as some say, to Portugal. We shall wait to see what other acts of hostility they shall perpetrate. We have said from the beginning that the French pretend to justify their sack of Rome by the slaying of General Duphot. We now add, that besides the fact that he caused his own death by his determination to force one of the quarters of our Civic Guards, every sort of satisfaction was offered to the French, but they, neither accepting such satisfaction nor refusing it, proceeded to immediate action, and committed those excesses which We have described, thus evidently proving that it was a mere pretext of which they took advantage to torment Us in every way.

" And now We give you from Our heart the Paternal Apostolical Benediction. From Sienna, the Church of the

Assumption, the 16th of March, 1798, and 24th year of Our Pontificate. Pius, P. P. VI."

The Emperor Paul I. of Russia had visited Rome, in 1782, under the name of Conte del Nord, his mother, the Empress Catherine, being then alive, and he had often visited the Pope, for whom he professed much affection. The letter now sent to him by Pius VI. gave an impulse to the sending of an army into Italy under General Souvarow.

Pius VI., in another letter to Erskine, dated from Florence the 28th of July, 1798, writes :—"The matrimonial dispensation, which was sent to you from America, We return to you herewith enclosed, but in all similar cases you must inform Us as to whom to send them for execution, for We, not having here the Penitenzieria, address them at hazard, and the more so as the handwriting of the missionaries and bishops are un-intelligible." The Pope next referred to the sudden death of Bishop Charles Berington, Vicar Apostolic of the Midland district in England, who, he supposed, had not before dying, signed the retractation required of him by Rome. The Pope thought that Erskine had taken the good part in agreeing with the three Vicars Apostolic for selection of a successor, delaying the confirmation of the choice until the re-establishment of the congregation of the Propaganda, unless indeed Erskine should confirm such successor in conformity with the sentiments of the Cardinal Prefect. Meanwhile, adds the Pope, there is no need to talk of coadjutors, for as the penal laws are abrogated, no district is left exposed to the risk of remaining without a pastor. He had not received from Bishop Douglas a request for a coadjutor. Erskine must have already received an answer "about the miserable affair of Monsignor Hussey. And We ask your advice how to get Bishop Douglas to yield" [in the matter of the Veto]. The Pope expressed his sorrow at the revolt in Ireland, deploring the necessity of bloodshed, although the Irish bishops, fulfilling their duty, inculcated on the Catholics the proper subordination. This letter shows that

Pius VI., in the midst of his sufferings and infirmities, even during his sore persecution, found time to give minute attention to ecclesiastical matters, and was not wholly absorbed in political affairs.

On the suppression of the Congregation of the Propaganda by the French Government, and the expulsion, or flight, of the Cardinals from Rome, Cardinal Borgia, the Pro-Prefect of that Congregation, managed to find a refuge in Padua, then fallen under Austrian domination. Erskine was enabled to communicate frequently with Cardinal Borgia *via* Vienna, and also with the Pope, first directly and afterwards through Monsignor Odescalchi, Nuncio in Tuscany, who gave his assistance until the French seized on Tuscany and carried the Pope elsewhere.

The blow given by the Revolution to the Propaganda and the Oriental and National Colleges in Rome, threatened to be a fatal one for the Missions to Infidels and Heretics. Erskine did his best to remedy the evil by opening correspondence with Missionaries in all parts of the world. He referred everything to the judgment of Cardinal Borgia, and he and Borgia, two persons only, transacted the entire business of Propaganda. Erskine opened a new correspondence with P. Giovanni Battista Marchini, Procurator of Propaganda, at Maccao in China; with Mgr. Luigi Maria di Gesù, bishop of Upsala and Vicar Apostolic in Malabar; with P. Arcangelo, Prefect Apostolic *per interim* at Martinique; with the Bishop of Baltimore; with D. Paolo Moretti, Missionary in Stockholm; with Mgr. Cortenovis, Vicar Apostolic of Ava and Pegù; and with many others. The French seized also all the revenues of the Propaganda, and Monsignor Erskine collected and administered funds for the Missions, and gave an exact account of his receipts and disbursements.

Monsignor Erskine now lost all his Roman revenues as *Uditore*, and as Papal Envoy, and got but little from his Canonry in S. Peter's, and from his pensions, owing to the enormous forced contributions levied by the French. His noble relatives, had they been called on, would certainly have given him pecuniary assistance. But there was no occasion for this, for George III. provisionally pensioned Monsignor Erskine during the time of the occupation of the Papal States. This spontaneous liberality was not unusually shown to other Diplomatists under similar circumstances, but was truly remarkable when shown to Erskine. This is undoubtedly the first and only instance since the schism, of a Papal agent subsidized by the British Government.

News of the death at Valence in France of Pius VI. on the 29th of August, 1799, soon reached Monsignor Erskine. The circumstances of this death of the Pope in exile, and after unparalleled sufferings and persecutions, excited in England extraordinary emotion, and Erskine determined to celebrate a sumptuous, and almost public, Requiem Mass in London. For this purpose he chose the Irish Catholic chapel of S. Patrick in Sutton Street, near Soho Square, which was in the Westminster district and in the same neighbourhood as the Spanish, French, Portuguese and Bavarian chapels, which were all under the protection of their respective Governments. In S. Patrick's, which had no Diplomatic protection, Monsignor Erskine was consequently more free to make his own arrangements. The mass was celebrated on the 16th of November. In the midst of the church rose a magnificent catafalque, surrounded by many rows of torches and covered by a richly adorned Baldacchino. On the top of the catafalque, on an ample cushion, reposed the Tiara, while at the two extremities were placed the family arms of the Pope, and at the sides the following inscription was seen :—" Pio VI. Pont. Max., Qui Christianæ Religionis odio in Captivitatem ductus, obiit Valentiæ in Galiæ D. xxix Aug. An. MDCCXCIX." Under the organ at the end of the Chapel and fronting the altar, was this inscription in English :—" Pius VI., born at Cesena 27 Dec., MDCCXVII., elected Pope 15 Feb MDCCLXXV, a just, munificent, magnanimous Prince, a Pontiff revered for his piety and zeal in the cause of Religion, led by his enemies into captivity. Whilst furnishing in the midst of adversity and sufferings the brightest example of Christian patience and unsubdued fortitude, He resigned his soul to the bosom of his God at Valence in France XXIX. Aug. MDCCXCIX; forgiving his persecutors, and praying for the restoration of tranquillity to the Church and to the World."

The Solemn Mass was said by Bishop Douglas, and the sermon was preached by Dr. O'Leary, and then five absolutions were given by the bishops of Lombez, Rhodez, Montpelier and Waterford, and Bishop Douglas. In the choir assisted the archbishop of Narbonne and the bishops of Nantes, Angoulême, Arras, Uzes, Cominges, Troyes, S. Pol de Leon, Lescars and Moulins. Three other French bishops then in London, were too ill to attend. The Ministers of Austria, Russia, Naples, Sardinia, Portugal and Bavaria were all present. As Monsignor Erskine was neither a priest nor a bishop, he could neither preach nor pontificate at the Mass. He published, however, a Panegyric on Pius VI. with an account of the Funeral.

The Conclave for election of a new Pope began in Venice on the 1st of December, 1799, and Cardinal Consalvi was Secretary to the Conclave, and received letters for Erskine, notably one dated on the 17th of December, containing the news of the allowance fixed for the Cardinal Duke of York. Doubtless Erskine lost no time in forwarding this news the moment he got permission, not only for sake of the attachment of his family to that of the Stuarts, but also out of gratitude to the protector of his infancy.

Cardinal Chiaramonti was elected Pope on the 14th of March, 1800, as Pius VII.; and five days later Consalvi, Pro-Secretary of State, informed Erskine that he had been confirmed in his office of *Uditore S. S.*, and sent him on the 23rd of March the Cypher for correspondence. Erskine continued to write his despatches, which were still forwarded by Mr. Canning, the Under Secretary of State, as well as by Count Woronzow, and the couriers of Lords Grenville and Minto.

On the 7th of May, 1800, Pius VII. sent to Erskine a Brief from Venice, saying:—" We are persuaded you will continue your services with the same zeal, fidelity and honour, as hitherto displayed, especially in conducting Our affairs with this generous government, for which We have the highest esteem and the most lively attachment, in this respect yielding nothing to Our Predecessor."

Pius VII., who left Venice on the 6th of June, 1800, and made his solemn entry into Rome on the 3rd of July, now restored ecclesiastical affairs, and Cardinal Gerdil, Prefect of the Congregation of the Propaganda, resumed his duties. Erskine now gave a full account of all his money transactions to the Economist of the Propaganda, and on the 18th of July, began to compile a book in which were entered all the receipts and disbursements, for use, in case of his death, of his executors. From this book it appears that from January, 1798, to the end of September, 1801, the total of the sums received and deposited with Coutts, the banker, was £27,259 16s. 8d. Of this sum, divided into four portions, no less than £26,065 16s. 8d. pertained to the private account of Cardinal Borgia, for each of the four portions had this note annexed to it:—" This sum does not belong to the Congregation, but stands to the credit of his eminence Cardinal Borgia, to whose disposal it is personally confided, and to whom alone I am responsible." The remainder—£1193 13s. 3d.—was received by Erskine in five portions, and was placed to the disposal of the Congregation and its Prefect.

The disbursements were:—To the French bishop of S. Pol de Leon, £124 7s. 2d. From August 27, 1799, to August 24, 1801, on eight cheques of Cardinal Borgia, £4927 18s. 6d. From June 18, 1799, to September 22, 1801, Erskine sent sums amounting to £7658 16s. to missionaries, as follows:—To G. B. Marchini, the Propaganda Procurator at Maccao in China, on 18th June, 1799, £1800; on August 25th, 1800, £900; on 10th March, 1801, £675; in all £3375. To M. Letondel,

Proctor of French bishops and missionaries at Maccao, £180. To M. Shwendinam, Proctor of French missionaries at Coromandel, Pondichery, etc., on June 18, 1799, £135. For the same, per Abbé Chaumont on 24th June, 1799, £45. For the bishop of Gortina, on 1st October, 1799, £112 11s., and an equal sum for travelling expenses of Signors G. B. Rabeau and Stefano Jourdain, for the Oriental Missions. To the same on 25th August, 1800, £472 11s., for missionaries at Cochin China, Siam, etc.; and £337 11s., to be sent to Monsignor Cortenovis, Vicar Apostolic of Ava and Pegu at Rangoon ; and on 10th March, 1801, £675 2s., for the missions of Tonquin, Cochin China, S' Tchuen, Siam, Coromandel, etc. In all was sent to Abbé Chaumont for transmission to aforesaid destinations, £1755 6s.

On 27th July, 1799, £112 11s. was sent to Most Rev. George Hay, in Edinburgh. To Monsignor Luigi Maria di Gesu, bishop of Upsala, and Vicar Apostolic at Verapolis, coast of Malabar, were sent on 7th October, 1799, £450 ; on 23rd August, 1800, £337 10s., and on 10th March, 1801, £337 10s. : in all £1125.

To Don Paolo Moretti in Stockholm, were sent on 25th August, 1800, £72 16s. ; on 27th February, 1801, £195 12s., and on 22nd September, 1801, £144 5s., in all £413 3s. To Monsignor Cortenovis at Rangoon, on 13th March, 1801, £337 10s. To R. D. Troyes, £225. All these sums make a total of £7658 10s, sent by Erskine to missions, exclusive of £325 7s. 10., paid on the order of Cardinal Gerdil, the Prefect, and making the gross sum of £12,911 16s., 4d., of which £12,587 18s., 6d. was set to account of Cardinal Borgia, and £325 7s. 10d. to the account of the Congregation. Receipts were entered for all these items, and for their transmission Erskine found a very good medium in a Jew, who gave him great satisfaction. The balance at Coutts, amounted to £14,347 13s. 7d., and of this, £13,477 18s. 2d. was put to the disposal of Borgia, and £869 15s. 5d. to that of the Prefect *pro tempore* of Propaganda.

Monsignor Erskine was one of the fourteen Cardinals reserved *in petto* in the Consistory held by Pius VII. on the 23rd of February, 1801, when thirteen other Cardinals were published. Erskine begged the Pope not to publish him as Cardinal as long as his Mission lasted in England, in order not to offend the susceptibility of a Protestant nation. His conduct in this respect gave great satisfaction to Mr. Pitt, to whom, as well as to George III., Erskine's creation *in petto* was made known. Indeed His Majesty asked him all about his dress as Cardinal.

At this time the Bali Ruspoli asked Erskine to get him a passport and license to reside in England. Erskine obtained it for him from the Home Minister, William Henry Cavendish, third Duke of Portland. In this passport Ruspoli was styled " a Subject of His Holiness the Pope," but the permission was only to travel or reside anywhere at a distance of ten miles from the coast. This limitation was perhaps because Ruspoli was a Knight of Malta, of which island the British had taken possession.

On the 6th of March 1800, Mgr. Agostino Valle was nominated as Erskine's coadjutor in his office of Consistorial Advocate, and Mgr. Lachini was made *Vice-Uditore* in room of Donati.

Erskine, in view of his departure for Rome to be proclaimed a Cardinal, wrote to Canon Preston on the 30th of May, 1801, as if he was then on the point of leaving London, but the affairs of France and the Holy See caused a delay of several months. The Concordat, which in September, 1800, had begun to be negotiated in Paris by Mgr. Spina, archbishop of Corinth, and Father Caselli, Superior General of the Servites of Mary, was already arranged in the principal matters ; and Consalvi, the Secretary of State, left Rome on the night of the 5th of June, 1801, and went to Paris to conclude it, and he signed it as Plenipotentiary of the Holy See, on the 3rd of July, 1801. The ratification, which was done by the Pope in

August, and afterwards by the First Consul, Bonaparte, completed all the formalities necessary to the validity of this Convention, which was subsequently published solemnly. The presence of Erskine in England was necessary for the carrying into execution parts of this Concordat.

For by the second article it was agreed that the Holy See, in concert with the French Government, should newly arrange the boundaries of the French Dioceses. By the third, it was stipulated that the Pope should notify to the existing occupants of French bishoprics, that he expected them, in view of the good and unity of the Church, to make every sacrifice of their personal rights, even to the resignation of their respective sees, and that in case of their refusal to resign, provision would be made, in any case, without regard to their resistance, for the government of the new dioceses by new bishops. By the fourth article, the new bishops were to be nominated by the First Consul within three months from the publication of the Bulls, and were to be canonically instituted, afterwards, by the Pope, according to the forms customary in France before the change of Government.

Pius VII., had now to ask all the old bishops to resign their sees, in order to effect this new organization of the clergy and church of France. It was a hard thing to ask, but necessary under the circumstances. Of all the French bishops, some were hidden away, and some re-entered France, when the persecutions ceased under the Consulate, but did not exercise, at least openly, their episcopal jurisdiction. Other bishops were dispersed in the Southern parts of Italy, or in Germany, or England. In England were three archbishops, those namely of Narbonne, Aix and Bourdeaux, and the bishops of Lescar, Arras, Montpelier, Angoulême, Nantes, Noyon, S. Pol de Leon, Usez, Perigeaux, Cominges, Lombez, Vannes, Moulins, Rhodez, Troyes and Avranche. From these prelates the strongest opposition was anticipated. They were in a country where resistance to French innovations was strengthened by national rivalry. The presence, moreover, of the Count d' Artois, natural heir to the Crown of France, re-animated their old sentiments of devotion and loyalty and tended to keep them back from any act signifying defection from their sworn fidelity.

To Erskine was left the task of confronting these difficulties. And to him were sent, in September, by the Papal Secretary of State, the Briefs for every one of the French bishops then in England, with the necessary instructions for accompanying each Brief with a letter from Erskine himself, to inform the recipient of the steps taken by the Pope in behalf of each prelate.

On the 16th of September, Erskine sent the Briefs to the bishops, along with a letter which he afterwards published in French and Italian, at the press of L. Nardini, A. Dulau & Co. Portland Street, London. Erskine's letter was as follows:—
"By express command of Pope Pius VII., I transmit to your Lordship the Pontifical Brief herewith enclosed, the receipt of which you will be pleased at once to acknowledge, and I pray you to send me without delay the convenient response.

"The Pope has not omitted to practise every possible endeavour to preserve to your Lordship your See, but had experienced most profound regret in finding your resignation, in these urgent circumstances, indispensably required for the good of the Church and for her Unity, and for peace and for the re-establishment in France of the Catholic Religion. His Holiness, moreover, has charged me to assure your Lordship, that he has in every possible way recommended you to the First Consul, whom he has asked to keep you in view in his nominations to the new dioceses, and at least to provide for your subsistence. And such is the anxiety of the Pope to contribute in every possible way to the relief of your Lordship, that he will not omit any favourable conjuncture for alleviating the burden of your situation and helping your personal needs.

"Having thus discharged the duty laid on me by the Pope, I

now proceed in my private character to offer my services to your Lordship, and to sign myself your Lordship's devoted and obedient servant—Charles Erskine."

Ths French bishops were dilatory, and instead of sending separate replies, met together at the house of the archbishop of Narbonne, to draw up a joint-letter to be sent in the name of all. Erskine, hearing of this, wrote to the archbishop, to remind him that a common answer would not satisfy the Pope, who had written to each prelate individually. This letter had its effect, and by the beginning of October, Erskine had answers from all the prelates, and he sent these answers in one packet, on the 6 of October, through means of M. Otto, the French Minister in London, to Monsignor Spina in Paris.

These bishops, for the most part, refused, on various pretexts, to resign the Sees which they canonically held. This opposition continued in spite of the execution of the Concordat, and only began to cease when Louis XVIII., after the Bourbon restoration, made a new Concordat with the Pope, amplifying the former one and improving it to the benefit of the Clergy, and to the better administration of the Dioceses. It is to be noted that the French bishops, who resisted the Concordat, and disobeyed the Papal Briefs, yet did no act to disturb the new bishops in the administration of their dioceses, either by way of protests or by declarations of nullity, so that the Concordat was tranquilly carried out in France. The only exception was that of the Bishop of Blois (whose name is not mentioned as one of the refugees in England) who carried his opposition to such a length, as to think himself authorized to exercise his episcopal jurisdiction in France, and even when he was abandoned by his brethren, in the time of Louis XVIII., reputed himself the only legitimate bishop of France, and so became the founder of *La Petite Eglise*, a schismatical church which caused no great consequences and became extinguished with him.

Five prelates, the archbishops of Aix and Bordeaux, and the

bishops of Lescar, Cominges and Troyes promptly resigned. The remaining, to the number of fourteen, refused.

Monsignor Erskine, for his part in executing the Concordat, was styled a Bonapartist, but his real sentiments on that topic were that Pius VII., in his fear of a new invasion of Rome on the withdrawal of the French Minister, Cacault, condescended too much. Bonaparte had more need for the Concordat than he chose to allow. Five days after the Battle of Marengo, Bonaparte told Cardinal Martiniana, bishop of Vercelli, that he had resolved to live at peace with the Pope, and come to an agreement for the restoration of Religion in France. The first advance towards this was made by Bonaparte, who, however, when the negotiations commenced, changed his conciliatory tone to one of bullying. Erskine knew that the French bishops in England were hardly dealt with, but his duty was not to indulge his own sentiments, but to execute the orders of the Pope.

There was now no further business to detain Erskine in England, and he was free to return to Rome to assume the dignity of a Cardinal. From the 4th of October, 1801, Cardinal Caprara, *Legate a latere*, was in Paris to publish and execute the Concordat. In the beginning of October peace was concluded between England and the allies with France, and it was agreed to hold a congress at Amiens to settle the basis for the general peace of Europe, and Bonaparte facilitated the return of the French emigrants to their homes. In England the penal laws against Catholics were relaxed, and Catholic worship was freely permitted within their chapels.

Eskine himself thus summed up his work in England :—

1. He obtained open communication—closed heretofore for two hundred years—between the Holy See and the British Government, and direct correspondence between the respective Secretaries of State, a thing vainly attempted on many previous occasions, and notably some little time before Erskine's arrival in England.

2. He gained the accordation to himself of all the privileges and Court distinctions given to Foreign Ministers, although ostensibly he had no public character, and thus secured the decorum due to the Holy See.

3. He obtained that in the constitution made by England for Corsica, nothing was fixed in religious matters without the approbation of the Pope.

4. He gained for the Papal Government freedom to act against those subjects of Great Britain who, when travelling or residing in the States of the Church, committed infractions of the laws.

5. He secured the aid of the British fleet in protecting cargoes of grain, etc., and in protecting the Papal coasts, which were infested by pirates in time of the late war.

6. He impeded the adoption, in the British Parliament, of the motion for the dissolution of the religious communities of nuns existing in many parts of England.

7. He opposed some noveles which ministers wished to introduce into Ireland, respecting bishops and parish priests, to the prejudice of the Holy See, and when the bishops gave their consent to these innovations he caused the execution of such measures to be suspended.

8. He secured that Ministers should not intermeddle in the choice of Vicars Apostolic in England, to which intervention they had been stimulated by some of the badly affected among the chief of the English Catholic gentlemen.

9. He appeased the great dissensions he had found existing among Catholics.

10. He prevented the scandal about to be produced by the excessive zeal of a foreign bishop, who was not acquainted with the English laws and customs.

11. He took part with Ministers in removing the impediments placed by the French *recusant* prelates in the way of the return to France of the French priests.

12. He obtained the open manifestation to the Emperor of

Russia of the intention of the British Government to restore the three Legations to the Holy See.

13. In each of the several treaties between Great Britain and France, including that of Amiens, he secured the support of Great Britain for the interests of the Holy See.

14. But for the insuperable obstacle of the King's scruples, he would have obtained the total abrogation of the laws against the Irish Catholics.

15. In the treaty of Amiens, the Pontifical States were named so expressly, by the British representative there, and of this there was no precedent since the schism.

16. He celebrated the public funeral of Pius VI.

17. He caused public prayers to be offered in all the chapels of the three kingdoms for Pius VI. in captivity.

18. He maintained correspondence with Nuncios and agents of the Holy See in all parts of Europe.

19. He contributed towards procuring from the British Government a subvention for the Vicars Apostolic in Scotland.

20. He spared much expense to the Holy See by his economy, and by his dispensing with the services of paid secretaries.

In reference to the proposed substitution of Titular Bishops for Vicars Apostolic—a measure above alluded to—which was strongly urged by several Catholics of rank, and was favoured by Pitt, Erskine was afraid that the free choice of the Holy See would be fettered. He said to Mr. Pitt:—"Are you content with the conduct of the Vicars?" The reply was:—"Yes, I have no reason to complain of them." "Well then"—rejoined Erskine—"I advise you to ask for no change, of which neither you nor I can foresee the consequences." Mr. Pitt then said:—"You are right," and he wholly abandoned the proposal, which he had probably entertained merely out of complaisance.

Erskine prepared for leaving England early in December, and wrote letters to the French bishops to announce his intentions. The archbishop of Narbonne, in the name of all of them, sent a courteous reply, dated the 9th of December, from Somerset Street. Monsignor Erskine chose to return to Rome by way of Paris, partly because it was the shortest route and partly because he wished to witness the solemn publication of the Concordat, and to observe the conduct of Bonaparte. In the passport enabling Erskine to cross to France, which was given him by the Principal Secretary of State, Thomas, Lord Pelham, was written, in the place for designating his quality, "Monsignor Erskine, *late Legate from His Holiness at this Court.*"

"I left London"—wrote Erskine in his Diary—"at 7 A.M. on the 12th of December 1801, and arrived at Dover after 7 P.M. Here, as the embarcation was not ready, I staid all the 13th at the Ship Inn. On the morning of the 14th, at 4 after midnight, I sailed in the Minerva Packet, Captain Hammond. The best wind prevailed and the sea was most tranquil for two-thirds of the passage; but then the wind changed a little, and the sea began to swell, with consequent nausea. I reached Calais at 8 the same morning. We would have taken an hour less in crossing, if the Captain, fearing the sand banks at the East of Calais, had not bent too much to the West, in consequence of which, when he perceived his mistake at day break, he had to tack back to regain the point. When we arrived at Calais, two Guards came on board to take the passergers' names. One remained on board until the other, after a long time, returned with licence for our landing. Then we went processionally into a miserable hole, where was a woman distributing national cocards, a pretext to get a present of 24 sous, and a dishevelled fellow who again wrote down our names, comparing them with our persons. Thence we went in procession once more to the Hotel de Ville, where we had more interpellations and exhibitions of passports. In mine was written:—*Chargé d' affaires à la Cour d' Angleterre.* After this I went to the Kingston Hotel, which had been recommended to me by Signor Masseria,* cousin of the First Consul, and who, for a long time preceding the secret negotiation afterwards carried on in London by the French Minister, M. Otto, Count de Mosloy, was passed forwards and backwards from Paris to London, and from London to Paris, to prepare the way for the said negotiation. The hotel is kept by Grandsir, a most excellent man, and his brave wife, who enlightened me about French money and the payments to be made for post horses, postillions, hotels, and all things concerning travelling."

Erskine had been treated in England by Customhouse and other officials with the respect due to his diplomatic character; and on his first arrival at Calais was disgusted and angry with the French douaniers for ransacking his carriage and tossing about everything in his imperial, trunks and boxes. The carriage, it may be noted, was made expressly to his order, and at much expense, by one of the best manufacturers in London, who, when Erskine asked whether it would bear a long journey, said:—"Your Honour may go to China; and dont pay me when you return if you find repairs necessary." This carriage did not go to China, but Erskine used it on his present journey and for many years in Rome, and on his last journey from Rome to Paris.

"After breakfast"—proceeds Erskine—"I went to the Commissary General of the Ports of the Straits and of the Harbour of Calais, named Mangaud, a man, to say truth, exceedingly brusque. On entering, I presented a letter from M. Otto, recommending the Commissary to pay me all the regards due to my public character and the good intelligence which passed between my Court and the French Republic. He had scarcely read it when he made me a thousand reverences

---

* This was Philip Masseria, a Corsican, who from 1799 to 1801, fought in the service of England, and died in London in 1807. His father was a Corsican adventurer and conspirator.

and compliments with all the French politeness, and at once restored my passport and was hardly prevented from accompanying me to the street door. I returned to my hotel, and soon after Father O'Leary returned also, with Mr. Macræ, Captain Portlock and his daughter and Mr. Garret. They all told me that because they were seen in my company they had their business speedily settled.

"During dinner a messenger came from the Mayor of the city to say that he and the chief municipal officials desired permission to pay me a visit. I replied that I was very sensible of the honour intended, but was unwilling to give them so much trouble, and that but for my unsuitable dress I had rather go to see them. About an hour afterwards, the Mayor, M. Michou, the *Juge de Paix*, the Commissary of the Executive, and the Head of the Tribunal of Commerce, arrived and passed a good half hour. The conversation turned chiefly on the return of religion. The Mayor seemed a very sensible man. Many compliments passed on both sides, with many eulogies of the First Consul. They rejoiced at the resurrection of France from the disorder to which she was reduced without religion, morality or restraint. They asked me if I believed the re-establishment of the Catholic religion would be quickly effected. I answered that there was no doubt of it, from the moment that on the part of His Holiness and of the First Consul there was established a mutual agreement in all good faith. Delay only arose from the necessity of previously systematising and regulating all the details for its accomplishment. I accompanied them to the door and they took leave of me with all sorts of compliments, and were, as I flattered myself, well contented with me. The Englishmen above mentioned were present during this visit and were most edified, taking it as a mark (and so it was) of respect to the Holy Father, and as an indication of the disposition of the French to return to the better way. Father O'Leary (the only Catholic among them) said that this meeting was ample compensation for his journey, even should he derive no benefit to his health, for the improvement of which he was travelling. In the evening, just as I was going to bed, M. Mangaud sent a note to apologise for not visiting me, as an accident had happened to him when out riding. I sent a proper answer."

Monsignor Erskine left Calais on the 15th of December, and when changing horses at Boulogne-sur-Mer, met a fat woman, who boasted of the reception there given to Lord Nelson when he attacked that place with his flotilla, and said the English lost in that affair near 600 men, mostly by drowning. The English confessed to a loss of about 300. Erskine slept on the night of the 15th at Abbeville, and reached Amiens on the evening of the 16th. In Amiens were then assembled the Plenipotentiaries of France, Joseph Bonaparte; of Great Britain, Marquess Cornwallis; and of Holland, Mr. Schimelpenning. They expected from Spain the Count del Campalanque. Erskine slept at the hotel *Éclaire*, where he found Mr. Merry, Secretary of the English Legation to the Congress. On the morning of December 17, after a good chat with Mr. Merry, Erskine left Amiens, and reached Paris on the 18th, some time before evening fell. He went to the Hotel de Rome, Rue S. Dominique, Faubourg S. Germain, and hired "a very convenient and decent" apartment, the same which Monsignor Spina had occupied.

In his diary Monsignor Erskine describes his first day in Paris thus:—

"December 19. This morning I went to visit Cardinal Caprara and then to leave a packet of Madame Osmond's with the Duchess de la Tremouille, whom I saw in a small and poorly furnished room with a mean looking bed in the corner. She was stitching at an embroidery frame. She was once the favourite of the Queen. *Che catastrophe!* She returned a month ago from Petersburg, to which city, on the invitation of Paul I., she had gone from London where I had known her. I found in the same house, and far better lodged, the Duchess

De Cruzolle, whom also I had known in London. I then went to Count Marcost and left him a letter from Count Woronzow; then to Count Philip De Cobentzel and to Mr. Krathoffer, secretary of the Austrian Legation, leaving for each a letter from Count Starhemberg : then to Marchese Lucchesini, and to M. Portalis, Councillor of State and Minister of Worship. Then to Mr. Fesch, uncle of the First Consul, leaving for him a letter from Signor Masseria. And then to Mr. Perregueaux, banker, with a letter from Mr. Coutts. In the evening I was visited by my old friends, the Marchese and Marchesa Lucchesini ; and then came in Cardinal Caprara and told me the First Consul knew of my arrival and would probably receive me in a day or two."

Monsignor Erskine used to say, in reference to his first interview in Paris with the Cardinal Legate, that the moment he saw him he recognised in Caprara a diplomatist whose entire business was to say and unsay, so that little or nothing could be concluded from his discourse. And he carried this system to the most trifling matters. For example, when inviting Erskine to dine with him whenever he pleased, he instantly added that Erskine would have so many invitations that it would not be worth his while to dine with him, but that Erskine would do well to accept the other invitations. The characters of Erskine and Caprara were entirely opposed, and there never could be anything between them save relations of mere convenience. As a matter of fact Erskine never once in his diary mentioned dining with Caprara, although he frequently met him at dinners.

On the 20th of December, Erskine went to Mass at S. Roch, which he thought "badly kept." He seemed surprised at some customs in this church. "You take a chair from a woman who keeps a quantity of them in a corner, and moves about collecting a sou from each person. Then a man decked in a short surplice with a hood shaped like a nautilus shell, and a purse in his hand, collects the alms, preceded by a boy in uniform like that of a hall porter, and with a staff similar to that of a running footman, who tells the people in a rather loud tone of voice to make room." After mass, Erskine paid visits to the Prussian Minister, and to Mr. Jackson, the British Minister, whom he had known in London, but both were out. He then went and talked to Cardinal Caprara, and then, at Caprara's suggestion, went to Cavalier Azara, the Spanish Minister. He then returned home, put on his boots and took a walk. In the evening he wrote letters to Cardinals Borgia and Gerdil, to tell them of the sums he had left with Coutts to their credit on the Propaganda accounts. Erskine now received a letter which had arrived in London the very day he left that city. It was a despatch from the office of the Secretary of State in Rome, and was dated on the 12th of December 1801. It mentions the dangerous condition of Cardinal de Zelada, who had a fresh attack of erysipalis. It says:—"The French Government has granted to Monsignor Spina the body of Pius VI., and Spina and Padre Caselli are returning to Rome with their precious deposit. The Holy Father enjoys good health and assists at all the Advent chapels and functions. It seems the French troops will soon evacuate the kingdom of Naples, passing by way of Fermo, Loreto, Ancona and Pesaro. The march of 12,000 men cannot but be severely felt by the Papal States in the present scarcity of provisions and in the miserable condition of the Treasury. On the completion of this march, Ancona will be evacuated."

. . " No further news about the Congress of Lyons."

Monsignor Spina had left Paris a little before Erskine's arrival, and had gone to Valence. On the night of the 23rd of December, they disinterred the case containing the body of Pius VI., which had already, by Bonaparte's order, been buried in the public cemetery. On the 10th of January, the body was formally consigned to Spina, who caused it to be carried to Marseilles on a car drawn by four horses.

The Pope gave earnest attention to the Congress of Lyons, to which had been convoked all the Deputies of the cities of

Lombardy and the Legations, and of other cities occupied by the French troops in Italy. The constitution for the new Republic in Italy was to be shaped in this Congress, and it was feared that danger to religion would result.

On the 21st of December, after mass at S. Valery, Erskine went to Caprara, and made appointments with him for the evening. He drew £100 sterling from the banker Perregaux, and bought a repeater from Lessine, the watchmaker, paying for it 50 crowns. He then called on M. Talleyrand, Minister of Foreign Affairs, who was not at his office, as the day was the *Decade*, the Republican substitute for Sunday. He then went home and had a long visit from the Russian Minister, Count Marcost.

In the evening, as previously arranged with Caprara, "I went"—relates Erskine in his diary—"to Cavalier Azara, who has got old in body and spirit, and at his house met the Princess Santa Croce, dressed in the extreme of the present Paris fashion; and the Cavalier Angiolini, formerly Tuscan Minister; and the Marchese Serristori, ambassador of the King of Etruria and his wife lately arrived in Paris. From thence Cardinal Caprara and I went to the house of Madame Grand, where, at my first entrance, I was introduced to Minister Talleyrand. Here were also the famous Prince of Nassau; the Count de Westfalen; the Count de Cobentzel; the Princess di Due Ponti, an old lady who played chess; the Count of Narbonne, whom I had met in Rome at *Mesdame's*; the Ligurian Envoy Frarega and Signor Sevra; M. Decre, Minister of the Marine; Signor Bouligni, formerly Spanish Minister at Constantinople, from whence he was sent away at the request of Paul I. and of England; two brothers of Talleyrand, his nephew and niece, and other ladies."

Of Talleyrand, Monsignor Erskine noted, but not in his Diary, that "Chenier presented Talleyrand, who had to emigrate in time of the Revolution, to the Convention, as a true Republican, and so caused his return from exile."

And of Azara, the Spanish Minister, Erskine narrated as follows :—

"Azara went to the Consul, Bonaparte, the same evening that the Preliminaries of peace with Great Britain were signed, and when Savary announced the Spanish Ambassador, Bonaparte discharged at him all possible expletives, approaching close to him with foam at his mouth."

On the same day, December 21, Erskine wrote to Cardinal Consalvi, Secretary of State, giving an account of his journey from London, and intimating his purpose of waiting in Paris before resuming his journey to Rome, partly to avoid the inclemency of the season and partly to see the publication of the Concordat and add one to the cortege of the Cardinal Legate on the day of that solemnity. Moreover, he wrote, "I shall not be wholly useless as long as the correspondence with the bishops in England continues." To this long letter is added the following postscript :—"In giving an account to your Eminence, in my letter of the 8th, of the result of the affair with this Mr. Fegan, I forgot to enclose the note of Lord Hervey, who is the intermediary link between my note and memorandum, and the reply which was given *viva voce*. I enclose meanwhile a copy with translation" into Italian. Lord Hervey means the Earl of Bristol and Protestant bishop of Derry, who was doubtless recommending some one for a vacant Catholic see in Ireland.

On the 22nd of December, "I went"—proceeds Erskine— "to visit, as advised by Caprara, the Ministers of War, Marine, Justice, Finance, Interior, Police and National Treasury. While I was out, M. Portalis, Prince Giustiniani, Cav. Angiolini, Count de Cobentzel, M. Krathoffer and M. Perregeaux called on me. And when I returned, Mr. Jackson came and remained some time. Card. Caprara with Monsignors Sala and Mazio also called when I was out. One of the Vicars General of the Archbishop of Aix, with M. De Boisgelin, one of the Archbishop's nephews, came to tell me that Madame de Grammont desired to pay me a visit. I said I would go to her. This morning the Minister Tallyrand left for Lyons."

December 23. "I went to M. Portalis and afterwards to the Cardinal Legate to inform him of the result of our conference. During my absence M. Fesch and General Berthier, Minister of War, called. I wrote to London to the Archbishop of Aix and to Bishop Douglas. I dined with the Prussian Minister. Then I went home and M. De Boisgelin came, and we went together to Madame Brunot, and at her house met Madame de Grammont and her daughter, wife to one of the nephews of the Archbishop of Aix." Monsignor Erskine, before leaving London, had been consulted by the Archbishop of Aix and the other French prelates who obeyed the Pope and resigned their sees, as to how they should behave in regard to returning to France. Erskine had then advised them not to stir from England until invited by the Pope himself, in order to shew that no personal interest or inconsiderate love of country had induced them to resign. They had followed this advice. Now, however, that Erskine was in Paris and plainly saw the good to be produced by their presence, he thought it his duty to write to the Archbishop of Aix and invite him and the other bishops who had resigned, to return to France as quickly as they could. Erskine added that the Cardinal Legate was of the same opinion. He did not of course introduce the name of Portalis, the Minister of Worship, though his letter had been agreed upon between Portalis and himself.

Dec. 24. "The Abbé O'Connor, Marchese Fonseca, and Princess Santa Croce paid me visits. I wrote a note for M. Portalis, and going to leave it with him, found him at home, and went to see him. He was engaged with Abbé Bernier. I afterwards left cards on Mr. Murphy and Mr. Parish who had called on me." The Abbé Bernier now mentioned in Erskine's diary, was Parish Priest of S. Laud d' Angers, and, together with Joseph Bonaparte and Emanuel Cretet, Councillors of State, was chosen to treat and conclude the Concordat in

Paris with Cardinal Consalvi, Monsignor Spina and Father Caselli, who were nominated by the Pope for this office. Bernier took also part in the execution of the Concordat, and finally was promoted to the Bishopric of Orleans, where he ended a career which once had a certain kind of celebrity.

Dec. 25. Monsignor Erskine went to Mass on Christmas Day at the church of S. Valery, and his diary contains a long description of the ceremony of the " Pain Benit," which was new to him. He was visited by Canon Welch and Abbé Bernier, and had a card from the Finance Minister. He dined with Cav. Azara, and met there Cardinal Caprara, Princess Santa Croce, a Spanish lady and her husband, General Pardo, the Secretary of Legation and others.

On the 26th of Dec., Monsignor Erskine, after Mass at S. Valery, took a long walk and then received several visits. He dined with Marchese Lucchesini and spent the evening with Cav. Azara and met the Abbé Sabatier, one of those who caused the re-union of the States General. Erskine notes in his diary:—" In Paris they do nothing but dance, eat, go to the theatre, and amuse themselves. Of politics one never hears a word. When the epoch of the Terror was over, there was a ball to which no one was admitted, who had not had some near relative guillotined, or was not introduced by some one who had, and this was called the Ball of the Victims. In London, the ladies who emigrated went with the head and neck *à la Guillotine.*"

"The Abbé Innes, Superior of the Scotch College," writes Erskine, "was with me on the 27th to consult on what steps should be taken for recovering the property of the said College formerly existing here. I advised him to draw up a memorial to the Marquess Cornwallis and present it here to the British Minister, Mr. Jackson. Principal Gordon is *malcontent*. All the interesting Manuscripts, so valuable for the notices they contained of the Stuart family, were sent by Abbé Innes to Mr. **Stapleton** (now Vicar Apostolic of the Midland District), then President of Douay College, to be sent to England. In that moment the embargo was put on. Stapleton consequently gave them (as he himself could not convey them) to the custody of a trusty person in Douay itself. This person not long after was arrested and thrown into prison; and his wife, fearing that these English papers, of the contents of which she knew nothing, might prejudice her husband, burnt them all. Some time previously £5,000 sterling had been offered for a copy of these Manuscripts."

M. Portalis came to see Erskine on the 28th of December, to tell him that the First Consul would receive him privately, and with pleasure, on any morning it might suit Cardinal Caprara to bring him. And on the 29th, Caprara notified that he would on the following day make the presentation. Erskine had in writing asked M. Portalis to procure him this audience, which he considered indispensable in consideration of the charge sustained by him in England, and the part he took in executing the Concordat. Erskine spent most of the 29th of December with Lucchesini, visiting the Gobelin Tapestry Manufactory, of which he entered a very long and minute account in his diary.

"This establishment," wrote Erskine, "was then emerging from the misfortunes it suffered in the Revolution. Even in the time of the Directory they one day promised protection and the next day carried off the workmen to the wars. The Director is M. Guillaumot, who, in 1750, took the first prize in Rome for architecture. The maintenance of the factory costs the Government 50,000 crowns *per annum*. Each workman gets three francs and ten sous a day, besides a dwelling and a small garden. The working hours are graduated according to the season, as they only work by day light. All are men who begin as boys, and it takes about twenty years to make a perfect artist. General Berthier went one day to see this manufactory, which before he thought was all done by machinery. The Director told him of the time and trouble it cost to train the pupils, and that six of them were at that moment actually serving in the army. The General sent an order for their return. The looms were at first placed horizontally, and were irremovable until all the work was completed. Under the web was the design, and behind the shoulders of the weaver the original was hung on the wall as at present, the loom being between the weaver and the light. They only work at one portion at a time, and the rest—already made or to be made—was rolled up on two cylinders, as was also the original: so that the workmen never saw anything but the reverse side, until all was finished. Subsequently the loom was made moveable on two pivots, so as to turn and allow the right side to be seen at pleasure of the weaver. Afterwards they employed the foot loom, which was less inconvenient for the workman, who was no longer obliged to stand bent, as over the other looms, and moreover the design, which previously was over a paper placed under the web, was now on the web itself, thus rendering the execution more exact. The same disadvantage remained, however, namely that of making the work by pieces, and the originals suffered by being wound and unwound as before. At present, in the gallery formerly set apart for pictures of the French school, which are now removed to Versailles, the present Director has erected a loom on which tapestries of any size can be worked. For the height of the room permits this, and thus the originals, of all dimensions, can stand entirely displayed on the wall. At first they used silk for the brighter tints, now they are beginning to use wool for all the tints. Notwithstanding the invention of perpendicular looms, they still continue to work occasionally on the horizontal. What beauty! What delicacy in the gradations of the tints, what vivacity of colouring, and what subtlety of work! In the Director's cabinet were two small tapestry pictures representing vases with flowers, and the head and half bust of a boy. One would swear they were paintings. There was also an oval piece, with the head in profile of the First Consul, marvellously imitating bronze. As regards the building, there is nothing grand about it, either within or without, nay it is less than grand or handsome. The taste for exterior show is reserved for Rome, where they employ in the appearance what might be better employed in the substance."

Erskine thus describes his first interview with Bonaparte: "On 30th of December, Cardinal Caprara came at 12 to bring me to see the First Consul in the Tuileries in the apartment on the first floor, the side of the *Pavillon de Flore*. At foot of the staircase where we dismounted is a hall for servants: inside the entrance door of the Palace were two Grenadiers, and two more were stationed above before the door of the apartment, and they presented arms to the Cardinal. On entering the apartment is a saloon, where were servants of the First Consul, dressed in grey liveries, with silver lace on the collars and on the turnings of the cuffs. We passed on into an antechamber, and found there the aide-du-camp, Lauriston (the same who carried to London the Preliminaries of the Peace, and who is of Scotch origin, and of the family of the famous Law, Minister of Finance), who went in to announce us, and a moment afterwards came out again, to make the Cardinal pass in. Some minutes afterwards M. Portalis, Councillor of State and Minister of Worship, came out to tell me to enter. In the midst of the room and standing up was the First Consul in a blue coat embroidered in gold, white waistcoat and pantaloons, half boots with spurs, his hair without powder and negligently drawn on to the forehead. His coat is always either blue or red, cut in military fashion with small collar turned back, and double breasts, which he keeps buttoned. His aspect is rather serious, but tempered with sweetness: eye somewhat sunk—nose aquiline—mouth small—complexion a pale dark. His face is less long than as represented in portraits; indeed, I have never yet seen any portrait which gave a perfect likeness of him. His stature is less than the mean, and, as it seemed to me, he is lean by nature and by fatigue.

"The Cardinal Caprara remained also standing, and M.

Portalis was present. He [Bonaparte] received me gracefully, and talked on various subjects, passing rapidly from one to another, and after about a quarter of an hour made me a bow, and I retired. Some moments afterwards the Cardinal and M. Portalis came out, and at the foot of the staircase we separated, and each of us went his own way. In the evening I was introduced to the house of Madame de Montesson, stepmother of Egalité, Duke of Orleans. There was good company and in good number."

Elsewhere Erskine wrote of Bonaparte :—" He lets no one at all into the secrets of his projects. He writes his own letters and gives his orders directly to Generals, Ambassadors, etc. Once a month he holds a Review, and afterwards a reception of the Foreign Ministers, whom he invites the same day to dinner. He goes to bed every night in the same bed with his wife, and here he sometimes receives the couriers, and she is obliged to hide herself under the sheets. . . . He was once on the point of divorcing her. The horses were put to the carriage that he might go to make his declaration at the Municipality. He was just issuing from the palace. Barras threw himself at his feet and calmed him." Bonaparte was not very tender towards the members of the fallen Directory, for " Barras lives in Brussels under surveillance ; Carnot in Flanders, on very limited means ; Seyes remains eclipsed, and lives in Paris ; Reveillere-Lepaux lives near the Jardin des Plantes. This man was the real persecutor of Pius VI., in order to found his religion of Theophilanthropists. The other Directors yielded to his severities against the Pope, as he refused on any other terms to assent to their measures." Apropos of Pius VI., Erskine says that "General Burgoin, now Minister in Sweden, who wrote a 'Report on Spain,' was the author of the ' Life of Pius VI.' "

Erskine observes on the conduct of Bonaparte with his Generals :—" The Generals who give him umbrage are sent away as Ambassadors. Massena was destined for Constantinople, but was unwilling to go there. When he was recalled from Italy, on the charge of pillaging, he withstood a fierce attack from Bonaparte in the presence of many witnesses." Regarding the jealousy and dissensions between General Moreau and the First Consul, Erskine has several notes, and writes :—" When news arrived in Paris of the decisive victory gained by Moreau at Hohenlingen [on 2nd of December, 1800] Madame Moreau went to congratulate Madame Bonaparte, saying that from this point every ulterior obstacle would be removed. She was received very coldly; and a similarly cold reception was given to General Moreau when he arrived." Much discontent was felt, according to Erskine, by Catholics and Sectarians, at the mode in which the re-establishment of religion was carried out, and many of the Generals and officers were disaffected towards Bonaparte. Among these was General Moreau, "who has many friends, and lives retired in a house near the *Invalides,* going often to the chase, but never to parade. He said openly at a dinner-table, in the presence of many persons, that if any one attempted to do violence to his conscience, he would rise against it and would have many followers." Erskine adds :—" When I was supping with Zalt, one of the Mayors of Paris, he told me that the suburb of S. Antoine and Moreau were ready to do again what they had already done." Moreau was subsequently condemned to two years' imprisonment, for participation in a Royalist plot, but was suffered to retire to America. In July 1813, he returned to Europe on the invitation of the Allies, was wounded mortally at the battle of Dresden, and died on 1st of September 1813.

"Bonaparte," observed Erskine, "makes bishops as he makes troops, and sends those of Brabant into Italy, and those of the Romagna into Brabant, and sends Frenchmen into Piedmont," etc.

Monsignor Erskine, according to his diary, went on the 31st of December, " to dejeuner at one o'clock to Madame Grand.

The company was limited," but included the Cardinal Legate and several ambassadors. The refreshments were " tea, coffee, chocolate, butter, *Pan di Spagna*, cold fowl and game." " M. Portal, the most celebrated physician in Paris came in." The same day Erskine dined with Mr. Jackson, the British Minister, and met among others, " Lord William Bentinck, son of the Duke of Portland, arrived a few days ago from Egypt, where he had been six months. He had previously made the campaign [in Italy] of 1799 with General Suwarow. He confirmed to me what Colonel Woronzow had told me about this General. Lord William hates Egypt, where, according to him, all is bad except its fertility. The English, moreover, never would have been able to carry out the expedition [under Abercromby] had General Menou made other dispositions." " Lord Colorain " was at this party.

On the 1st of January, 1802, Erskine "went with Cardinal Caprara to be introduced to Madame Bonaparte. She was out. We left our names." On the same day Erskine received *via* London, duplicate despatches from the Cardinal Secretary of State, Consalvi, and thus replied :—

"Signor Cardinal, Secretary of State: From London have been sent to me despatches of your Eminence, dated the 7th and 14th of last November, and as the first of these needs no answer, I pass on to the second. And here first of all I return to your Eminence very many thanks for your kindness in assuring me that my conduct in London, in the affair of the French bishops, has met with the benign approval of His Holiness.

" As regards the package, of which your Eminence reminds me, containing Briefs of the Pope and a letter in his own hand, which in my letter of the 21st of last month, I told you that I knew, at my arrival in Paris, had been sent to London by Cardinal Caprara, in consequence of which, I wrote to the Vicar Apostolic of that district, I now add that the day it reached me, being sent back from London, and on the following day, the 23rd of December, I re-directed it to the said Vicar Apostolic, enjoining him to distribute the letters without delay, and give me an account of it. I cannot but admire the paternal clemency of His Holiness in the style adopted in his letter to the archbishop of Narbonne. I desire it will have effect, but I don't know how to hope for it in the case of those who have transformed an affair of Religion into an affair of Chivalry, and are proud of it.

"By the same despatch I received the *Pro-Memoria* of the Commissary of Antiquities on the attempt of this Banker, Sloane, and the orders of your Eminence to get a sequestration put, in name of His Holiness, on the monument so stealthily carried off by the said person. Now, even had this order reached me in time, yet I could not have executed it, nor could the Ministry have helped me. For the laws of the country prevent this—a country where once persons or things are landed, they cannot be called on to give account of any crime committed by them in foreign dominions, nor has the Ministry the least arbitrary power. It is necessary to exercise all the care in Rome, but on this topic I will not enlarge, and will only repeat that which I had the honour to write to you some time ago, and recently in reference to the affair of Mr. Fegan, namely, let your Eminence execute the laws rigorously, without partiality, or exception of persons or Nations ; and, allow me to add that the pecuniary penalty will be the best of all ; not, however, left to the arbitrary will of the Judge, but fixed by the law itself. As to the monument in question, I already knew it was in London, and I marvelled when I reflected on the little vigilance and fidelity of those persons on whom depends the execution of the laws which prohibit clandestine exportation of such things. The delinquency of such persons should be most severely punished. I knew also that in London nobody came forward to purchase the said monument, sculpture being no longer in fashion, and paintings being more sought after. So that diligence in respect to pictures ought to be redoubled. It seems, then, to me that it would be much better that Signor Conestabile should make an offer to Mr. Sloane to redeem the said monument, at the price paid for it, or, if necessary, at a higher price, he undertaking also the cost of the return carriage which cannot be very much.

"Apropos of this Mr. Sloane, I had the honour to write to your Eminence to say that I was informed there was some thought of nominating him British Consul in Rome, and I said I would write to know whether he would be approved of by my Court. I now desire that your Eminence should write me an answer to the effect that he is one of those persons who give trouble to the Pontifical Government by aiding in transgressions of the laws, and seeing that such is his conduct in a private station, and thence inferring what might be expected from him if invested with a public character, I should notify to the British Government that he would not be agreeable to the Pope, nor a help towards maintaining that good intelligence which it is desirable to preserve between the British Government and the Pope's. Your Eminence will know the proper terms to adopt. I only venture to make the suggestion. I also venture to say that there is in Rome one Mr. Moire, a Scotchman, who lives near the Cavalletto, who seems well adapted for the post. Your Eminence can procure information about him, and if the result be satisfactory, you can write to me, as if for my private instruction, that I may send your letter just as sent to me, that is with the answer about Sloane and the suggestion about Moire, to the Minister who spoke to me in London about the said intended nomination to the Consulate. I remain etc. Paris, 1st Jan. 1802."

This Mr. Sloane or Sloan was Alexander, son of William Sloane and Sara Macloun, of Glasgow diocese, born in 1754. The Catholicity of his parents as well as his precise age was uncertain, but he himself abjured the errors of Calvinism, and was admitted at the age of 18 years into the Scots College, Rome, on the 17th of May 1772. Of his own accord, and without having taken any holy order, he left the College in 1774, and eventually became a Banker in Florence and Rome, realizing a large fortune. He married Aloysa Hayes, and had several children. One of his sons, Francis, built the Facade of the church of Santa Croce, in Florence, and his name is thereon inscribed in memory of his munificence. He died at Rome on the 8th of November, 1802, and was buried in the Scots College with the following inscription :—

D. O. M.
ALEXANDRO SLOANE
SCOTORUM HUJUS COLLEGII ALUMNO BENEMERITENTI
QUI VIXIT ANNOS L.
OBIIT V IDUS NOVEMBRIS A.D. MDCCCII.
ALOYSA HAYES UXOR ET FILII MOERENTES
CONJUGI ET PATRI OPTIMO
HOC PIETATIS ET GRATI ANIMI
MONUMENTUM POSUERE.

The Earl and Countess of Mountcashel were now staying at the same hotel as Monsignor Erskine, and some other English people. On the 3d of January, Erskine went to Abbé Bernier and gave him two cartouche boxes, which had been given by the Grand Lama to Sir John Macpherson when he was Governor General of India. One of these boxes contained powder of gold, and the other had goat's hair scented with musk. They were intended for a present to the wife of the First Consul from Sir John, but Erskine thought they should first be submitted to Bonaparte to decide whether the horrible odour of musk could be adventured for presentation to Madame Bonaparte. The cold was now intense, and the Seine had overflowed. Erskine that day, the 3rd, dined with Madame Laborde, whose circumstances were not so good as in former days. He met at dinner General Ventimiglia, " who was in the service of Naples in the famous expedition against the French in Rome, and he met also Signor Lachene, a Piedmontese gentleman, who, by his singing, got married in London to an ugly rich woman, whom he treated, as was reported, very badly. He sang with Madame Noaille, daughter of Madame Laborde, who sings exceedingly well." News came of the "death of [Visconti] the archbishop of Milan, suddenly, in the arms of M. Talleyrand, at whose house he was at dinner—a large party of 80 persons—on the 30th of December. An old man of 82 years, he had travelled to Lyons in spite of the severity of the weather." The next day, Erskine had a visit from Canon Welch, "who was born in France of an English family, and was made by Pius VI. a Canon of the Vatican Basilica, so that he used to boast of having three nationalities at the same time—English, French, and Roman. He was now attached without special title to the Legation of Cardinal Caprara.

Erskine, on the 5th of January, met with a disappointment. The Abbé Bernier was to have called for him at 11 to bring him to the parade at the Tuileries, but broke his promise and sent an excuse at half-past 11. Consequently he went alone and was late, and, although furnished with a ticket from General Duroc, could hardly get in, and got such a bad place that he could see nothing. He went afterwards to the church of the Carmine, celebrated for the massacre of three bishops and over two hundred priests, on the 2nd of September, 1792.

"Every 15th of the Republican month," writes Erskine, "the First Consul holds a review or parade, and afterwards receives the Foreign Ministers in public, standing in the middle of the audience chamber, between the two other Consuls, with a crowd about him of Generals, who pay court to him. On these occasions he receives also the credentials of any new Foreign Minister. The new Minister steps from out the diplomatic circle, and presents his credentials to the First Consul, who at once passes them on to his Secretary of State, and the affair is over. This morning this function was performed by Mr. Jackson, the British Minister. The First Consul then, leaving the other two Consuls erect on their feet at their posts, advances a few paces to talk briefly with each of the Foreign Ministers, who then present their countrymen. The Foreign Ministers—and sometimes some of those presented—are then invited to dinner. At the dinner are present Madame Bonaparte, the three Consuls, the Generals, ambassadors, officials of State, and those soldiers, who at the parade had received the distinction of valour—the musket, sabre, or other gift. And to these the First Consul, in the course of the dinner, pays especial attention. Generally the First Consul and Madame Bonaparte sit at the middle of the table at opposite sides. The First Consul sits between the Presidents of the Consulate and of the *Corps Législatif*, and Madame Bonaparte sits between the two other Consuls. The Foreign Ministers are shewn to their proper seats by a chamberlain. The rest of the guests take places where they can. There is only one hot course, and desert. The dinner is quickly over. All agree that Bonaparte has no passion for the table, nor for women, gambling or hunting. It is only the passion for glory which fills his mind."

"Yesterday evening after 11, Cardinal Caprara privately married, in the rooms of the First Consul, Louis, brother to the First Consul, and Madamoiselle Beauharnais, daughter of Madame Bonaparte, and General Murat and the younger sister of the First Consul. The last couple had been married some time previously with the civil forms only." At this nuptial benediction were present, " besides two or three other persons, Bonaparte himself, his wife, his mother, his uncle, his brother next to him in age, and his elder sister with her husband, and his third brother. For the last couple the ceremony was *convenient*. A temporary altar had been erected."

The First Consul left Paris on the night of the 8th of January, 1802, for Lyons, attended by a splendid company, and he was shortly nominated by the Congress to be the President of the new Cisalpine Republic. " Bonaparte had a fixed desire for this nomination, but at first did not wish to say so. The Congress did not, or would not, understand his hints. Different proposals were made, and Bonaparte got into a fury. At last he unbosomed himself to Melzi [Count Francesco Melzi, the Vice-President] and Marescalchi [Count Ferdinand Marescalchi, Minister of the Republic], who exerted themselves in his behalf, and the affair was settled to his satisfaction."

Erskine, on the 12th of January, paid a "visit by appointment to the Second Consul, Cambacérès [afterwards Duke of Parma], and was well received. There were several persons in the antechamber. Immediately when I was announced, I was introduced to the Consul, with whom were a General, four or five other persons, and M. Portalis. The Consul kept me about half an hour in conversation, such as is customary on such occasions, asking whether I had had a good passage to Calais, if I was going to make any stay, if I had been ever before in France, if the climate suited me, if I had begun to see the sights of Paris, if I had found acquaintances, and so on." On the 14th, Erskine paid a visit to the Third Consul, Le Brun [afterwards Duke of Placentia], and dined with Cambacérès. Almost all the Ambassadors and Ministers were present. "The dinner was magnificent and excellent, served in the best manner: exquisite ices, coffee and liqueurs." The same evening Erskine went with Lord and Lady Mountcashel to a party given by Mr. Smith, a rich American, and met there Madame Stäel, "Lady Cayer," and a host of notables. Cambacérès always had a reputation for loving a good dinner. "In a Council of State, after a long sitting protracted to 7 P.M., two plans were proposed about cod-fishing. One plan, proposed by Admiral Brueys, was adopted, and contained thirty-three articles. Bonaparte said: "Let us proceed now to the discussion of the articles. What—exclaimed Cambacérès—the articles—and when shall we dine! It is now seven o'clock! Bonaparte took a violent fit of laughing which alarmed Cambacérès, and the sitting broke up. Bonaparte, as far as he was concerned, would have sat till morning without thinking of dinner or anything else. He is indefatigable, and works fifteen hours a day."

Among the persons now met in society by Erskine, was the Minister of the Treasury, Marbè Marbois, one of those who returned from transportation in Guiana.—The Calvinist Haller, the French Commissary, who went to Pius VI. on the 15th of February, 1798, to announce the establishment that day of the Republic, and that the Pope's reign was over, and who on the 17th February brutally compelled the Pope to give up the rings off his fingers and surrender the Vatican treasures,—Baron Denon, who accompanied Bonaparte to Egypt, and published a most valuable account of his travels,—Madame Neckar,—General Marmont [Marshal and Duke of Ragusa], noted by Erskine as "a young man of very obliging manners, married to a daughter of Perregeaux the Banker,—" M. De Burk, of Irish origin, who was Danish Minister at Stockholm, and thence passed in the same quality to Spain,"—Barthélemy, " formerly Minister in England, afterwards in Switzerland when the Revolution was formed there, author of the treaty of peace with Prussia and Spain, afterwards member of the Directory and exiled to Guiana. He is tall, pale, and of prepossessing aspect, and by his discourse one would believe that he disapproved of Revolution. In London he left various opinions about him. Mallet du Pin says that in the Swiss Revolution he had no bounds. His banishment to Guiana after the 18 Fructidor of the year 8 is in his favour."

Erskine dined once (January 28), "with Marbè Marbois, and met Barthélemy, two priests, and another person, lately returned from Guiana, to which place they had been transported after the affair of 18 Fructidor. Thus there were at table five who had experienced the same lot. The whole way from Paris to their embarcation they were transported in a cage with iron bars, and at sea they were treated as slaves and fed on putrid fish and biscuits rotten with weevils. At Guiana, where the

Governor is Victor Hughes, noted for his horrible wickedness in Guadaloupe, these five, with others to the number of 300, were dispersed here and there. A few had something of their own and fared less badly, and others found a benevolent receiver and were fairly well treated. But others, and that by far the greater number, were crowded together and were very badly off. The air is the worst possible. There is only one village, called Guiana, on the sea-side, and containing about 400 inhabitants. The country has here and there dwellings, or rather huts, for Europeans. There are some wandering tribes of natives, formerly instructed by the Jesuits, who are peaceable, and as far as concerns the baptizing of their children, are Christians. The soil is most fertile, but uncultivated. Excellent coffee is produced."

Miss Helen Maria Williams, an authoress who favoured the doctrines of the Girondists, attracted the notice of Erskine at a party given by Lady Mountcashel, and is thus described in his diary:—" One lady was all in black, with spangles of jet and silver, with a veil in same style, covering all one side of her face and descending from her head upon her arms ; and as she excited my curiosity by the singularity of her dress, I found her to be Miss Williams, who has published many little books on the French Revolution—works similar to her attire."

On the 31st of January, "about 6½ P.M., the cannons announced the return of the First Consul from Lyons, and I went to welcome back M. Talleyrand. The emigrants who have returned, seem resolved to get themselves into trouble. They wont associate with the others, and have adopted a coceard in which the national colours, except the blue, can be hardly distinguished. It is said they talk indiscreetly, and do not treat with civility the members of the Government when they meet them in society. It is certain that the Government has given them to know that it is not content with them."

On the 2nd of February, the son of Consul Le Brun left Paris for Rome to carry the demand of the First Consul for the archbishopric of Milan for Cardinal Caprara, and this request was acceded to.

On the 4th of February, Erskine "saw the review or parade at the Tuileries from the windows of Maret, Secretary of State," and was highly delighted with the magnificent spectacle. "The parade is really well worth seeing. Prussians, Austrians, and Russians, all are enchanted by it. The Consular Guard is surprising. What splendid men, what precision and facility of movements! The uniforms of the soldiers are simple, but elegant and commodious, while those of the Generals and heads of battalions and squadrons are rich with gold embroidery and in exquisite taste. There were Grenadiers on foot and on horseback, Fusiliers, Chasseurs, Pioneers and Horse Artillery with six pieces of cannon. Bonaparte—on a beautiful white horse, in midst of Generals and Aides-du-camp—was dressed in the uniform of the Consular Guard, *i.e.*, blue coat, white vest and breeches, with half boots and hat without plume, and passed along the front and then through the lines of infantry and cavalry. Afterwards he stopped at the left wing, and all the troops filed past him." "When I returned to my hotel at 4 P.M., I found an orderly had come with a letter from one of the Prefects of the Palace, inviting me to dine with the First Consul." Erskine, of course, accepted this invitation, and thus describes the dinner :—

"In the first room were servants and Grenadiers at the doors, as well as on the stairs and at the Palace entrance : in the second room a numerous guard of Grenadiers : in the third the military band : in the fourth, which is very large, were Generals, State Officials of all kinds, Foreign Ministers and distinguished strangers just presented. I was the sole and only person in ecclesiastical habit, and I had been invited without previous presentation in public audience. There were arm-chairs at either side of the chimney piece, which was opposite the entrance door, and a line of stools removed from the walls on the side opposite the windows, and to the right of the entrance door. Four ladies came, the wives of members of the administration. After some time Madame Bonaparte with her daughter, wife to Louis Bonaparte, and Madame Murat. This last lady sat down on a fauteuil between the door and the mantelpiece. On the other side of the chimney-piece sat Madame Bonaparte, and next to her was another lady. Next came Madame Louis and then the three other ladies. I was presented to Madame Bonaparte by a Prefect of the Palace. After some time the Minister of State came in by the same door, then, after brief interval, the Second and Third Consuls, and finally the First Consul, who went to compliment the ladies, and afterwards put himself with his back to the fire-place. Shortly the door was again opened, and the announcement was made, *Madame est servie*. Thereupon the Second Consul took the hand of Madame Bonaparte and they walked on, the First Consul following by himself. Then the ladies followed, and then all the rest without order and as best they could. It was fully half-past six when we entered the Gallery and found a long table for about two hundred persons. In the middle sat the First Consul, with the President of the *Corps Législatif* on one side and the President of the Tribunate on the other. Madame Bonaparte was opposite her husband and between the two Consuls. Then the other ladies, Generals, Ambassadors, High Officers of State, etc., took their places. Then all the others took places at hap-hazard and without distinction.

"I found myself not far from the middle, between Marbois, Minister of the Treasury, and General Mortier, Commandant of the Paris Military Division. But one hot course, followed by desert, all excellent and well served. At half past seven we had already left the table and gone to the next room for coffee. The company was now dispersed between the coffee-room and that in which we had been assembled before dinner. In the latter was the First Consul, the centre of a group. I placed myself at a little distance towards the door. Bonaparte saw me, and soon moved towards me and spoke to me very courteously, saying he had doubted whether I had already left Paris. He then discussed my appointment to the Cardinalate, my relations in Scotland, how I came to be a Catholic, and to be born in Rome, and lastly he asked the age of the Cardinal Duke of York. He then, after a few words with the Ministers of Denmark and Russia, turned into the other room where the rest of the company was."

On the 14th of February, Erskine received a visit from Eugene Montmorency (second son of the Duke de Lavalle) and his sposa, Mademoiselle de Bethune; and in the evening he went to a splendid conversazione, given by Madame de Montesson. Madame Bonaparte, and her daughter, wife to Joseph Bonaparte, were present. Madame Bonaparte wore a magnificent dress, "with two rows of stupendous pearls falling on her breast." Madame Visconti had superb diamonds and a "golden cord round her waist, a long piece of which hung down at one side, with here and there olive-shaped buttons, which were made to open. Each button contained a different scent." Count Marcost was covered with diamonds. He had been offered 204,000 lire for one hat ornament, given him by the French Government. There was also a ball and supper, for which Erskine did not remain.

Peace was concluded at Amiens on the 25th of March, 1802, and was celebrated in Paris on the 26th by discharges of cannon from the *Invalides* and the Tuileries, with illuminations in the evening. Erskine walked out to observe the effect on the people, and writes that the pronouncement of peace produced "nothing. They tell me it is always so."

"In Amiens the conclusion was very similar to the preliminaries. England proposed to recognise the King of Etruria and the Italian Republic, on condition that the King of Sardinia should be restored : and insisted, similarly, on the restitution of the Legations to the Pope. France insisted on maintaining a number—no matter how small—of troops in the States of

Naples and the Pope. Every day a new pretension was advanced under a new shape. England did not profit by the situation of the fleet in their power at S. Domingo. Lord Cornwallis was identified with Joseph Bonaparte. It is said they had a project to open the navigation of the Black Sea, and that on this condition France would not oppose the views of Britain and Russia upon Turkey."

"The Concordat was submitted on the 5th of April to the Legislature by M. Portalis, Minister of Worship, who also proposed the organic laws for Catholic and Protestant worship. He spoke two and a half hours. The propositions passed in the affirmative, and the discussion was remitted to the Tribunate; and on the 7th the Tribunate passed them by 78 votes against 7. Simeon spoke, and the President was Girardin. On the 8th, the resolutions of the Tribunate were brought to the *Corps Législatif.* The hall was thronged, and the galleries were crowded by spectators, men and women. The Deputies of the Tribunate, Simeon, Lucien Bonaparte, and Jocourt, entered the hall at 2 P.M. Lucien Bonaparte spoke; and afterwards Jocourt, a Protestant, made a brief speech upon the regulations fixed for the Protestants. The Government orators did not ask to speak. The voting was 228 for and 21 against the measure. In the hall the result caused a sensible feeling manifested by sneers, laughter, and disgust. The Convention or Concordat and the organization were now become law, and so the President, Marcorelle, proclaimed."

"The next day, the 9th, Cardinal Caprara, Legate *a latere*, paid his first public visit to the Government. He left his house, Rue Plumet, Hôtel de Montmorin, about half-past one. The carriages of the three Consuls came to fetch him, which with his own made ten carriages. One carriage led the way with Cross-bearer and Chaplain and the Cross inside; and a detachment of gendarmes, trumpeter, and officers at the head. The carriage of the First Consul came next, containing the Legate, myself, and a Prefect of the Palace, with mounted officers riding beside the windows, and at the back of the carriage. Then came the carriages of the second and third Consuls, and of the Cardinal, all containing the suite. Gendarmes on every side, and lastly another detachment of gendarmes followed by two detachments of dragoons, each a hundred in number.

"The route was by the Boulevards des Invalides, Rue Grenelle, the Palace of the *Corps Législatif* (*olim* Bourbon), the Bridge and Quay of the Revolution and the Grand Carrousel, to the great gate of the Tuileries. The Legate, on arrival, found the Cross-bearer already standing with the Cross raised. At the entrance and along the staircase were Grenadiers and officers lining the way and presenting arms. The Cross preceded as far as the door of the Council chamber on the first landing, and the Legate passed to the second landing place, with the same Prefect of the Palace ever on his left. At the outer door of the apartment, a General met the Legate, and there was still the same accompaniment of grenadiers, presenting arms, with beating of tambours. The Legate was met at the second door by General Duroc, Commandant of the Palace, and at the third by the Prefect of the Palace on duty. The fourth door was shut. The Prefect passed in through it and closed it behind him. Then on a sudden the door was thrown wide open, and we entered the audience chamber.

"At the end of this chamber were three chairs with four aides-du-camp behind them, and the three Consuls stood in front. At the sides stood the Ministers of State, Prefects and Councillors. On the entrance of the Legate, the First Consul advanced to the middle of the room to meet him. Here the Legate interchanged compliments in French with the First Consul. Then a chair was brought and placed opposite to the chairs of the Consuls, but no one sat down. Then the Legate read in Latin a formula of oath, the reading of which had all the air of a surprise. In fact, half-an-hour before the Legate left his house, Portalis went to him on this subject—although the Legate had told me that an agreement had been made that no oath was to be read. Portalis brought a formula which the Legate could not approve. Portalis then departed, but returned at the very moment when the Legate should have mounted his carriage, and Portalis and the Legate were together some minutes in private.

"After the reading of the oath, the First Consul talked with the Legate on common matters, and asked the names of those with him. He asked me after my health. He then asked the Legate if he had brought Theologians. The Legate pointed out one Theologian whom the First Consul addressed, telling him to hold fast to sound doctrine and the true spirit of the Gospel, which meant peace and charity. To this the Theologian replied, '*Maxima Sana.*'

Those accompanying Cardinal Caprara, and by him presented in this public audience, were:—Monsignor Erskine, Uditore S.S.; Monsignor Sala, Secretary of Legation, and Signor Mazio, Canonist; Signor Welch, Canon of S. Peter's, and Maestro di Camera to Caprara; Abbé Valdorini, private Secretary; Messieurs Jarry, Le Surre, and Lecotte, the French Secretaries; Abbé Ducci, Secretary for Ecclesiastical Affairs; and the Abbé Rubbi, Theologian.

"The Legate then went to see Madame Bonaparte, who was sitting in a room and was near the fireplace. They rose when the Legate entered and when he left. They sat and talked some time. The seat of the Legate was half turned to the side of that of Madame. The procession on returning from the Palace and the route were the same as in coming."

On the 11th of April, Erskine wrote in his diary:—"This morning the Cardinal Legate went with the usual cortege (myself excepted) to Nôtre Dame, where he consecrated the Abbé Cambacérès, archbishop nominate of Rouen; the Abbé Bernier, bishop nominate of Orléans; and Abbé Pancemont, parish priest of S. Sulpice, bishop nominate of Vannes; and he installed the archbishop of Paris, Belloy, formerly bishop of Marseilles." This is the last entry in Erskine's diary.

Monsignor Erskine, when keeping this diary, by no means confined himself to notices of breakfasts, dinners, and visits to and from great men, and public functions and receptions. On the contrary, his longest entries are descriptions of the principal churches and establishments in Paris, the catacombs, Botanical and Zoological Gardens, manufactories, etc. His remarks on scientific subjects were very minute, and he filled some pages with a detailed account of a watch with a new escapement. But although he discontinued his diary, he did not omit to make occasional notes on persons and things.

On Easter day, April 18, the same year, 1802, the Legate, to solemnize the Concordat, celebrated High Mass at Nôtre Dame with great pomp, in presence of all the great dignitaries, civil and military. After the gospel, the new bishops took the oaths, according to the stipulations of the Concordat. The day was kept as a public festival by order of the Government. But many persons were by no means contented with the terms of the Concordat. On the day of the celebration in Nôtre Dame, Erskine says that "Augereau, Macdonald, Massena and Bernadotte, retired to the end of the church during the sermon, and talked to each other with manifest signs of displeasure." And "on the day of the publication of the Concordat many military men at the Bureau of War made such a rumpus, that several of the clerks took their hats and went away."

Even before Easter Day, when the Concordat was celebrated, dissensions had arisen between the French Government and Rome about the appointment of bishops. The Pope required a satisfactory retractation from the "Constitutional" bishops before giving them institution to the new sees under the Concordat. The terms of this retractation were difficult to settle. Erskine says that, "On the evening of the 15th April, every negotiation was nearly broken off. Portalis had a violent altercation with the Legate, during which he insulted the Legate to his face and abused the Pope. The subject of this quarrel was a letter which was to be signed by Rich, a 'Constitutional,' nominated to a see by the First Consul. The Legate was under the impression that he would have to depart, and therefore gave the necessary order to destroy the Papers. The following morning Bernier came. Another letter was drawn up, and more than this, the bishops were to make a private retractation to be united to the latter, and then the Profession of Faith might be considered to be satisfactory."

Erskine says that "Camus [Armand Gaston] is the man who directs Portalis." Camus was a chief promoter of the Civil Constitution of the Clergy; and Portalis, by the Organic laws, endeavoured, as far as possible, to replace in vigour the "Constitution" under the cloak of the Concordat. "From all the Departments," wrote Erskine, "came declarations that the *Constitutionals* were not wanted as bishops." The Second and Third Consuls and some members of the Tribunate were "against the adoption of the *Constitutionals*." And finally, "The Legate little by little is reduced to humiliation and to nullity."

That the Legate was himself somewhat to blame, is shewn in a memorandum written by Erskine, with the heading:— "*False steps of the Legate.* 1st. In the Bulls for bishops, a retractation and satisfaction were required from the *Constitutionals*. The French demand the omission of this, and the Cardinal Legate consents. 2nd. The Government sends a note to the Legate, and asks him to forward it to the Pope. The note was to ask the Pope's consent to the nomination of some *Constitutional* bishops. The Legate refused to send it on, and tells the Government to send it themselves. And so they did. The Legate sent no notice in advance to Rome, and sent his despatches by the courier of the Government. 3rd. The Legate declared that he could not give institution to the *Constitutional* bishops elect, without their declaration that they were adherents to the Holy See; would accept all the decrees against the Civil Constitution of the Clergy; and would be submissive and obedient to the Pope. They were to sign a letter to that effect. On Good Friday (April 16) they refused to do this. Another letter in general terms was proposed. The Legate consents that they should make a declaration and retractation in the presence of Bernier and another bishop, and receive the absolution. 4th. The declarations were made and Bernier alone bore witness to them. The Constitutionals denied that they ever made these declarations and were not publicly contradicted by the Legate."

"As it was known that the Constitutional bishops denied having made any verbal retractation before Bernier, it was judged necessary that they should append their signatures to their own proper retractations. Portalis after some difficulty consented to this course. A formula for this purpose was sent by the Legate to each bishop on the 7th of June, the day after Pentecost. The First Consul sent to summon the Legate, and another messenger, an hour later, notified the Legate to bring Sala with him. They found Bonaparte furious. He said the Legate was a perjurer for having written a circular to the bishops without previous communication to the Government. He told Sala that the Court of Rome had sent Seminary boys to cross with subterfuges the operations of the Government. Several times he rose from his seat and went towards him as if to beat him. He broke a vase in his rage. He said the Constitutionals had the merit of having preserved Religion, and that they could not make any retractation. The Legate hardly spoke a word. Sala made some little answer. Then Bonaparte asked the Legate if he had anything to say on the part of His Holiness, and enquired after the Pope's health. The Legate replied that the Pope was ill and suffered from weakness of the head, and recollected with difficulty. Bonaparte turned again to Sala and said:—This means that the Pope wants a modification of the organic laws, and I cannot see why these laws should displease His Holiness as they were made to protect Religion, which in this respect will be under the influence of the Civil power."

Monsignor Erskine had intended to leave Paris after the functions of Easter Day, but was detained waiting for a farewell audience of the First Consul. This was the reason assigned by him in a letter to Cardinal Consalvi, dated the 8th of May. Again, on the 25th of June, he was still expecting his audience. He at last got one, but on what day is not stated. According to Moroni, Bonaparte told Erskine, on his taking leave, that " he would be happy to do him a service, for he esteemed him highly."

Finally, after a sojourn of eight months and a half, Erskine left Paris on the 29th of August, 1802, at 4.30 A.M. He travelled in his good English carriage, and by easy stages. On the 2nd of September he reached Lyons, stopping in the Hôtel d' Europe, and remained there four days. He writes of Lyons :—" The number of inhabitants is diminished by one third. There are not 80,000 at present. The looms before the Revolution were 14,000 : two years ago they were reduced to 6,000, and now are 9,000. . . . The churches were despoiled and half ruined as at Paris. Five churches are in the hands of " Constitutionals "—Jansenism has made strides here."

On 6th of September he set out for Turin, where he arrived on the 12th, and lodged in the Albergo Nazionale, thus spending six days in his second stage. The passage of Mont Cenis must have taken up some time. He was charmed by the views. " On Mont Cenis were planted Crosses, and General Jourdan [Marshal and Peer of France], caused the arm of one to be cut off." Leaving Turin on the 13th, he reached Milan on the 15th, and stayed there two days. He gave up the post horses, and bargained with a vetturino to take himself and carriage to Florence in six days. He went by Lodi, Piacenza, Fiorenzuola, Parma, Reggio, and Modena to Bologna, where he stopped to visit Don Gregorio Chiaramonti, the Pope's brother, and he arrived in Florence within the time agreed on with the vetturino, on the 22nd September.

In Florence he remained some days, and met many friends,

notably the Princess Corsini and her son Don Neri, and Don Orazio Borghese, and met also some English travellers, among whom was Lady Cooper. From Florence he went with post horses to Siena, which city he had not seen before, and where he was charmed with the Cathedral. Going on by Radicofani, he arrived at Viterbo in the end of September.

At Viterbo, Monsignor Erskine received a surprise, which was by no means agreeable. He there found a person awaiting him, commissioned by Consalvi, Secretary of State, to give him notice, that as he was soon, in the very next consistory, to be published a Cardinal, and as already Monsignor Lacchini had for eighteen months performed the duties of *Pro-Uditore*, it was thought opportune for the despatch of public affairs, that the discharge of the Auditor's business should be continued by the said Lacchini, while to Erskine would remain merely the title and honour of Auditor, and the usual residence in the Quirinal or Vatican palace.

It may well be imagined what effect such unexpected news must have produced on the vivacious temperament of Erskine. He must have considered it the highest honour to discharge the duties, were it but for a few days, of an office which in his absence from Rome, had been conferred on him by two Popes, and therefore he regarded as most injurious to himself this hindrance now opposed to him. The first resolution which he took in the burning heat of his resentment, was to stop in Viterbo and there await his promotion to the Cardinalate. But when his effervescence had calmed down, and he had considered the matter in reference to public opinion, which he knew would be in his favour, he determined on continuing his journey to Rome. He was, however, so painfully affected by this severe blow that for the rest of his life the remembrance of it always revived his sense of the injustice done to him. He used to add that by this blow were scattered to the winds all the magnanimous intentions of Pius VI., who had ordered the fees of the Auditorship to be funded and placed in deposit to meet Erskine's expenses when he should be proclaimed a Cardinal. Erskine took this misfortune as a manifest sign that under Consalvi, he would never, even though he were a Cardinal, be promoted to any of the great offices of State, nor be called on to take part in the grand affairs of the Papacy, internal or foreign. Nor was he far wrong in his anticipations.

Erskine reached Rome on the 1st of October, 1802, and the Roman *Diario* of the 4th, announced his arrival, giving him the title—as was due to him—of *Uditore SS.* The Pope gave him audience very soon, and received him with his usual kindness, giving him many signs of his particular esteem. He even took him in his carriage, along with the Majordomo, Monsignor Gavotti, on the occasion of his visit to Castel Gandolfo, on the 18th of October.

On his part, Monsignor Erskine was anxious to give His Holiness a token of his filial attachment, and he presented him with a case, expressly brought from London, containing eye-glasses and spectacles of all kinds, with a set of lenses graduated to every kind of sight, the whole being mounted in gold and of exquisite workmanship. His Holiness was much pleased with this valuable present, which he greatly admired, although he had no personal occasion for it, his eyesight being good. The Pope subsequently, about 1808, gave it to Lucien Bonaparte, who made constant use of the glasses, and was in the habit of exhibiting the case and its contents to his visitors, as a gift from His Holiness, of English and very precious workmanship.

Monsignor Erskine was now residing in the Auditor's apartment, in the Quirinal palace, which Pius VII. had chosen for his habitation this year. It was now suggested that this apartment should be given to some one else, as the Vice-Auditor preferred, even after becoming Auditor, to occupy his old rooms in the Spada palace in the Corso, a situation more convenient for his legal business. It distressed Erskine to find these indelicate attempts to anticipate his departure. The coolness towards him displayed by Cardinal Consalvi was also annoying. It was the custom for papal nuncios or envoys on returning to Rome, to give to the Secretary of State a verbal and confidential account of their mission. When Erskine discharged this duty, Consalvi gave little attention and evinced no anxiety for information. Erskine failed not to shew his disgust at this apathy exhibited by Consalvi to the affairs of England, and told the Pope that his Secretary of State did not even condescend to ask him about the weather in London.

Much of this strange behaviour of Consalvi may be explained by the fact that French influence was rapidly becoming ascendant in Rome. Bonaparte no longer intended to observe the Treaty of Amiens. And owing to the circumstances of Italy and the position of the Pontifical States, the Roman policy was almost entirely, and of necessity, the policy of the French. Monsignor Erskine, though born in Rome, yet by his nationality and temperament, and by his inclination reinforced by his many years of residence in Great Britain, was, and was considered an Englishman. He could not therefore figure prominently in the Roman government without hurting the susceptibilities of France which, in spite of the Peace of Amiens —soon broken—maintained always a national antipathy to England. On the other hand, Pius VII. recognized in Erskine a man of high genius and experience in business, and did not omit to consult him in various matters, especially in such as related to the internal administration of the Papal government.

On one occasion during an audience with the Pope, the conversation fell on the subject of various administrative disorders and irregularities. The tenants of the lands of the *Camera Apostolica* had got into the habit of offering for long leases of these lands such sums as rent, that the other competitors were driven away. But after getting into possession, they importunately demanded reductions of rent, which they managed to obtain by persistent applications and by pathetic representations of the harshness of the terms of the contracts into which they had inconsiderately—as they pretended—entered. The abatements, sometimes exceeding all fairness, proved detrimental to the Papal treasury. The Pope asked Erskine for his opinion as to the best way to put a stop to this abuse, which had long become habitual. Erskine replied promptly, that he had ready two distinct plans, one, which he knew beforehand would not commend itself to the Pope's kind heart, and another which possibly might please him. The first plan was, that as these abatements were very common, inasmuch as every tenant counted on them as a certainty, it was necessary to make an example which would stop these irregularities once for all; and he proposed on the next appeal for abatement, to refuse it, and exact the entire payment by seizing the securities taken by the Government for due execution of the contract, and to do this without regard to the consequences of such a proceeding to the tenant. The tenant ought to know his own business and to calculate his own interest: nothing was concealed from him in his preliminary investigations, and the offers of rival competitors shewed him the true value of the lands. But he wished to triumph over the other competitors and to cheat the Government. Let him pay the penalty. One such example would suffice to prevent recurrence of similar disorders. The Pope at once shewed repugnance to this proposal, and then Erskine set forth his second plan in which would be found the mercy so dear to His Holiness.

This second plan was to accord a carefully calculated abatement to the tenant, and to admit that the tenant's mistake in concluding the contract arose from unforeseen circumstances. But the abatement was to be only for the past years, and from the date of the concession the contract was to be considered as rescinded and null, and a fresh letting was to be held with observance of greater regularity. This second plan pleased the Pope and was approved by him, but was never put into execution, in consequence, probably, of the opposition of those whose duty it was to carry it out. The tenants continued to obtain enormous abatements and to enjoy long leases to the immediate loss of the Treasury and consequent detriment of the Public.

Notice was now given to Monsignor Erskine to be ready for the consistory to be held in January, 1803, and which was actually held in the Quirinal on the 17th of that month. Erskine and two others, Locatelli and Castiglione, all previously reserved *in petto*, were created Cardinal Deacons. Among the seven Cardinal Priests now created were four French archbishops, namely Jean Di Dieu Raimond de Boisgelin, archbishop of Tours; Jean Baptiste de Belloy, archbishop of Paris; Stephen Humbert de Cambacérès, archbishop of Rouen; and Joseph Fesch, archbishop of Lyons. The hat was given to Erskine three days afterwards. And in secret consistory of the 28th of March following, he was granted for his title the church of S. Maria in Campitelli. This church was selected in recognition of Erskine's attachment to the Stuart family, for it had given his first title to the Duke of York, when he was made a Cardinal, at the age of twenty-three years. The Congregations assigned to Erskine were the Council, Propaganda, Rites and the Fabbrica.

One of the first duties the new Cardinal had to perform was to notify, on the forms prescribed by the Secretary of State, his appointment to all the reigning Catholic Sovereigns of Europe, including the First Consul of France. Erskine also sent congratulatory letters to the absent Cardinals who were appointed in the same consistory as he was, and notably to his personal friend De Boisgelin, formerly a refugee in London. De Boisgelin replied on the 5th of February, expressing his pleasure that both of them were together in the same list of promotions. "We were so long," he says, "in accord with each other in the course of a difficult negotiation that it seems as if Divine Providence designed to crown together our constant union." The "only bitterness is that, while we are united in participation of the same dignity, we are separated in society. Your Eminence will be kept in Rome to enjoy the advantages due to your merits and services, and I must stay in my archbishopric to discharge my duties." De Boisgelin also wrote a long letter on the 16th of April to Cardinal Erskine, from which it may be gathered that he did not wish the Pope to forget his past services to the church, nor to assume that his promotion ought to be ascribed solely to Bonaparte's nomination. De Boisgelin asserts that he had been ever obedient to the Popes—to Pius VI. in the time of the Revolution, and to Pius VII. at the time of the Concordat. He had at the Pope's bidding resigned his See of Aix. Yet he always retained affection for the old dynasty. The sentiments of loyalty to the Bourbons were shared by all the members of the De Boisgelin family, to whom this promotion to the purple was so little pleasing, that the only portrait of the archbishop to be found in the family is one—a whole length and full size—in the dress not of a cardinal but of a prelate.

Among the earliest letters of felicitation received at this time by Cardinal Erskine was one from Sir Francis Burdett, dated London, April 23, 1803. It begins by commendations of one Mr. William Clossé, and then proceeds:—" Pray accept my congratulations upon your new honours, and believe me a sincere partaker in whatever can add to your comfort and happiness." Sir Francis had married, in 1793, Sophia, youngest daughter of Thomas Coutts, the banker. Mr. Coutts himself, towards the end of May, wrote his congratulations to his old friend, and alludes to the unusual Spring, and the consequent bad effects to be feared on the harvest. All this—he says—is nothing compared with the renewal of the war, which he considered inevitable and the greatest calamity.

Prince Woronzow wrote thus, from London:—

"*Harley Street, 5 Aout, 1803.*

"C' est avec un plaisir inexprimable que j'ai reçu votre aimable lettre, Cara Eminenza. Ce souvenir d' une Persone si estimable et a la quelle je suis si attaché, m' est bien précieux.

"Le retard de ma response, ne provient que de la difficulté de faire passer une lettre d' un Pays si heretic, dans celui de la Sainteté. Vous nous voyez peutêtre prêts a etre envahis et exterminés, vue la Puissence de celui qui se prepare a notre extermination, aidé des mandemens des Saints Eveques de l' E'glise Galicane et des veux des fidèls de cette même E'glise; mais John Bull est un heretic obstiné, qui a l' air de vouloir mourir dans une impénitence finale. Aussi il se prépare a bien recevoir les aimables uisiteurs qui viendront pour le convertir à coup de canons.

"En attendent je vous prie de bien recevoir notre Ministre le C$^{te.}$ Boutourlin, qui va résider à Rome. Il est mon neveu; c' est un homme d' esprit, d' instruction, d' une caractere franc et honet et d' un fond de gayeté, qui rend sa societé très aimable. Je vous suplie de lui accorder votre amitié et je vous répond d' avance qu' il la meritera. Ne vous attendez pas de trouver en lui un Diplomâte fin, astucieux et fort occupé d' affaires. Celles qu' il y a entre nos deux cours, ne sont ni frequentes ni dificiles à s' arranger. Il s' occupe plus des auteurs classiques, des beaux ars et de tout ce qui regarde l' antiquité, que de la Politique, que d' ailleurs est devenue tout à fait inutile depuis la recente découverte si philantropique qu' on a fait d' abreger et simplifier les negotiations en introduisant la methode d' argumenter par de bouches à feux, qui eclaircissement tout ce qui est douteux et finissent par prononcer victorieussement tout ce qu' on avance. Ce sont là le vrais arguments ad hominem.

"Ma fille et M$^{lle.}$ Jardine, sensibles et reconnaissentes de votre obligent souvenir, vos prient de le leurs conserver. Mon fils est dans son Pays assidue à s' instruire dans cette nouvelle maniere de negotier, si eloquente et si prompte. Il brule d' envie de pouvoir aussi argumenter en compagnie de quelque milliers de es compatriotes, contre ceux qui s' exercent déja dans ce grand genre d' eloquence.

"Tous nos amis comuns se portent bien.

"Adio Cara Eminenza: portez vous bien: conservez moi votre amitie' qui m' est chère et voyez que la mienne vous est voué pour toujours."

Count de Bouterlin was in this year, 1803, appointed by the Emperor of Russia, Alexander I., to be his Envoy Extraordinary at the Holy See with Count Cassini, the former Charge d' affaires, as Councillor of Legation, but very soon afterwards, in consequence of the arrest in Rome of the French emigre Vernègues, who was attached to the Russian embassy in Rome, and was therefore under the protection of Russia, the Emperor broke off all diplomatic relations with the Pope.

Cardinal Erskine about this time, out of good-feeling and kindness of heart, took upon himself a troublesome duty, more properly to be discharged by a British Representative in Rome had there been one. Frederick Hervey, Earl of Bristol, and protestant bishop of Derry in Ireland, died on the 8th of July, 1803, in Albano, having had none but hired servants and salaried persons at his deathbed. This wealthy but eccentric Peer had passed five years in Rome or Italy, and being passionately devoted to the Fine Arts, gave commissions to artists, and made large purchases, and left not a few debts at his death. In this disorder of his affairs, and in the absence of his son who lived in England, Cardinal Erskine came forward, and being uncertain whether there was any will or testamentary document, took, on the 2nd of July, provisional possession of all the property of the deceased, and employed his own Auditor, the Avvocato Celestini, to compile an inventory of everything belonging to the late Earl, and to collect and transport all the articles to Rome. Erskine also secured the safety of all the property of the deceased which remained in Florence in the Villa Strozzi, which the late Earl had taken on lease: and this was done by getting Duke Strozzi to serve notice on the keeper of the Villa not to allow the least thing to be removed by any one who was not legally authorized.

Meanwhile the creditors, clamourous for settlement of their claims, and unwilling to abide the result of proceedings in England, or to wait for the arrival in Rome of the heir, petitioned the Pope to nominate Erskine as guardian and administrator of the inheritance. The Pope desired his auditor, Monsignor Lacchini, to communicate with Cardinal Erskine, and ascertain his wishes on the subject. The Cardinal in reply told Monsignor Lacchini that he could not accept this charge, and that his exertions had been only for the purpose of securing the property and preventing dilapidation and pillage. He therefore took the liberty of suggesting Celestini, who had hitherto acted in the affair, and knew all the circumstances of the case, as a proper person to be made Administrator. Now, however, as his object of saving the property had been attained, he resigned all superintendence over the late Earl's affairs, and declined all further proposals to assume the management or distribution of the assets.

The manner in which the new Earl of Bristol regarded the conduct of Erskine on this occasion will be best seen from the following letter, which is still preserved :—

"*Tunbridge, August 29, 1803.*

"My Dear Cardinal,

"It is quite impossible that I should ever be able to express how deeply and sensibly I feel your kind and friendly conduct on the late melancholy occasion. No words can convey it, so I will not attempt it, but trust to your doing justice to feelings which it is out of my power to describe. May we some time or other meet at Rome, and you will then be in some degree a judge of the impression which your real kindness has made upon me.

"Since I heard from you I have had a letter from Torlonia, who I find is in considerable advance, both during my poor father's life and since, for the various expenses which have arisen. I answered it by general civility, but could take no step respecting the money till I know whether there is a will amongst the papers at Rome.

"This letter is, of course, entirely for yourself. The last will which has been found in this country was written at a time when I was not on good terms with my father, and leaves all the personalty—to the amount of near two hundred thousand pounds—to a distant relation. If unfortunately there is no subsequent will in Italy, it will fall to the person who gets the personalty (a Mr. Henry Bruce, in Ireland) to pay all the debts in all parts of the world. All the landed estate was entailed upon me, and therefore comes to me without being subject to his debts of any description: and if the personalty is left away from me, as that is more than twenty times sufficient to discharge his debts, I shall leave the law to take its course, and pay nothing but those expenses, of any sort, which your Eminence may have order'd, and which of course will be an exception to my general rule. You see, my dear Cardinal, that this is a letter of perfect confidence, intended for your own eye. Torlonia need be under no uneasiness. As soon as we know whether there is another will and who are the executors, immediate steps can be taken to pay all debts of every description without an hour's delay. Adieu, my dear Cardinal, and believe me to be, with the most sincere attachment, your truly obliged and affectionate friend and servant.

BRISTOL."

This letter, stamped by the foreign office postal stamp and sealed with a black seal with the Earl's arms, was directed in French :—

"A Son Eminence Monseigneur le Cardinal Erskine, etc.,
En son Hôtel, a Rome."

Among his English friends who rejoiced at the promotion of Erskine to the purple were his kinsman, the Earl of Buchan, and the members of the Coutts family, with whom Erskine was in correspondence long before his visit to Great Britain. The following letter, which was printed by the Scottish Antiquarian Society, and copied for the author by Lieut.-Colonel Fergusson, was written to the Earl of Buchan by Erskine some years before his mission to George III. :—

Rome, June 6th, 1785.

My Lord,—I am quite ashamed, on having delayed so long to give an answer to the letter with which your Lordship was pleased to honour me in the last year. Although I may have wherewith to excuse my silence; yet, I must confess, it is quite out of my power to justify it: nevertheless, I will venture to produce what may in some measure apologize for my fault; relying for the rest on your humanity and good nature.

When I received your Lordship's letter, I was seized with a weakness in my eyes, to which I have been subject for some years past, during the heat of summer, which almost entirely hinders me from reading or writing. In that situation, although I attempted it several times, yet I was obliged at last to give over the thought of answering your Lordship's letter for that season; especially in a language, to which not being used, it required some better application: for although you was so kind as to put it in my option, to write to you either in Italian or Latin, I looked upon it as disgraceful for me, considering myself as Scotch, to make use of any other language but that of our own country. Being obliged on the said account to put off writing to your Lordship, I thought to make some atonement for it by exerting myself, in the meantime, in preparing those measures which might forward your researches, that in the end I might show, that if I had been silent I had not been idle. To that purpose I addressed myself to the keeper and clerks of the Vatican library, but as I could have no satisfactory answer from them, I applied next to the keeper of the Secret Archives, where all the old bulls and letters, and other such papers, are preserved; and as he flattered me with the hopes that such things might be found there as might prove useful, providing I could obtain a leave from the Pope for the extraction of such notices as I should require, I made my petition to His Holiness, by whom it was graciously granted. You may easily see, my Lord, that the bringing about this work with different persons, and the waiting for the proper opportunity to speak to the sovereign, took up more time than I had imagined at the beginning; but as I had gone so far, and was fixed on the scheme of accounting in some measure for my dilation, I still expected, until I should be favoured by the gentleman keeper, who being occupied about the publication of some work, could not comply with my demands neither so soon nor so fully as I desired. At last I received from him the enclosed note [of twelve Papal Bulls relating to Scotland of dates 1216-1261]; but another unexpected accident retarded my furthering it to you. Mr. Gavin Hamilton, who had been long thinking of returning to his native country, being at last resolved to undertake that journey in the beginning of the late spring, I thought of sending my letter by him; but, as it happens, having put it off from one week to another, he did not set off until some days past, and I don't know for what accident he forgot to acquaint me with the day of his departure. So that also on account of this unexpected combination, my letter set out some days later than it should. This is what I may say in my behalf. Unexpected circumstances, and perhaps a premature desire to show to your Lordship my will to serve you, have produced my fault, for which I beg your pardon.

Now, late indeed, but once at last, I render to you my Lord, and to all the gentlemen of the [Antiquarian] Society [of Scotland], my most humble thanks for the honour bestowed on me, by giving me a place in your learned Society. I am so much the more sensible at it, as it flatters me with the thought, that although so far removed, yet by this means I have acquired a new connection with the country from which I draw my origin. It must give to your Lordship a particular satisfaction to have been the promoter and founder of a Society so beneficial to Scotland ; which entitles you to the gratitude of all those who love their country ; and I am proud, that so generous an institution should be owing to the patriotic spirit of a person to whom I have the honour to be related. As much as it depends on me, I shall leave nothing unattempted, by which I may be useful to the object on which our Society has been erected. To that purpose, I shall not cease to insist on the gentleman, the keeper of the Archives ; and since the Pope was so gracious as to give leave to copy any papers I should ask for, if your Lordship thought proper to write to His Holiness a letter on that account, I believe it would be very well received by him, and if you would mention in it my connection with you, it would be honourable to me. Besides the note which I send enclosed, of such Bulls as have been found hitherto, the keeper has shown me a muniment on parchment, of which, if you desire it, I may likewise send a copy. It is an oath of allegiance of John Baliol to King Edward the First. It begins by narrating, that on the death of King Alexander, several pretenders to the Crown of Scotland appeared ; that they agreed that the question should be decided by Edward ; that he had declared for Baliol as next heir. To show his right, there is a kind of genealogical tree from Alexander the First down to him : then it is said, that Baliol had attempted to revolt from Edward, contrary to the oath taken at his election, and now apprized of his fault, he renews his oath of allegiance, which is set down *per extenso*. This is a part of history well known ; but if your Lordship should choose to have a copy of the said paper, I can further [forward] it to you. In the meantime, other researches shall be made : and I hope they shall not be useless. In order to draw more the keeper in our interest, I think it would not be improper to make him an honorary member of the Society. His name is *Abbate Gaetano Marini, Prefetto dell' Archivio Segreto Vaticano*. As to the collection of Bulls you have mentioned to me, there is such a thing, but I do not think it worth purchasing for the Society, since it could draw no advantage from it, for its interest. In the Vatican Library, perhaps, something might be found: but in that unsafe chaos, to which the keepers themselves are strangers, it will be a mere accident if anything be hit upon; and I doubt very much if Assemani [Stephen, Custos of the Vatican Library] could ever have been able to fulfil what he promised. Nevertheless, I shall use all my endeavours, that proper researches may be done [made] there.

By Mr. Gavin Hamilton you will receive my portrait, which I had sent to him beforehand. It will gain an additional merit to the original, to have it placed in so good company as you hinted to me. The names of Mr. Henry and Mr. Thomas Erskine had already reached to this town by the public papers; and by several of my acquaintances here, it had been reflected on the singularity of three persons of the same name, being in the same profession at the same time, in three so distant countries. But your brothers, my Lord, have a more ample and more luminous scene where to exert themselves, and talent more apt to fill it. I must be satisfied, that born at a distance from the country of my fathers, if I have added no lustre, I have at least done no disgrace to our family. This is the aim which I proposed to myself from the beginning, and although deprived of many subsidies, I hope I have attained to it. As to Mr. David Erskine, I was always of your Lordship's opinion, but I have heard since that he is gone to the East Indies. I thank you for the account you was so kind to give me as to my other relations, and am glad they have begun to repair the losses sustained by our family at other times. But, my Lord, must I despair of ever seeing you or your worthy brother in this country? I daresay that you would find in Italy, and especially in Rome, many things not unworthy the trouble of a journey; and it should be the greatest happiness I could ever enjoy in my life, to be here for some time in your company. In the meantime, if it were not too much liberty for one portrait to ask three, I should be very happy to have in my possession the portraits of persons that I so much admire.

Mr. John Geddes, by whom I received your letter, will be the deliverer of this. I heard from him with pleasure the regard which your Lordship has for him, who well deserves it. I have been very happy with his acquaintance and company in my younger years, and have always had a particular esteem for his virtues and merit.

I have the honour to be, with the greatest respect,
My Lord,
Your most obedient and most humble servant and kinsman,
CHARLES ERSKINE.

From a letter to Lord Buchan, written from Rome May 1, 1790, by Monsignor Erskine, it appears that Mr. and Mrs. Coutts, and their daughters, visited Rome in that year, and brought to Erskine a letter of introduction from Lord Buchan. Erskine showed the Coutts family all the attention in his power. From the same letter it appears that the Cardinal Duke of York, had promised, on Erskine's request, to send to Lord Buchan portraits of the Cardinal's family. (*See* the life of Hon. Henry Erskine, by Lieut.-Colonel Alex. Fergusson. Edinburgh. 1882.)

Mr. Coutts, the banker, wrote on the 31st of October, 1803, to Erskine, stating that the Rev. Henry Hervey Bruce, the heir to the personalty, had given him an order to open in his name a credit with Torlonia for £14,000, with which to satisfy the debts due to Torlonia, and to all the other creditors of the defunct Lord Bristol. This fortunate clergyman was created a Baronet on the 9th of June, 1804.

As a member of the Congregation of the Propaganda, Cardinal Erskine naturally took a leading part in discussions upon affairs concerning Great Britain and Ireland. This appears from his votes in Propaganda in this year, 1803, in the matter of the ecclesiastical jurisdiction of the Vicars Apostolic. These Vicars in times of persecution acted independently each of the other, with extraordinary faculties in points of discipline, and with free expenditure of the funds entrusted to their administration. This independence, so useful to the Church in past times, might degenerate into despotism very dangerous in times of peace. At present the Church in England enjoyed peace and freedom of worship. But certain inconveniences had arisen between the vicars and their clergy, and it would be better to re-enter into the jurisdiction of the Common Ecclesiastical Law, according to the decrees of the Council of Trent, as far as the execution of such decrees may be permissible. Erskine proposed to the congregation to order the Vicars Apostolic to meet together for joint consultation at least once a year, and to hold their first meeting as soon as possible, and, in this first meeting, to consider the erection of a general Seminary; to provide for impeding publication of pernicious books and pamphlets; and to arrange a system to be followed for good administration of the mission funds.

In the Propaganda congregation, held on the 2nd of August, 1803, to take into consideration the claims of the President and Superiors of Maynooth College to send up candidates for ordination without consent of their diocesans, it was unanimously decided that the old concession by which students of colleges might be ordained by any bishop, without dimissory letters from their diocesans, and with testimonial letters from the rectors only, was now out of date; was originally granted for times of peril and necessity; and was now abrogated in times when the profession of the Catholic faith was free, and when Maynooth itself was founded and subsidized by the Government.

Erskine was now made Protector of Scotland, where the Catholic Faith languished more than in other parts of the British

States, and where Catholics were few and scattered. He was also made Protector of the Scots College in Rome, in which he had been once a student. Immediately upon his appointment as Protector, he called upon the Rector of the College, the Rev. Paul Macpherson, a Scotchman, and agent of the Scotch bishops, to furnish him with a report upon the condition of the College, pecuniary and otherwise. This report is still extant. Macpherson had come forward spontaneously to assume direction of the College at a time when the former Superiors or Rectors had abandoned it, and he endeavoured to save it from total ruin. The report gives a lamentable picture of the past management, and suggests as the best remedy for past evils the establishment of a Superior or Rector of the Scotch nationality, to direct and administer it under the sole control of the Cardinal Protector. A Scotch Rector knew the habits and dispositions of his fellow-countrymen much better than Italians, for, in the past, the Italian Superiors, by hurting the susceptibilities and opposing the national inclinations of the students had occasioned quarrels, resistance, disorders, and sometimes scandals. A Scotch Rector would exert himself to maintain as large a number as possible of students for the mission, and would also, indirectly, assume a certain responsibility towards the Scotch Vicars Apostolic, a responsibility of which the Italian Rectors shewed themselves completely independent. From this time forth a Scotch Rector has always been at the head of the College. Cardinal Erskine endeavoured to restore the finances of the College, and with partial success.

By the Bull of Foundation of this college, Clement VIII. granted it the Abbey of S. Elia in Mellicuca, in the diocese of Mileto in Calabria, and by another bull of January, 1603, gave it the Abbey of S. Mennato, in the diocese of S. Agata dei Goti, in Terra di Lavoro.

These two abbeys had been enjoyed for many years peaceably by the college, but as Clement had entrusted to the

Jesuits the direction and administration of the abbey lands as well as of the college, the two abbeys, on the suppression of the Jesuits in the kingdom of Naples in the last century, were seized and alienated by the Royal Court, on the plea that they belonged to the Jesuit Order and not to the Scots College. The then Cardinal Protector of the College protested against this usurpation and was told by the Royal Court that the abbeys would be restored to the College when the Jesuits ceased to be its directors. This condition became fulfilled in 1773, but the promise of restitution was not kept, and owing to the circumstances of the time, no further steps were then taken. Cardinal Erskine, on becoming Protector, revived the claims of the College by an able statement, corroborated by documents, to be presented to the Naples Court in the name of the bishops and clergy of Scotland, and the support of the British Ambassador at Naples was promised. But for various reasons the application was not renewed till the year 1805. Before the end of that year the second invasion of the Naples States by the French, and the installation of Joseph Bonaparte as the new king of Naples, destroyed all hope of recovering for the College, the lost abbeys.

Cardinal Erskine was more successful in the case of the bequests left to the College by Cardinal Giuseppe Spinelli, formerly Protector of Scotland and Prefect of the Propaganda, who, by his will dated June 28th, 1759, ordained that a sum of money, amounting to ten thousand Roman scudi should be kept by a trustee, to be employed for Scotch missions, and also declaring that for the same purpose he had constituted in Rome a *censo* or mortgage with the Jerusalem Order [of Malta] at $2\frac{1}{2}$ per cent. The annual receipts were to be applied to maintain three additional students in the Scots College. Cardinal Spinelli gave also, for Scotch missions, fifty policies, or "*Luoghi di Monte S. Pietro,*" of which the interest was to be at the disposal of the Cardinal Protector of the College *pro tempore*. These Spinelli bequests incurred, at the time of the French invasion, the fate of all properties of Religious Foundations. And even when the Pontifical Government had been restored, the *Luoghi di Monte* had to submit to reductions. But the *Censo*, or Mortgage, made with the Order of Malta, was fully re-established, and secured for the College, after an attempt, defeated by Cardinal Erskine, made by Bali Buzi to obtain a reduction of twenty-five per cent. on the payments.

The Scots College also regained full possession of its valuable vineyard near Marino, which had been alienated and declared national property by the Revolutionary Government. Cardinal Erskine, in December, 1803, by a strongly worded letter to the Conestabile Colonna, the Governor of Marino, caused that functionary to put a stop to the injuries done to the vineyard by evil-disposed neighbours ; and he also opposed and finally silenced the unjust claims upon the vineyard, put forward by one Giuseppe Brancadoro and his heirs.

The Vicars Apostolic of Scotland sent their thanks to him for accepting the Protectorship of Scotland and of the Scots College in the following letter :—

"My Lord,

"The pleasure and satisfaction which we felt upon the news of your Eminence's being appointed, by the Holy See, Protector of these our Missions, could not, with propriety, be expressed by an individual. It was for this reason that none of us hitherto took the liberty of troubling your Eminence upon that occasion. But being now assembled with the principal members of our Clergy, this was one of the first objects which fixed the attention of all. It is in the name of the Scots Mission, at the request of the Scots Missionaries, and we have reason to believe we might add, with truth, it is with the approbation and applause of the whole nation and of every Scotsman, that we express our joy upon an event which will form an epoch in the Ecclesiastical history of this country. Whilst we look forward, with well founded hopes, to the effects of your powerful and zealous patronage, we must beg leave to offer your Eminence our grateful thanks for your generous and kind attention, which our College and Agent in Rome have already experienced. We have not to inform your Eminence of the difficulties, in which we are constantly involved: they are well known to you. It is a comfort to us to reflect, with confidence, that you will neither lose sight of them nor omit anything which can extricate us from them or alleviate them.

"We have the honour to be, with profound respect, My Lord, your Eminence's most obedient humble servants,

* Geo. Hay, Bp. of Daulia, V.A. in Scotland.
* John Chisholm, Bp. of Oria, V.A.
* Alex^r· Cameron, Maximianopolit. Coadj^r·
* Æneas Chisholm, Diocesar^s· Coadjutor.

Preshome, 14th Aug^t· 1804."

The endorsement on this letter contains the following:—"Sussidio mandato ai detti Vicarii Apostolici dalla Congregazione di Propaganda nel 1807." The subsidy was 1,000 Scudi.

A certain Monsignor Antonio Scarpelli, a man of some literary merits, had published the first of a series of letters on Economy, Political and Agrarian, and had sent a copy to the Pope. He received encomiums for his first letter from the principal Economists of Italy, and was about to publish further letters, when to his surprise he received, on the 27th of June, 1803, an intimation from Consalvi, Secretary of State, that he was not to proceed further with the publication of his letters, either in his own or any other name; inasmuch as they directly attacked the system established in the Pontifical States, were injurious to Monsignor Vergani, the Secretary of the Congregation for re-ordering the State, and were dangerous in the way of prejudicing public opinion against certain measures about to be taken by that Congregation.

Scarpelli from the 23rd of January, 1803, had been writing to

Erskine to tell him of the efforts he was making to fix Prince Stanislaus Poniatowski in Rome, by getting the Prince to purchase certain of the State lands, and notably Castel Gandolfo and the Lake of Albano. He complained of the tricky and annoying manner shown towards him, the Prince's agent in these purchases, by the officials, and was particularly severe, and bold almost to impertinence in his remarks upon Consalvi, and upon Lante, the Treasurer General, whom, in his letters to themselves, he taxed with bad faith. He was determined to resist the attempt to stop his writings and sent to the Pope a petition energetically drawn up, and demanded as Censors for his future publications, two personages, of rank not to be imposed on by the Authority of any Minister, who had no private prejudices or interests to serve and who were capable of feeling what was due to the Pope, namely Cardinals Erskine and Pacca. The first knew the English system of Political Economy—the second was acquainted with the North and South of Europe. The pope assented to this petition on the 20th of July, 1803, and copies of the supplica and rescript were sent on August the 1st to both Cardinals, who accepted the charge, and when Scarpelli sent the proofs of his letters for examination, he received them back through Cardinal Erskine who wrote his full approval, adding that Cardinal Pacca was of the same opinion. Scarpelli succeeded in publishing his works, but from the style of his correspondence was evidently, like many reformers, a disagreeable sort of man.

In February, 1803, the city of Cingoli, in general council, chose by acclamation Cardinal Erskine as *Com-Protettore*. And by Brief of 11th of October, 1804, Erskine was made Visitator Apostolic of the Monastery of S.S. Augustine and Rocco in Caprarola, then reduced to a pitiable state of poverty. The Abbess set forth in a petition to the Pope that each nun had only half an Italian pound of meat per diem, and on maigre days one egg, and half a pound of ricotta. The whole daily cost of each person in the monastery could not exceed five Bajocci—less than twopence halfpenny ! In December, 1804, Erskine was elected Protector of the Ven. Hospital of S. John the Evangelist, in Caprarola. In August, 1805, he became Protector of the Monastery of Monte Luce, in Perugia, where he re-established the annual Fair, conceded to that Monastery by Benedict XIV. And, in 1807, the Municipalities of Castiglion on Lake Trasimeno, and of Proceno, near Viterbo, elected him their Protector.

A few months after his publication as Cardinal, Erskine was appointed by Pius VII. to be administrator and Economo of the Giraud patrimony, consisting largely of lands held under the Pope, but the Cardinal by letter of August 7th, 1803, to Mgr. Lacchini, the *Uditore S.S.*, declined this charge, under the plea of want of leisure, but asked that his resignation should be kept secret until the appointment of a successor in that post, lest the creditors should rush in and press their claims to the ruin of the property and of the heirs, the Counts Giraud. But Erskine's resignation was not accepted, and he continued to manage the property until he finally resigned his charge in March, 1806, having at that time provided for all payments on the estate, leaving the brothers, Counts Pietro, Giovanni, Francesco and Giuseppe Giraud to arrange their own private debts. The Duke of Sermoneta, Prince Don Francesco Caetani wrote to the Cardinal on the 11th of January, 1804, to settle his disordered affairs and arrange with his creditors. Erskine by letter of the 13th of January, accepted, but only on the condition that all the Duke's ministers should thenceforward be dependent on him alone. Yet on the 27th of January, same year, the Cardinal told the Duke that some unforeseen circumstances had happened which prevented him from further administering the property. Then in same year, 1804, at the request of Count Tiberio Soderini, the Cardinal was deputed [rescript dated 16th September,] administrator of the Soderini property, a charge which he fulfilled until he resigned it on

17th of February, 1807, by letters to Soderini and the Papal Auditor.

In this year, 1804, Cardinal Erskine received from the Vice-Gerent the orders of Deacon, and he officiated as Deacon Ministrante on the Feast of S.S. Peter and Paul in the Basilica of the Vatican at the High Mass celebrated by the Pontiff.

That Erskine amid such manifold occupations did not lose sight of his Scotch relations appears from the following letter from the Earl of Buchan :—

"My dear Cardinal Cousin,

"I have had lately the great satisfaction of marking to our good Cousin, the Earl of Kellie, in the strongest manner, the influence of esteem, friendship and kindness upon publick conduct, in refusing on the most earnest sollicitations of the Prince of Wales, to lift up my hand against an Erskine.

"Nothing could be more magnanimous than the conduct of Lord Kellie towards me since when he really thought himself in danger of losing his election as one of our sixteen Peers : he abstained even from asking me to support him !

"Your Eminence mentions, in your last letter to me, the declining state of your brother Cardinal, my Stuartine kinsman, to whom, I hope, you will have the goodness to renew my request for Portraits of himself and his unfortunate Brother.

"As the Lenoxian race of Princes must end with the Cardinal, the line of Buchan is indisputably in the next degree of male representation of the Family, of which the Cardinal is the present Heir.

"I have reason to believe that both by Battoni and Mengs there are more than one portrait of each of the Royal personages, and I earnestly sollicit to be gratifyed with such of those originals as his Eminence may select, to be placed in my Hall of Kindred.

"What your Eminence says concerning the beautiful works of Michael Agnuolo and Raffaelle, Antonio Tempesta and others, on the walls of the Vatican, is consolatary, though I cannot digest the barbarity of removing a Brutus from the Capitol of Rome, where only it was significantly classical. It is much worse than removing a Sun dial which marks only ignorance, whilst the other deed is high treason against the golden rays of Apollo.

"Duppa has, from tracings, beautifully and correctly engraved the heads of Michael Agnuolo and Raffaelle, with which I mean to adorn the walls of my Abbey at Dryburgh.

"Your good Cousin, my brother Henry Erskine, has lately married a most worthy and amiable lady of a highly cultivated mind and of dispositions perfectly suited to his age and circumstances: you will rejoice with me on this event.

"Lady Buchan desires to join in best respects and good wishes, and I remain cordially,

"Your affectionate Cousin

BUCHAN.

Edinburgh, January 22d. 1805."

The writer of the above letter was David Stuart, 11th Earl of Buchan, who was indefatigably devoted to literary and scientific pursuits, and who may be considered the founder of the Antiquarian Society of Scotland. His brother Henry married for his second wife, on the 7th of January, 1805, Erskine, daughter of Alexander Monro, Esq., and widow of John Turnbull, Esq.

The next letter is from Frances, daughter of Mr. Thomas Coutts, the great Banker, who on the 7th of September, 1800, had become the second wife of the first Marquess of Bute :—

"Mount Edgcumbe, March 20th, 1806.

"Caro Amico, My Lord Cardinal,

"How grateful it is to be remembered by those we esteem and for whom one feels an affectionate regard, whatever distance may be between us, whatever circumstances this chequered life may offer. Your Eminence, I am confident, is certain that the friendship of Lord Bute and myself can never alter towards you, and therefore whenever you can, pray do not omit making us happy by telling us you enjoy good health and everything you can desire.

"Alas: my health is worse and worse, and the Physicians all agree that nothing but a warm climate will restore me entirely. Your acceptable letter and very valuable Medallion only came to my hands a few days ago: the date of your letter is April the second, 1804, so where it has been all this time I know not. I cannot give you a greater proof of its resemblance to *l'Isola Bella* than the following. I received the letter and parcel in Cornwall, at the seat of Lord Grenville, Boconnoc,* where we have been all winter on account of my health. There was nothing to lead Lord Bute to think of your Eminence at that moment, or of Mount Stuart, yet before I had read the letter he at once exclaimed ah! this is Mount Stuart. Pray express this to Madama Dionigi, and say how much we have both admired it. I cannot say how much I value it, or how much pleasure your recollection of that place affords us both. Ever since my Physicians have urged a warm climate, and now have declared such to be necessary, I have, I own, encouraged a hope that some accident might give us an opportunity of visiting once more Cara Italia : and the idea of seeing you, my dear Lord Cardinal, once more, is truly most grateful. Yet I hardly know we can hope for so great a pleasure. Meanwhile I am much weaker and certainly must not pass the next winter in England.

"I forget if when you were in this country you saw this place. It is uncommonly beautiful, almost unlike every other. We do not think it absolutely without resemblance of Bute, tho' superior in cultivation and beauty.

---

* Boconnoc [near Lostwithiel, Cornwall, now the property of Lady Louisa Fortescue].

"The weather has been very severe—cold East winds, a great deal of snow and frost.

"I hear constantly from my dear father who is well, as mamma and my two sisters are very well. I believe I need not say we often talk, and oftener miss the amiable and agreeable society of your Eminence. Indeed, indeed we can never forget and must ever remember with heartfelt pleasure the happy days we have passed with you. How delightful to talk over all those times would it be, and I will still flatter myself we may yet have this happiness.

"My little girl is now four years old, her brother three, and I think you would like to see them. The boy is the image of his father, and she, I am told, is like me. They are everything I can wish at present, and enjoy robust health.

"If I knew how, I would apologize to your Eminence for the length of this letter, but that you have taught me to feel so lively a sense of your goodness that I feel it would be formal and unnecessary. I will therefore conclude this with all manner of warm regards from Lord Bute as well as myself, and with the assurance of unalterable regard and affection I am, my dear Lord Cardinal, your sincere friend, FRANCES BUTE."

This letter was addressed: "Al Sua Eminenza—Il Cardinale Erskine—Roma."

The Madama Dionigi mentioned in this letter was Marianna Dionigi, a well known authoress. She published: "Viaggi in alcune Città del Latio, che diconsi fondate dal Re Saturno." 1809. Roma. This work contains numerous and valuable engravings. She was an intimate friend of Cardinal Erskine. The late Monsignor Angelini, archbishop of Corinth, Vicegerent of Rome and Canon of S. Peter's, wrote on the cover of his package of Erskine papers, a few lines upon Erskine, and there states that to the house of Marianna Dionigi used to resort the flower of literary society, Erskine, namely, who brought epigraphs, which Enrichetta, daughter of Marianna, and then but nine years old, translated into Italian; Cunich

[Raimondo] who also brought epigraphs to be similarly treated; Visconti [G. B. A.] the famous Antiquary, who composed metrical epigraphs to be put into verses by Enrichetta; and Morcelli, Stefano Antonio, who discussed, before it was engraved, the inscription afterwards placed at the foot of the obelisk at the Quirinal, beginning with the words, "Me quondam Egypti dilectum," etc. In this house also they lamented the death of Winkelman, assassinated, in 1768, by Francesco Arcangeli. The infant prodigy, Enrichetta, is now the Contessa Orfei, and an esteemed poetess. Erskine was about twenty-five or thirty years of age when he first began to frequent the casa Dionigi, and his friendship with the Dionigi family continued to his death.

The Emperor Napoleon, who had hitherto forced by threats Pius VII. to comply with his wishes and adopt the French policy, determined to proceed further, and either to make the Pope his complete slave in all matters, civil and ecclesiastical, or to deprive him of his temporal power, leaving him the name merely of Bishop of Rome. Accordingly Napoleon wrote on the 13th of February, 1806, to the Pope setting forth his determination in harsh language; and Cardinal Fesch, on the 2nd of March, drew up a note in softer terms, but to much the same effect. Pius VII. was invited to break off communications with all the other European Powers, to shut his harbours against the Russians, Swedes and English, and to expel them from Rome and the States of the Church. The Pope was to be at peace with France and her friends, and at war with all the enemies of France. For the Father of the Faithful thus to become a French satrap was impossible, yet Napoleon's demands were not to be rejected without deliberating on the consequences. Pius VII. convoked all the Cardinals in Rome, to the number of thirty-two, to assemble together on the 8th of May, 1806, and he laid the matter before them, requiring each Cardinal to take two days to consider the letters of Napoleon and Fesch, and then to give his opinion either in writing or *viva voce.* A second Convocation of Cardinals was held on the 8th of June, to consider the recognition of Joseph Bonaparte as King of Naples. Pius VII. was supported by all the Cardinals in refusing to obey Napoleon, but to please him, accepted, on the 17th of June, the resignation of Consalvi, Secretary of State. The King of Naples he would acknowledge, provided he sought investiture from the Holy See.

Meanwhile the French troops, which had seized Ancona in October, 1805, had by the following year occupied all the harbours of the Pontifical territory in the Mediterranean as well as the Adriatic, and on the 1st of November, 1807, the French General Lemarrois proclaimed himself Governor-General of the provinces of Ancona, Macerata, Fermo, and Urbino, which he had already sometime occupied by his troops, and by decree of Napoleon of April 2, 1808, all these provinces were united to the Kingdom of Italy.

Cardinal Erskine felt the effects of this invasion, for his own income was chiefly derived from abbey and church lands situated in the usurped provinces. In June, 1808, his abbey of S. Maria di Lastreto, near Fossombrone, was sequestrated, and the sequestrator, the Marchese Giuseppe Capalti, seized the private property of the Cardinal, such as his cattle, the arrears due by tenants, and the wool, grain, etc., already stored. Erskine succeeded in getting restitution of his personal property so illegally confiscated, but when he proceeded to sell his cattle he was met by a prohibition, based on the plea that the cattle might be wanted for the use of the farmers! He got this prohibition removed, but lost all his revenues from the abbey of Lastreto and from the Priory of S. Domenico Loricato.

Rome itself was occupied, on the 2nd of February, 1808, by French troops commanded by General Miollis, who planted eight pieces of cannon against the gates of the Quirinal Palace.

In February and March fourteen Cardinals were forced by Miollis to depart from Rome, and among these were Doria, Pro-Secretary of State; Somaglia, Vicar of His Holiness; and

Braschi, Secretary of Memorials. The Pope nominated Gabrielli as Pro-Secretary; Despuig, Pro-Vicar; and Antonelli, Pro-Secretary of Briefs. But on the night of the 18th of June, 1808, Cardinal Gabrielli was seized in the Quirinal Palace and deported to his See of Sinigallia, and on the night of September 6, Cardinal Antonelli, the Dean of the Sacred College, and Pro-Secretary of Briefs, was forcibly carried away from Rome. Cardinal Pacca was now nominated Pro-Secretary of State, and Cardinal Erskine was made Pro-Secretary of Briefs in room of Antonelli.

Cardinal Erskine might have effected, on the first entrance of the French troops, an escape to England, to which course he had been previously strongly urged by his cousins in Scotland and his friends in London. He was known to be a foreigner, of a nation hostile to France, and was therefore exposed to the enmity of Napoleon. But he resolved to remain at his post and to help Pius VII. in his sore tribulations. When appointed Pro-Secretary of Briefs, he at once set to business and called for exact information concerning the state of his office, the number of the clerks, and its financial position. This information was supplied to him. As his new duties necessitated constant attendance on the Pope, and as he feared that, as had happened to other Cardinals, he would be violently removed, he requested permission to follow the example of Cardinal Despuig, and to reside in the Quirinal. The Pope consented, and Erskine went into the Auditor's apartment, which had remained vacant ever since he had left it to become Cardinal. His removal was effected with all secrecy and caution. For the Quirinal Palace since September, 1808, was virtually blockaded by French sentinels and Gendarmes. The great gate giving access to the Piazza had only the small wicket open, and carriages were no longer admitted within the Court-yard. The very domestics and others in the Papal service who had to pass in and out, were liable to be arrested and carried for inspection to the nearest French Police Station. Erskine managed to escape the notice of the French sentinels, and entered the Quirinal to reside, some days subsequent to the proclamation of the new Government, and the consequent publication of the Excommunication in June, 1809.

There were now shut up in the Quirinal along with the Pope, three Cardinals, namely Pacca, pro-secretary; Despuig, pro-vicar; and Erskine, pro-secretary of briefs; and there were also Mgr. Naro, majordomo; George Doria, master of the camera, with the officials and the members of the Pontifical household.

It might have been supposed that the three Cardinals would have formed a convenient council for joint consultations on affairs in this critical conjuncture, but on the contrary, Pacca alone was the guide of his Holiness and directed everything. Only occasionally and in private was Erskine consulted by the Pope. Two nephews of Pacca who had voluntarily accompanied their uncle, gave themselves great airs, and offered to interfere in matters which did not concern them. Although Pacca and Erskine had much esteem for each other, yet there existed no such intimacy between them as to lead to confidential interchange of advice and opinions. Pacca thought Erskine timid, because he was reserved and did not disclose his sentiments on useless and inconvenient occasions. Erskine was silent, because things were not directed according to his ideas. He was aware that Pius VII. was profoundly humble, and too much inclined to under-estimate his own talents, and to depend on the advice of others. Pacca set this down to natural weakness of character. Erskine urged the Pope, that in necessary matters he should indeed avail himself of the judgment and information of others, but that afterwards he should adopt those resolutions which were dictated by his own sagacity and by the Holy Spirit from above which would always aid him.

Erskine's residence in the Quirinal palace did not last long.

On the evening of the 5th of July, 1809, the three Cardinals were assembled in the rooms of the majordomo, with the chief officers of the household. Their conversation naturally fell on the circumstances of the moment and the news from the city, when it was interrupted by a domestic, who said that he and his companions, who had been standing at one of the windows of the same apartment to get fresh air, had observed two men who, in the extreme quiet and solitude of the street, were passing, and talking to each other with a pre-occupied air. Perceiving persons in the majordomo's windows, which looked toward the *Quattro Fontane*, they stopped precisely on the footpath beneath, and with a stick struck with some force the curbstone of the footpath to excite the attention of the folks in the window. Then one of them, without raising his head, said in a very clear and distinct voice:—*Keep well on guard this night, for surely some great blow is in preparation against the Pope.*

Such an announcement caused great agitation. Cardinal Pacca at once sent for Pfyffer, Captain of the Swiss, who maintained relations with friends in the city, to ask whether he had heard anything, and to charge him to procure some certain information. The Captain assured his Eminence that he had received no communication of any importance from his friends, and that if any suspicion had been hinted to him he would not have failed to report it. But he promised to go and do what was possible at that hour to provide further news.

Captain Pfyffer after a good half hour, returned and reported that no movement of troops could be noticed at any point of the Palace, as far as could be observed, and that everywhere supreme tranquility prevailed, it being now near midnight. He added that his news from outside was that no military disposition—to be feared in the Palace—was on hand. Only he heard that some Neapolitan troops—as was already known—had arrived on the day before, and were to be employed by General Miollis in the garrison of Rome, which was now almost entirely unprovided with French soldiers. From all this, from the complete quiet which prevailed, and from the hope which all persons naturally entertain that bad news may be ill-founded or at least exaggerated, they began to think it was a false alarm, such as had happened on other occasions, and having remained together until after midnight, they resolved to go to bed, and wished each other good night as tranquilly as usual. Before separating, Erskine turned to Pacca and asked whether he, as one ready for all events, had thought of what was to be done concerning the sacred person of His Holiness. Pacca replied *we will think about it.* Erskine rejoined with some vivacity : *We will think about it ! It ought to have been thought about already*, and went to his room.

Erskine, when he reached his own apartment, could not rid himself of anxiety, in spite of the reassuring news which Pfyffer had brought, and in spite of the prevailing silence and quiet. In the agitation produced by the uncertainty of an event which might have fatal consequences, he could not bring himself to go to bed to seek repose. He therefore kept watch vigilantly, and heard at two o'clock in the morning a certain regular tread under his windows which looked out on the *via della discesa di Monte Cavallo.* He went at once to the window to find out whence this sound proceeded, and notwithstanding the obscurity of that hour, was able to ascertain distinctly that a good many troops in all silence were assembling on the Piazza of the Quirinal. He then no longer doubted the truth of the warning given in the early hours of the night, and while he stood hesitating what to do, he became aware of some noisy movements within the Palace itself. There was now no room for doubt or hesitation, and he resolved to proceed to the Papal apartments and share the danger menacing the Pontiff. It was necessary to pass to the Cortile of the Palace through a gate on the side of the Panetteria, which was always guarded by a Swiss. But to his horror he found the gate shut, and, in spite of the efforts of his servant, who knocked at it and shouted, could find no means to open it, and therefore was compelled to go back to his room. Cardinal Despuig, whose apartment was at the same side as Erskine's, was more lucky, for he had passed through a little time before, at the very moment when the Swiss, obeying the orders of the French, suddenly shut the gate and retiring from his post, threw the key away, so that to re-open communication it was necessary to break down the door.

One can but imagine the desolation and agitation of Erskine thus cut off from his colleagues and the Pope, and fully ignorant of what was happening, although he heard the tolling of the Bell of the Quirinal, the ever increasing noise of confused movements, and the sound of the blows with which the French, already admitted into the Cortile, were breaking down door after door in order to have free passage everywhere. The Cardinal remained a prisoner in his own apartment, for sentinels were posted in all parts to prevent all circulation of the inmates. The servant of Erskine said he saw his master striding up and down his room in an indescribable state of agitation, and exclaiming every now and then, *What has happened to the Pope? What will become of him?* The same servant used afterwards to assert that from that time forth the Cardinal never was the same man. From being robust and hearty he began to decline in strength and health, and probably then was laid the foundation of the malady which in little more than two years brought him to his grave.

At last, on the morning of the 6th of July, Cardinal Erskine became aware of the forced departure of Pius VII. and of the principal circumstances of the breaking into the Palace, and the irruption of French soldiers into the Pope's apartment. A French officer notified to Erskine that he was at liberty either to remain in the Quirinal or to go to his own house. The Cardinal at once removed to his apartment in the Capranica Palace near the Valle theatre. Cardinal Despuig also left the Quirinal on the same day.

Cardinal Erskine was now free, so far as appearances went, but was in reality closely watched. He was moreover very poor. He had been dependent, for his education and means to pursue his studies, on his mother's family and on the Cardinal Duke of York. He inherited no property from his father, who had abandoned his own country in order to remain faithful to the Stuarts. As an advocate he might have realized a fortune, but his career as a lawyer, when most profitable, was cut short by promotion to the Prelacy. He was always reckoned among the poor Cardinals, for his income was only 4,000 scudi, about £800 per annum. Now he had lost all his ecclesiastical income, which was seized by the usurpers, and he was almost reduced to beggary. Under these circumstances he resolved to avail himself of the proposals formerly made to him by his cousins in Scotland, and who had lately, through Mr. Coutts the banker, repeated their offers of a home and money in case of his finding himself ill-treated in Rome. But Napoleon's blockade continued. English ships especially were excluded from all Italian ports. The transmission of letters was difficult, and even bankers' despatches were rigorously examined.

Cardinal Erskine, however, wrote two letters—one to Lord Kellie, the other to Coutts, disclosing his condition. He asked Coutts to communicate with Lord Kellie, in the event of the loss of his letter to his cousin. Torlonia, with much kindness, undertook to cause these letters to reach their destination, as far as lay in his power.

Meanwhile, to economise, Erskine gave up his horses, and as he could not, being a Cardinal, walk in the streets of Rome, nor mix with the multitude and so excite the suspicion of the French, nor yet stay at home in perpetual imprisonment, he determined to retire to Caprarola or to Castel Rubello. He chose Castel Rubello, a place belonging to his relative, Salvatori, and there he hoped to find cheapness, quiet and repose after his trials. The French made no objection to his change of residence.

The removal to the country at first did him good. He enjoyed the healthier air and the long walks, and felt relieved from his troubles, and restored to quiet and freedom. But in a month or two the charms of rural retirement began to pall upon him. He sighed for more society than that afforded by his two domestics and the parish priest, a worthy, but rough sort of man. He had no library and no visitors, for his Salvatori relatives were seldom in Castel Rubello. Cardinal Erskine now fell into low spirits and thought himself neglected by his cousins, because he had as yet received no answers to his letters. In the month of September he wrote again to Coutts the banker. But no letters from England arrived, and Erskine felt broken down in spirits and in health. In October symptoms of some internal disorder appeared, and the Cardinal was afraid of a sudden attack of paralysis or apoplexy. He said to his servant, Lorenzo :—" Lorenzo, if ever you should perceive that I can't speak, don't get me bled, but rather give me a purgative."

While in this melancholy frame of mind, and in this deplorable state of health, Erskine was surprised on the 23rd of November, by a messenger from General Radet, Inspector General of Gendarmes at Rome, who brought a despatch from the French Minister of Worship, Count Bigot de Priameneu, enclosing a command to proceed to Paris, a passport and a written order to the Imperial Gendarmes to furnish His Eminence with the necessary escort from Orvieto to Paris. The letter, dated from Paris, the 30th of October, 1809, was as follows :—

"Monsignor Cardinal, I am charged, by His Majesty the Emperor and King, to give you in his name the order to remove to Paris. I am authorized to render you the treatment accorded to French Cardinals. I pray your Eminence to acknowledge to me the receipt of this present letter and to give me notice of your departure. Receive etc., Bigot de Priameneu." The passport, written in the usual form, prescribed the route from Orvieto, and was available up to the first day of the next year. Cardinal Erskine was determined not to go to

Paris except by compulsion, and as this determination could be better evidenced in Rome than in a country place, and as necessaries for the journey could be better provided in Rome, he told the bearer of the despatch that he must first go to Rome, and he refused to acknowledge the receipt of the letter, lest by so doing he should seem to give his consent to this forced journey.

Cardinal Erskine now returned to Rome, but not to his own apartment in the Capranica palace, which he still rented, but to a palace in *Via di Aracoeli*, once the abode of Cardinal De Zelada. On the second floor of this palace, lived Monsignor Pio Ferrari, the husband of his only sister, Clementina Erskine. A married Monsignor, as appears from Sala's *Diario*, was not uncommon in Rome in those days. Certain offices in the Legal Department of the Papal Government were held by married men with the privilege of the title of Monsignor. Or perhaps Ferrari's wife had died before her husband bore this title. Be that as it may, the Cardinal's health demanded special assistance, more easily to be obtained in the house of a relation than in his own. On arriving at Ferrari's, the Cardinal fell ill and remained in bed some time.

A great and sad change in Erskine's appearance was now observed by his friends. But some persons deemed his illness to be diplomatic only, and simulated in order to avoid the Paris expedition. The French police were of this latter opinion, for suddenly, on the 8th of December, General Radet sent him the following letter, dated at "*one* o'clock of the afternoon":—

"Eminence, The orders of H. M. the Emperor and King, Napoleon, which have been transmitted to me by His Excellency the Governor-General, are that your Eminence must leave within twenty-four hours for Paris. In notifying to your Eminence these orders of the Sovereign which do not admit of delay or illusory excuse, I am charged to recommend you to make known to their Excellencies the Ministers of General Police and of Worship, the habitation which your

Eminence shall choose in Paris on the moment of your arrival. I offer to your Eminence the means of security for your journey. I have the honour to be, with most respectful consideration, your Eminence's most humble and devoted servant, Radet."

The Cardinal did not obey this command, and the French took no immediate notice of his delay, probably finding his illness not so illusory as they had imagined, and waiting for his recovery. Erskine, however, made preparations for leaving and provided warm winter clothing, getting a box seat put to his English carriage for his two domestics. The next question was who was to accompany him? Orazio Celestini, his Auditor [who died Auditor of the Rota], promptly offered his services. Erskine did not doubt his personal affection but declined his offer with thanks, because he was of too vivacious a disposition and occasionally imprudent; and Erskine gave as his reason that he wanted a Priest to be his companion, as more becoming in the case of a Cardinal. Signora Marianna Dionigi, by means of Count Antonio Bentivoglio, recommended the Abbate Michel Angelo de Medico, who was accustomed to much travel and was at that time free and disengaged.

Meanwhile the Cardinal's illness, apparently of a rheumatic character, proceeded with various alternations, until at Christmas a decided improvement set in, giving hopes of a rapid and permanent restoration of his health. An Aide-du-camp of General Miollis, sent under pretext of polite enquiries after the condition of the Cardinal, now paid a visit, and reminded him of the intimation already twice given for leaving Rome, insisting that as soon as possible he should start on the journey. The Cardinal calmly and politely replied to the Aide-du-camp, asking him to make General Miollis reflect that to a man advanced in years, and not yet recovered from an illness of about a month's duration, it could not but be extremely inconvenient and perilous to health to undertake a journey in the rawest part of the cold season: and therefore he begged a respite at least until the opening of Spring. When the Aide-du-camp replied that General Miollis was not quite assured of the reality, or at least the seriousness, of the illness, the Cardinal, all inflamed with resentment, rose and sat up on the bed where he had lain, and with his natural impetuosity said to the Aide-du-camp : *Tell the General that honour is hereditary in my family*—an expression which signified much and was faithfully reported to Miollis, who complained of it and was very angry.

Erskine knew now that the violence about to be done to him was inevitable, he yet yielded to the remonstrances of his friends and consented that one of them should interpose and try to obtain a delay until the Spring. In order to strengthen this petition by authentic certificates concerning his health, a consultation was held by three of the most eminent Roman Doctors, including the Physician in attendance, who on the 30th of December unanimously signed a certificate, attested by oath, that Cardinal Erskine was seventy-one [sic] years old, of most delicate constitution, and now confined to bed for thirty-five days with lumbar rheumatism, and consequently was not in a condition to undertake in that season any journey which would expose him to the danger of very grave exacerbation. A favourable response to this petition was confidently expected by Erskine's friends, and he himself had some, but not very strong, hopes that he would be allowed a further delay. That very morning the Abbé Del Medico, who had accepted the situation of Companion to the Cardinal, was introduced to Erskine by Count Bentivoglio, and after conversation on other matters the Cardinal told him that his duties would begin on their leaving Rome, and probably in Spring, but that it would be well that Del Medico should arrange to be ready at any moment for departure. The Cardinal repeated the same advice on the following morning.

Nor was Erskine deceived, for on the 31st of December, just after his talk with Del Medico, an aide-du-camp of Miollis came to intimate an absolutely immediate departure, although the Cardinal was still kept in bed. This officer, either spontaneously, or by suggestion of Miollis, did much to soften the cruelty of this order, for while exhorting the Cardinal to comply without further resistence and to exert himself to begin the journey, he told him he might linger on the road at his pleasure, make stoppages whenever and as long as he might choose, and affirmed this to be the precise instruction of the General and of His Imperial Majesty. As another inducement not to remain longer in Rome, he reminded him that at the commencement of the new year the provisional government in Rome would cease, and the new government, entirely on a French footing, would be established, and that scenes would have to be witnessed which would necessarily be most painful to him. Finally he told him that the same orders had been given for the other two Cardinals who yet remained in Rome, namely Vincenti and Della Porta, both of whom were to depart, although Della Porta was in a very bad state of health.

Cardinal Erskine had no difficulty in admitting a further delay in Rome to be most painful to contemplate, and that Paris would afford a more pleasant residence as a city which he had already known, and in which he might meet many influential friends who formerly professed great attachment to him. His present reluctance to set out arose from his infirmities, his need of repose, and the want of pecuniary resources for such an expensive journey. Finally he promised to use all possible haste, and as for money he would travel as long as his means held out. As the Officer did not mention the usual twenty-four hours, Erskine thought he would be let alone for at least a couple of days. But alas! two hours had not elapsed when the Officer returned before 4 o'clock P.M. to notify his departure the following night, and by way of securing obedience posted a Gendarme in the anti-chamber. He demanded the names of the persons and domestics who were to accompany Erskine, for insertion in the new passport to be given before starting, and then went off to give similar intimations to the other two Cardinals.

The French Government in Rome was known for its art of vexing and worrying, so Cardinal Erskine bent to circumstances, and gave directions to pack the trunks, and sent to Del Medico to come quickly, ready for travel, and to forward his luggage. The Cardinal himself arranged the packing of his travelling case, sitting up in his bed, from which he thought he would only rise to get into his carriage. By four o'clock P.M. on the day appointed, all was ready for starting except the passport and to send for the horses. By midnight the passport had not arrived. The other Cardinals, Vincenti and Della Porta, who were similarly treated, had gone to bed. Cardinal Erskine thought it wise to do the same, especially as the Gendarme had asked for a bed for himself, and he sent word to Del Medico, that in case of leaving during the night or early the next morning, he would call for him at his house which lay directly in the route.

The passports did not arrive that night nor yet on the following day, which was New Year's Day, so that they spent that solemnity in tranquility. Cardinal Erskine profited by the delay to arrange better his travelling necessaries. He had to complain of his servants for not having got the tailor to make him a suit of garments to wear over his ordinary dress. They had only bought the materials and packed them in a trunk. Many Roman friends and a few prelates who were still in Rome, came to visit His Eminence, and to all of them the Cardinal seemed wonderfully recovered. The Cardinal went to bed early, to save his strength as much as possible.

On the 2nd of January, 1810, at about 8 o'clock A.M. the passport was brought, and the Cardinal fixed midday as the time for setting out. When Del Medico arrived at 10 o'clock, ready for the road, he found a French Officer with Erskine, who had brought from Miollis 3,000 francs, to pay for expenses. This was not a gift, for as such it would not have been accepted, but an advance of the allowance assigned by Napoleon to all the Cardinals he deported. General Miollis was very anxious that Erskine should receive this money, lest there should be a repetition of the scandal which happened in the case of Cardinal Fabrizio Ruffo, who when forced away from Amelia, to which place he had retired, had to stop at the first town on his way, for absolute want of money to pay for post horses. Erskine, in fact, had only funds to bring him as far as Bologna, so that this advance of money was most convenient. Del Medico took charge of the 3,000 francs, for which Erskine gave a receipt. General Radet sent along with the passport a written order to be presented to the Imperial Gendarmes at any place where His Eminence desired an escort for security. This apparent act of civility and respect was an empty form, for the Cardinal was in reality a prisoner and bound to obey the orders of the Gendarmes, as was soon proved. All was now ready and the Cardinal was about to send for the post horses, when he was informed that the Gendarme in the anti-chamber would not allow them to depart until the arrival of the other Gendarme who was to be their escort. In fact the French police were arranging matters for the departure on the same morning of the three Cardinals, who were to go in the following order;—first Vincenti, secondly Della Porta and last of all Erskine. But it was impossible for Erskine to foresee this arrangement, and it so happened that he only got his chocolate in the morning, and had to wait until evening for refreshment.

While the Cardinal—in company with some intimate friends who had come to say farewell, such as Mgr. Pio Ferrari, Orazio Celestini, Count Alexander Cardelli and others—stood waiting the order for departure, he was astonished by the entrance of Luigi Chiaveri,* stepson of the Banker Torlonia,

---

* Anna Maria Schulteis, born 1760, married Guiseppe Chiaveri, by whom she had three children, Carolina, Luigi and Agostino Chiaveri. Her husband, Guiseppe Chiaveri, died in 1783, and ten years later, in 1793, she took for her second husband Duke Giovanni Torlonia, the great banker and founder of the Torlonia family.

who presented him with letters just arrived from England, and informed him that £400, by commission from Coutts, lay in the Torlonia bank at his disposal. This was truly consoling news for Erskine, and such as to cheer him in the midst of the troubles which arose from illness and vexations. How long had he desired answers to his letters to England and expected them in vain? Now, on the point of stepping into his carriage, he learnt that his cousins had not forgotten him and that the remittance at present received was an earnest for future succour. Had he known this a few hours earlier, he would have rejected the money sent by Miollis. Yet he felt this providential relief to be very timely. He had debts at Rome. He must not abandon some old servants whom he could not take with him. And therefore he resolved to leave the £400 in Torlonia's bank at present, to discharge his obligations in Rome. It must not be forgotten that some days before he had received from Torlonia a circular letter, addressed to the Bankers in the several towns in correspondence with Torlonia, charging them to supply the Cardinal with whatever money he might want. Even although Torlonia might have been certain of eventual re-imbursement, yet he was none the less entitled to praise for his forethought and kind interest displayed towards his old friend.

Before proceeding further it may be proper to give the purport of the letters* now received from England. They were three in number, and two of them were from Mr. Thomas Coutts to the Cardinal. In the first Coutts tells Erskine that he had received his letter of July 12, 1809, and that as far as he could look into the future, the Cardinal's position was a critical one. Yet he had entertained some hope that out of respect for his rank there would be given him in Rome suitable means of subsistence, without reducing him to such a state of humili-

---

* It is to be regretted that the original letters have been lost. They are here reproduced from Del Medico's Italian version.

ation and need as was disclosed in his letter, which had smitten him to the heart. He assures him that he had forwarded the letter which had been enclosed for Lord Kellie, his cousin. He adds, "when I reflect that the death of this Peer and of his brother would raise you to so high a rank among the most ancient and respectable names of Scotland, I see clearly that your present position is all the more hard and cruel and the worthier of pity and compassion. If we had now the former Ministers Pitt and Fox, or men like them at the head of the public affairs of our Government, I would not in the least doubt that your position would be at once taken into consideration and alleviated in the proper manner, but it must be confessed that in the actual state of things I must not nourish the smallest hope. You may be quite certain, my dear Cardinal, that I shall neglect no means to serve you, and that I shall work with Lord Kellie as far as may be in my power. Meanwhile I have given directions to Torlonia to furnish you with a credit for £200 ster. which will serve to extricate you from your immediate embarrassment, and afterwards I shall write again on the earliest opportunity."

In his second letter dated, September 30th, 1809, Mr. Coutts writes: "I hope the letter will have arrived safely to you, which I wrote, and the duplicate or triplicate, to inform you of the commission given to Torlonia, and I will give orders to furnish you, if you desire it, with a second sum of £200 sterling, so that £400 may be at your service if necessary. You can judge better than I can, what situation suits you best; either England or some country where the English are in force, and where the most secure protection may be afforded to you, if some remote part of Italy cannot be found to present an asylum more advantageous to your health and more suitable to your habits. Here we are threatened with a change in our Government, I mean in the Ministry. If this should happen, your friends may have offered to them an opportunity of getting you such a pension as may put you into the independence of deciding whether you will come to England or remain on the Continent. Be very sure, my dear friend, that nothing will be more warmly at my heart than the rendering to you some essential service. It seems to me that your cousin is really most anxiously exerting himself for the same purpose."

The third letter was from Lord Kellie, written on September 30th, 1809, from his residence near S. Andrews, and was in answer to that of the Cardinal which had been sent through Coutts. Lord Kellie began by saying that he had written by way of Portugal, and under cover to the Advocate Lupacchioli, as if directed by the Nuncio of that realm, a letter dated 30th July, 1809, which, to judge by Erskine's silence had not reached its destination. Nor had Erskine received a previous letter of July 20th, 1808, in which Lord Kellie had given Erskine power to draw on Coutts for £200 sterling, whenever he might have occasion. Lord Kellie, in November, 1808, had sent another letter to the same effect. He then proceeds: "Our friend Coutts writes me word that he has now sent a credit on Banker Torlonia, which I hope will soon reach you. Be certain of my affectionate attachment, and that as long as I have means to succour you, you shall never find yourself in indigence. My interest in you will never cease under any circumstances." Finally in a postscript he adds: "I have submitted to Mr. Coutts' opinion, whether it would be proper to write in your behalf a Memorial to the King upon your unfortunate situation. His Majesty was always gracious to you when you were in England. Addio."

The non-arrival of those letters may be accounted for by the supposition that they were intercepted by the French Police, and withheld on account of the suggestions that Erskine should take refuge in England.

Cardinal Erskine was waiting for the Gendarme, who came at 12 o'clock, and it was expected they would start at once. But no—the Gendarme had not had his breakfast, and they must wait until he got a *dejeuner à la fourchette*. At last, at half-past 12 o'clock, the Gendarme got into the saddle, and the Cardinal entered his carriage, after embracing Ferrari and his friends, amid the cheers of the people, who crowded about the door wishing him a happy journey and a speedy return. He was much moved by this demonstration of respect. The route lay through the *via del Gesù*, piazza Venezia and the Corso. The day was fine, and many persons in the streets saluted the Cardinal with signs of their dissatisfaction at his departure. In the Corso they met General Miollis in a carriage coming from an opposite direction. The General took off his hat and made a profound salutation to the Cardinal, who considered this mock attention as an act of derision and a fresh insult. They then passed the *Porta del Popolo* and were out of Rome, the carriage being followed by the Gendarme.

Rome was now despoiled of all its old ecclesiastical splendour. Not a single Cardinal was left in the city. Not even a Bishop was spared to guide religious affairs. Monsignor de Gregorio, then a simple priest, was appointed Apostolic Delegate, and Monsignor Atanasio, then only a priest, was the acting Vice-Gerent, with faculties also of Vicar of Rome.

Just after leaving the gates, the Cardinal desired the recitation of the " Itinerary of Clerics," and afterwards eight *De profundis* for souls in Purgatory. The *De profundis* were repeated at every change of horses, and as they were changed at intervals of eight Roman miles, they recited one *De profundis* for each mile. The daily routine during the whole journey, which took up twenty-four days, including the whole day they stopped at Châlons-sur-Soane, was as follows :—They travelled generally from morning till evening, and as they went recited at intervals the Divine office for the day, according to the order of the Vatican Basilica, of which the Cardinal had been Canon. The *De profundis* was said at the proper intervals, and the *Rosary* towards the evening. The rest of the time in the carriage was spent in talking of the affairs of the day, or of events in the past career of the Cardinal, who was very eloquent in praise of England, to which country he longed to return. Erskine sometimes read Horace, especially the Odes. When evening fell they put up in the best inn they could find, and after supper went to bed. Each morning Erskine took chocolate made by his own servant after the Roman fashion.

At Storta, their first change of horses, the Postillions came to the carriage door to express their sorrow at having been employed to carry off a Cardinal. Tears were in their eyes, and they never even looked at the *mancia* when put into their hands. The Cardinal was much moved, but this demonstration on the part of the Postillions was not repeated at any other stage within the Pontifical States. When they reached Monte Rosi, and were waiting for fresh horses and a fresh Gendarme, a sub-officer of Gendarmes came to the carriage door, and talked to the Cardinal about the carriage, which he much admired, and about the journey. The Cardinal said he would like to stop the night at Nepi, and the officer remarked, but without the least appearance of dictation, that he could easily push farther on to Cività Castellana.

At Nepi, the Cardinal stopped the carriage at Casa Betti, where he purposed to sleep, and went to the room shown him by the Padrone. But when the servants were taking out the luggage, the Gendarme, who kept in his saddle close to the carriage, shouted to them to say they should not remove the trunks, for they must resume the journey. In vain Del Medico remonstrated. He told the Gendarme that General Miollis had given the Cardinal permission to stop where and when he liked, and that General Radet had provided the escort for security not for surveillance. Finally he said that the Cardinal had had nothing since his chocolate, and was in need of refreshment and repose, having only risen the day before from his bed to which he had been confined for thirty-five days. The Gendarme would listen to nothing, and raised his voice as if to threaten force. There was no help for it. They had to go on. But the Cardinal got a soup, and also had some conversation with Cardinal Della Porta, who was in that very house. It seems the police had directions not to allow two Cardinals to meet together in any town in the Pontifical Territory. It was very late when they arrived in Città Castellana, and were allowed to stop and rest in the only inn, and that a bad one, in that city.

The next morning they left Città Castellana at 6.30 A.M., and soon found, to the Cardinal's great joy, that no Gendarme accompanied them, and that consequently they would be more free to select their stopping places. In fact when nearing Terni, the Cardinal recollected that a Convent of Discalced Carmelites was but a little way off the main road, and that there lived Cardinal Trajétto Carafa, who in consideration of his age (over eighty) had, when driven from Rome, been dispensed from proceeding farther. Erskine resolved to pay a short visit to Carafa, and when near the Convent, got down from his carriage and with his valet walked to the Convent, sending on the carriage with Del Medico to Terni, with instructions to hire a conveyance in Terni to bring the Cardinal in half an hour to rejoin his travelling carriage at Terni, intending to proceed thence to Spoleto to pass the night. The French police were accurately informed of all this, but there was no Gendarme to interfere, and Erskine, being not prevented by force, visited every Cardinal he found on his route. The Bishop of Terni, hearing of Erskine's position, drove in his own carriage to find the two Cardinals at the Convent, and after an hour's visit brought Erskine back with him to Terni. This delay was very fortunate, for no fresh post-horses were to be had in Terni, and the tired horses required a rest before starting for Spoleto.

The journey to Spoleto was slow and tedious, and no oxen were to be found to drag the carriage up the hill of Somma. They did not arrive in Spoleto until half-past six in the evening. Cardinal Erskine availed himself of an invitation given in Rome to make use of the Pianciani palace. The

Count Pianciani was not of course in Spoleto, but had given Erskine a letter to his *Maestro di Casa*, who hastily prepared a repast. The Cardinal found compensation in this lordly dwelling for his miserable treatment and bad night in Civita Castellana.

Near Spoleto, on the road to Foligno, is a Convent of Discalced Augustinians, in which resided Cardinal Antonelli, Dean of the Sacred College, who was compelled by order of General Miollis to leave Rome on the 6th of September, 1808, but by reason of his age, which was eighty, was permitted to retire to this Convent, where he lived a solitary life. Erskine spent half an hour with him on the morning of the fourth of January, and the poor old Dean parted from him with tears.

They arrived in Foligno at mid-day, and here the Cardinal resolved to sleep and get the overcoats and trousers for himself and servants, which had been forgotten to be done in Rome, made up by a tailor, who was recommended by his old friend the Marchese Gilberti, and who promised to have them ready early next morning. Erskine stayed in the inn—a bad one—all day, close to the fire, and was visited by the bishop, Mgr. Moscardini. Marchese Gilberti remained with him and shewed him every attention. The tailor was not very punctual, and they did not leave Foligno before half-past nine the following morning. Some miles beyond Gualdo, the frontier, dividing the Pontifical States from the Kingdom of Italy, was reached, and passports were demanded at both Custom houses. There was no examination of luggage. At six p.m. they arrived at Sigillo and sought for the Augustinian Convent, having got a letter to the Prior from the Father Provincial. The Prior was delighted to see them, and prepared rooms for them at once. The Cardinal begged to be allowed to enter the room where the Fathers assembled in common, thinking it would be warmer, and also wishing to give time for heating his own apartment. Erskine was then brought to a roughly furnished hall on the ground floor, and was glad to find great blocks of wood blazing in a huge fireplace such as those once used in old Roman palaces. Erskine liked this room so well that he asked leave to sup there with the Friars. The request was granted but the Cardinal and his Secretary had a special supper.

Next morning at daybreak, the Feast of the Epiphany, the Cardinal went to Mass with the Friars. Del Medico said Mass at the High Altar, and the Church was full of people, all coughing very much. Afterwards Chocolate was served for Erskine and Del Medico, the servants got breakfast, and they left at 9 a.m. On their onward route they passed a spot on the hill side where the Marchese Lepri's carriage, being covered with snow, was overturned, and the Marchese himself was with difficulty rescued by the people of Sigillo. There was now a bright sunshine and no snow. At Scheggia, the postillions stopped the carriage to give opportunity to view the bridge, which is of singular and ingenious construction, and after Cantiano the road among the Appennines became most enchanting. Erskine's astonishment was increased on nearing the Furlo Pass, for there the chain of mountains closes in on both sides, leaving only a narrow passage for the torrent. The darkening of the air towards sunset gradually inspired a feeling of horror, which came to a climax in penetrating the tunnel cut in the living rock. The prospect on emerging from the tunnel was marvellously beautiful. They passed the night at Fossombrone, and in the morning (Sunday, January 7) drove to Fano, where they changed horses, and got out to admire the calm and placid sea. They now saw a ship, which Erskine pronounced to be an English one, and said to Del Medico: How gladly would I leave all this beautiful country if I could only save my person and remove myself from the insolent domination of Napoleon! He then talked of the freedom of travel in England, the absence of the passport and dogana nuisances, etc. They passed on through Pesaro and Cattolica and reached Rimini in the evening. Here Prince Spada sent his compliments to Erskine, apologizing for not coming in person as he was fatigued. Spada was returning from Paris, where he had been figuring as a member of the Deputation sent from Rome, with Duke Braschi as President, to thank the Emperor for all his benign doings in Rome! Spada by his message to Erskine shewed that he wished to keep well with both sides. The Dukes Braschi owed their all to Pius VI., the uncle of one Duke, and to Pius IX., the patron of another Duke, who was as anxious to welcome Victor Emannuel as his predecessor was to curry favour with Napoleon.

At 8 A.M. on next morning (January 8) they resumed travel, but the atmosphere had changed, and the cold and frost caused Erskine great suffering. At Cesena they visited Cardinal Braschi, who by reason of gout and other ailments, had been allowed to stay there. Braschi gave them a cordial reception and refreshments. The conversation fell on Paris, which city Braschi had visited on two occasions, the first in 1778, when he went as Ablegate to carry the Berretta to the two Cardinals, De la Rochefoucauld and De Rohan, and the second time when he was present with Pius VII. at the Coronation of Napoleon. On taking leave, Braschi burst into tears bewailing the unhappy state of affairs. They next went to Faenza, where they arrived in the evening and were visited by Cavalier Dionigi Strocchi, the Sub-Prefect. This was not a visit of formality or out of mere respect, but was one of friendship, for Erskine and Strocchi had been intimate friends years ago in Rome, in the house of Signora Marianna Dionigi. It was a most pleasant evening for the Cardinal. The conversation fell on old times, the poets and especially Horace. Strocchi made Erskine a present of the Hymns of Callimacus, translated and published by him in Milan, 1808; and of a *Canto Genetl'aco* composed and published in 1807, for the *Vicino parto* of Agosta Amalia, Vice-Queen of Naples. This visit caused the Hotel people to be very civil and also moderate in their charges. Monsignor Zauli, who was living in Faenza on account of the troubles in Rome, came to see Erskine and evidently wanted to talk politics, but was prevented by the presence of the Sub-Prefect.

On the 9th of January they arrived at Bologna, at half past one o'clock P.M., and stopped in the Pellegrino Hotel to pass the night there, as they had business to transact, and the Cardinal needed rest. In the evening Monsignor Scarpelli, the Marchesi Boschi and and other friends came in and paid a very long visit. The next night they slept at Parma at the Imperial Hotel, where they found Cardinal Vincenti, who had left Rome the same day that Erskine left it, and had hitherto been always in advance, but from Parma onwards was always behind Erskine. The two Cardinals were glad to meet. On the 11th of January they passed through Piacenza and slept at Castel S. Giovanni. They had a tedious journey, for the roads were covered with ice. At Borgo S. Donnino the Cardinal had put some questions to the Postmaster, who in answering addressed him by his family name. Erskine then asked him how he knew it? The Postmaster frankly said:— "From yesterday it was known here that your Eminence was to pass, as also the other Cardinal who remains behind, and I can also assure you that already at this hour it is known in Milan that your Eminence has left Parma to pursue your journey." This was a convincing proof to Erskine that although he was not attended by a Gendarme, yet all his movements were watched. Much snow fell this night.

Erskine on the 12th of January, arrived at Alexandria, and lodged in the *Albergo d' Italia*. In the same hotel were staying Duke Braschi, Cavaliers Falconieri and Palombi, who along with Prince Spada had been sent by General Miollis to thank the Emperor, in the name of the Romans, for having destroyed the Pontifical Government and reduced Rome to a simple French department. Duke Braschi was named President of this deputation, which had presented its homage to the new Sovereign of Rome, with all the formalities and solemnities prescribed by Bonaparte. In the morning they came to visit Erskine, who only received Braschi and Falconieri. Palombi was left in another room to talk to Del Medico. The conversation was brief, and only on matters of travel. Erskine, when on the road, could not keep from telling Del Medico of the painful impression produced by seeing Braschi, the nephew of Pius VI., at the head of such a scoundrelly deputation, and apparently content with his ignominious mission. At four o'clock on this day (the 13th) they reached Turin and went to *La Bonne Femme*, an hotel recommended—and justly so, as events proved—by a passing traveller for its good fare and moderate charges.

Immediately on arrival, the Cardinal sent a note to Signora Deodata Saluzzo, a literary lady of much celebrity at that time in Turin and in all Italy. She soon came to see His Eminence. Then came a Gendarme to restore the passport which had been given up on entering the city, but instead of giving it, as is usual, to the servant, he insisted on consigning it to the Cardinal himself, perhaps to make sure of his identity. The then Governor of Turin was Prince Camillo Borghese, who kept his post with almost sovereign magnificence. He knew of the Cardinal's arrival, but paid him no visit, although he usually shewed that courtesy to all the Roman travellers. Perhaps he was afraid of causing suspicion by politeness to a Cardinal. On the next morning (Sunday, January 14th, Erskine went early to Mass at S. Lorenzo, which was near the Hotel. Del Medico was the celebrant. The Padrone had sent notice the evening before to the Sacristan, so that all was found ready, and two very neat and polished seculars made excuses to Del Medico for not using those distinctions proper to a Cardinal, giving him to understand that they were sorry for the omission, which was intentional, and not an over-sight. There was nothing but a cushion placed at the rails for the Cardinal, and a common chair if he wished to use it. After mass they left Turin at 9 A.M. for Susa. The costumes of the Contadine on the Sunday were very pretty.

At Susa, where they arrived at half-past 3 o'clock in the afternoon, they expected a refreshing rest as a preparation for the passage of Mont Cenis. But the only hotel, the Post, in Susa, was the worst they ever met. The dinner was bad and disagreed with the Cardinal's stomach, though he had little appetite and ate little. The beds were so bad that Erskine was kept awake all the night. At five next morning (January 15) they left Susa to make the ascent of the mountain. Erskine seemed in bad condition for exposure to fatigue, and indeed from the snow, the cold and hardship, had now lost all the vigour which he had gained by the earlier portion of his journey. The snow was falling, but there was no wind. The Cardinal now felt the benefit of having his good London carriage, which closed perfectly so as to exclude the cold air from without. The movement of the carriage was like that of a litter, easy and most comfortable; the lining was warm, and the cushions were much softer than the bed at Susa. For additional heat they afterwards lighted two wax candles and kept them burning within the carriage.

In two stages they reached S. Martino, to change horses. It was usual for travellers to dismount here to put slides under the carriage, but the Postmaster told them that they might go on as they were to the top of the mountain, as the road had been kept free of snow by a number of men in expectation of the arrival of some great personage who was to come from Italy to pass into France. He said also that he would attach to the carriage two horses in addition to the six which they had employed from Susa. They would however be obliged to travel slowly for the remaining three French stages between S. Martino and the plateau. Erskine was glad not to be required to leave the carriage. At mid day they reached the plateau which terminates the ascent. Not far from the entrance of this plateau is the Hospice established by the Monks with the permission of Napoleon. The postillions had asked whether Erskine would stop at the Hospice, and at first received an answer in the negative. But shortly afterwards the Cardinal, who had occasion to get down from his carriage, got such a fit of chill and trembling that he changed his mind. The Monks gave him a cordial reception and put him in a room with a blazing fire, as they perceived from his pallor that he badly wanted warmth. They also gave him some hot broth.

The Superior, Dom Michel Angelo, in the Abbot's absence, prayed the Cardinal to stop for dinner now, at their usual hour, either in the general Refectory or in his own warm room to avoid changing the air. There would be plenty of time to travel after dinner. The Cardinal consented, and the table was prepared. At dinner were present two French Commissaries, sent to maintain the road and keep it fit for the passage of King Murat, who was expected from Naples. Before dinner they were presented to the Cardinal, who talked with them on general subjects. Erskine now learned of the publication of *Les Martyrs*, by Chateaubriand, a work—said the Commissaries—of greater fame to the author than even his *Génie du Christianisme*. The dinner was good, and the trout from the lake exquisite, but Erskine had no appetite, and his illness was so apparent that he was prevailed on by the Monks to stay the night, and at once to go to his bedroom and try to sleep.

Del Medico took a short stroll outside, and then went to the room of one of the Monks, with whom he talked, but always with great caution and reserve, inasmuch as the two Commissaries were devoted to the French Government; and a single word, if overheard, might seriously compromise the Cardinal. The Monk, noticing this reticence, took down an octavo volume and asked if the things therein published about Rome, Miollis, and the seizure of the Pope, were true. Del Medico read a few pages and was astonished to find printed in French that which, if only written in manuscript in Rome, would be most compromising and sufficient to cause the arrest of the daring writer. He came to the conclusion also that

Monks living in retirement might be better informed about affairs than folks living in the world.

To the surprise of Del Medico, the Cardinal now came in and brought him to visit Dom Michel Angelo, the Superior, a man of good presence, fresh for his age, and of polished manners, fitted for one who had to receive many guests of rank and position. Erskine after his two hours of sleep had regained a little of his vivacity. This Hospice was like that of S. Bernard or S. Gothard, and was endowed by Napoleon with 30,000 francs annually, with liberty to cut timber for fuel, on condition of giving shelter and food to all travellers who demanded hospitality. They kept a register of all their guests, and shewed the autograph signatures of many Cardinals and of Napoleon, who had twice been there. The Superior shewed them Napoleon's room, which was well but plainly furnished. The Superior little thought that in three years time he would be called on to receive Pius VII., on his forced journey from Savona to Fontainbleau.

They supped with the Monks in the Refectory, and trouts were again cooked at the request of the Cardinal, who had eaten so little at dinner, but now had a good appetite. He slept well that night.

They rose early the next morning (January 16), and in the chapel, which was not very warm, Erskine heard Mass said by Del Medico. After coffee and milk they left the Hospice at 8 A.M. The Head Inspector of roads, who resided at the Hospice, sent a number of men to accompany the carriage to be ready to help the Cardinal in any difficulty. The greater number of these men were dismissed with gifts by Erskine, and with directions to thank, in the Cardinal's name, the Head Inspector for his courtesy. He retained only four of these men, and it was well he did so, for, when turning a corner, so violent a gust of wind met them that the carriage would certainly have been overturned but for the four men on foot, who were prepared for the emergency, and by force of their hands and arms kept the carriage from falling over. At Lans-le-bourg they entered Savoy, and they slept in a good inn at S. Jean de Maurienne.

They passed the night of the 17th at Chambéry, and resuming their journey on the 18th, found the weather excessively cold. In vain they lighted four candles inside the carriage. They pitied the poor servants on the box-seat and would have brought them inside had there been room enough, but the carriage was built for two only. At *Les Echelles* Del Medico and the servants had to get down and walk, for the old road was precipitous and steep, as if going into an abyss. Here two men with ropes and chains made the hind wheels of the carriage immoveable. At Pont Beauvoisin, the French frontier, they got sunshine, which they had not enjoyed for a long time. They slept at Bourgoin, *Hôtel de la Poste*. In this hotel, Erskine, noticing some small hammers or maces on the mantelpiece in the dining-room, asked the landlady what they meant. She, with an air of great satisfaction, said there had been that day a party of Freemasons, who used the hammers to mark applause, etc. Erskine told Del Medico he did not expect much from such an hotel, and he was right in his judgment, for they were charged double prices and got very inferior treatment.

At 2 P.M. of the 19th they arrived at the Hôtel du Parc in Lyons. The landlady observed the miserable state to which the Cardinal was reduced by the extreme cold, and advised him for his health's sake to make a short stay, and offered to send for the Vicars General to visit him. But Erskine refused, and said he only wanted rest, and he went to his room where there was a blazing fire. Yet the cold was so intense that water froze near the fireplace. At 7 P.M. on the 20th they arrived for the night at Mâcon, and after mass on the 21st, set out for Châlon-sur-Soane, which they reached in the evening, and put up at the Hôtel du Parc.

Erskine was surprised when the landlady, meeting him at the

carriage door, called him " Eminence," and when he enquired the reason, she said she knew his quality from the arms on the carriage. But she probably got her information from the police. In the same hotel were some Spanish prisoners of high rank. They were six in number, and came after supper to Erskine's room to pay him a visit, staying half-an-hour. They were all military men, some of them Generals, and strongly attached to Ferdinand. They said they were content with their treatment by the French Government, and promised to see the Cardinal off in the morning. Erskine invited them to a Chocolate breakfast at 9 A.M. They came punctually. Erskine apologised for the Chocolate which was not prepared in the Spanish fashion. French Chocolate pleases neither Italians nor Spaniards. They chatted pleasantly until the hour for departure had passed, and the carriage had been some time waiting at the door. Del Medico reminded His Eminence of this, and the Cardinal said he was sorry to go. If you are sorry—said Del Medico—there is an easy remedy. Let the horses be taken off, and defer departure till to-morrow. The Spaniards also urged the delay, as snow had fallen in the night and the cold was intense. The Cardinal consented to remain, and invited the Spaniards to coffee after the three o'clock dinner. The Spaniards regarded Erskine as a British subject, and both Spaniards and Britons were then intolerant of the French power. The Spaniards also visited Erskine in the evening, and presented to him a young Englishman, a prisoner of war, who had taken service in Spain; and the Cardinal spoke to him kindly, and in the English language. But when alone with Del Medico, Erskine said he did not like this introduction of the Englishman in an hotel which was doubtless watched by the police, and he determined to go away in the morning, and gave orders accordingly.

They departed at 8 A.M. on the 23rd of January, saluted by the Spaniards, but the Englishman did not appear.

When in the carriage with Del Medico, the conversation fell

on the conduct to be observed in Paris, and the Cardinal said :—

"I am now about to arrive in Paris, the last, or the last but one, of the Cardinals, Vincenti alone arriving afterwards. It may be said that the whole of the Sacred College is assembled there, for only four or five are wanting who are disabled, by age and infirmity, from travelling. Now I know for a certainty that all the Cardinals get pecuniary support from the French Government; that they all are presented at Court and generally assist on Sundays at the Emperor's Mass; and finally that they all get apartments, carriages, servants, and everything which would be suitable to their rank, if they were in free and untrammelled circumstances, and if the Church were happy, and if the Holy Father were joined with them, exercising in freedom his full and independent authority. What ought I to do, when I find them unanimously agreed in maintaining such a course of behaviour?

"To oppose them and adopt a different mode of life would tend to nothing save to get myself obloquy, and the reputation of being imprudent, ridiculous, and fantastical. And I would place myself in complete disunion from my colleagues, who, after all, would not go back or change their conduct in the least. It was our duty to make the Paris public see plainly that we did not come to France in answer to a simple invitation of the Emperor, as they wished to have it understood, but because we were really carried off by force. We ought to have made it patent to the world that we were in a state of mourning, as truly the Catholic Church is, by reason of the outrageous violence committed on the person of the Vicar of Christ, and his strict imprisonment at Savona. This is why we should from the first have rejected the pecuniary assignment under any title, and afterwards we should have passed a retired life in strict privacy, occupying modest habitations, without carriages or ostentation of luxury, as is suitable to prisoners and persons violently deported, and living each on his own private resources

—all our Ecclesiastical incomes being sequestrated—and the richer fraternally assisting the poorer. Then there would be little difficulty in abstaining from going to Court, in refusing invitations, and in declining distinctions only granted to illude the public. This in fine was the proper behaviour to be shown by persons who yielded only to force. But the Cardinals in Paris, and among them the most venerable of the Sacred College have adopted quite another course. They go to Court, and they assist at the Emperor's Mass, and if now they do not see anything in it save the simple assistance at the Divine sacrifice, the day will probably come when this assistance will become problematical, and then, but too late, they will learn the error they committed from the first." By this last observation Erskine probably alluded to the Emperor's second marriage, as a step to which, measures were already taken for the annulment of that with Josephine, a marriage which was indeed a cause of schism among the Cardinals.

They halted on the night of the 23rd at Autun, on the 24th at Avallon, and on the 25th at Sens. On the 26th of January, 1810, at 4 o'clock P.M., they entered Paris by the Charentin Barrier.

They drove first to the Hôtel de Rome, but found it full. Cardinals Doria and Gabrielli and other persons from Italy were there. Then by advice of the well-known Courier, Livio Palmoni, they tried the *Hôtel des Ministres* which also was full. They then, as night was coming on, told the Postillions to drive to any hotel which they knew had accommodation, and they were brought to the *Hôtel d' Autriche*, Rue Traversiere S. Honore. It was necessary to accept here, at a very dear price, two rooms on the third floor with a small bedroom for the servants. On the following morning [January 27] Erskine was going to call on Cardinal Doria for advice, when Doria's servant, Carlino, who had been before in Paris with his master when Nuncio in France, and who knew the French language and the city well, came, in his master's name, to invite Erskine and Del Medico to dinner, and to offer his services in finding a lodging. Del Medico and Carlino went together on this quest, and hired an apartment on the first floor of the Hôtel Taranne, Rue Taranne, an apartment tolerably convenient, but not to be ready for occupation until the day after the morrow. The carriage was also hired. There was great affluence of strangers at that time into Paris and little choice of apartments. Cardinal Despuig the same morning had taken a first floor in the same hotel. In the mean while the master of the *Hôtel d' Autriche*, hearing of their intended departure, offered at same price a first floor apartment, but Erskine refused it.

Erskine and Del Medico at the hour appointed went to dine with Cardinal Doria. No one was at the table save the three Cardinals and their three Secretaries. They were surprised to find a meat dinner on a Saturday, but they were informed that in all French dioceses where the Cathedrals were dedicated to the Blessed Virgin Mary, it was the privilege to eat meat on all Saturdays between Christmas and the Purification. Some other Cardinals came in to see Erskine. Before they went away, Cardinal Doria invited Erskine to attend Mass on the next day (Sunday, the 28th) in his—Doria's—chapel. The Cardinal accepted the invitation, and went the next morning and returned after Mass to his hotel, and received visits from several Cardinals and Romans, who were then in Paris.

Among the first to visit Erskine was Cardinal Consalvi, whose visit was necessarily brief, as he was to be presented the very same morning to Napoleon by Cardinal Fesch. This limitation of time was not accidental in a statesman like Consalvi, but was premeditated in order to avoid a long conversation with Erskine. In fact, Erskine and Consalvi saw little of each other afterwards, and were now no better agreed in their views than they had been in past years. Visits to Erskine were made even after mid-day, by Cardinals who had assisted at the Emperor's Mass and at a Reception generally held in the Imperial Palace, and these visits were so frequent that

Erskine had to put off his dinner, which had been fixed for 3 o'clock P.M. The landlord was distressed that so many visitors had to climb to a third floor, and again, but in vain, pressed Erskine to descend to the first floor.

Cardinal Erskine, on the 29th of January, went to reside in the Hôtel Taranne, which was in fact an hôtel *garni*, for the letting was for furnished rooms only, and without food of any kind. They at first got their dinners sent in from a restaurant, but afterwards, they hired a kitchen and a French cook, as the Cardinal's health suffered from the restaurant diet.

The owners of the hotel were Monsieur and Madame Follet, a very religious couple, just suited for ecclesiastical lodgers. Madame used to tell how in time of the Revolution and the Terror, she always had a priest to stay in the house, who often, without being discovered, had celebrated mass and administered sacraments in Erskine's apartments. The Cardinal was now quite content. He had his intimate friend, Cardinal Despuig, on the same floor with him, and at Despuig's request, heard Mass in Despuig's chapel; thus saving the trouble of erecting a private chapel for himself. He was also near to the S. Germain quarter of Paris, where most of his friends lived.

For a month or two, Cardinal Erskine seems to have been in tolerable health, with only occasional ailments. He was also without any pecuniary anxieties, thanks to the kindness of his cousins. Early in February, he received from Rome the following letter :—

"*Rome, January, 24, 1810.*

"MY LORD,—Although deprived of your direct accounts, [letters from Erskine himself] I have heard with great satisfaction [of] your arrival at Bologna in good health.

"A few days after your departure, we [the Bank of Torlonia] received another letter from your friend Coutts, which we sent to Messrs Perregaux at Paris, who will have remitted [it] to your Eminency upon your arrival. Along with it was a new credit for [a] further two hundred pounds sterling, making together six hundred pounds; however as you have signed the receipt for only four hundred, if your Eminency should be disposed to make use of the whole sum, I beg you will acquaint me with it, that we may send your Eminency the receipts duly made out, and give proper orders to Messrs Perregaux that the sum may be at your disposal.

"I am so much taken up with business that I have no time to entertain me longer with your Eminency. I'll procure myself that pleasure at the first leisure moment.

"I'll end my letter by assuring your Eminency of the very great interest all my family takes to [in] your wellfare and happiness. My mother [Duchess Torlonia], the Duke and my brother, every one [who was] informed that I was going to write [to] you, have desired to be kindly remembered to your Eminency and to assure you of their most perfect esteem and friendship.

"I remain with equal sentiments and with due regard, My Dear Sir, your Eminency's Most Obb[t] h[ble] servant and affectionate friend, Lewis Chiaveri." This letter was addressed:—A Son Eminence Monseig[r] Le Card. Erskine, à Paris.

On this letter was written in Italian by the Cardinal:—"Answered the 6th of February, that I had left with Mr. Coutts the last £200 st. placed in his Bank to my credit by my Cousin Stewart Erskine [the Earl of Buchan?], not having occasion for it at present, and in order to draw it afterwards with less loss [on the exchange]; and that of Lord Kellie's £400, I had here drawn from Mr. Perregaux only 70 louis, which made 1680 francs; and that for this sum, united to the sums which I had had from him in Rome, Signor Torlonia could re-imburse himself by drawing the equivalent out of the said £400 from the Bank of Coutts, leaving there [*i.e.*, with Coutts] the remainder for me to draw it directly from thence [London] whenever I may have occasion; without making it make the useless and detrimental circuit of causing it to pass by way of Rome."

This and the following letter are taken from the originals in the extensive and very valuable Collection of Autographs formerly belonging to the late Monsignor Angelini mentioned on page 121, and now in the possession of Cav. Giancarlo Rossi, a well known collector who kindly lent them to the writer. The Angelini-Rossi Collection consists of about 250 cases of autographs of sovereigns, popes, princes, cardinals, artists, illustrious men, etc., and is well worthy of a visit.

The Cardinal, who wrote on the 6th of February to Chiaveri, received the following reply :—" My most respectable Lord, I have received with an infinite pleasure the letter you have done me the honour to write [to] me from Paris, the 6th inst., as it informs me of your safe arrival and gives me the most satisfactory accounts of your health, which I have communicated to my family, who takes the greatest interest to [in] your welfare, and every member of it, beginning by my Mother, the Duke and my brother, desire to be remembered to your Eminency.

"I hear with pleasure that upon your arrival Messrs. Perregaux remitted you Mr. Coutts' letter which I had forwarded to them for your Eminency.

"I see that you prefer to leave in Messrs. Coutts' hands the two hundred pounds which [they] had ordered me (I mean the Duke) to pay you, as you suppose the exchange you will get a better exchange at Paris than at Rome. For this same reason you wish that the remainder of the former four hundred pounds should be left also by [with] Messrs. Coutts in London, which [wish] shall be complied with, less the sum of the 70 louis, which you have disposed of, as well as the other [sums] your Eminency received at Rome which are put to your debit. We shall write in consequence to Coutts by first opportunity.

"This is the first day of Carneval. The weather is shocking, rainy and cold. We have had a severe frost these three days past, as severe as you may have it at Paris. Our Governor General gives this night a *bal masqué*, as he has already given two that have been well attended. We shall have the usual ones at the theatre, and if the weather favours us every thing promises a brilliant Carneval.

"Chev^r Albert, Crivelli and Monsignor Haeffeler, the three last Diplomatics that remained at Rome, have received orders to depart. The first went off this morning. The others remain as they have demanded their retreat. Crivelli has been dispensed to go. I have thought these accounts might be agreeable to you. I shall say no more upon these subjects.

"I remain entirely disposed at your commands; with sentiments of a most sincere esteem and regard, My dear Sir, your most obb^t and h^{ble} servant and affectionate friend, Louis Chiaveri. Rome, February 24, 1810."

"P.S.—Your Eminency may be sure of doing me the greatest pleasure whenever you will favour me with your news."

This letter was addressed: "A Son Eminence Monseig^r Le Card. Erskine, etc. etc., à Paris," with "Rue and Hotel Tarenne" written over it.

At foot of this letter, Erskine wrote, in Italian:—"Answered that he should let me know with precision how much of the £400 s^t I have drawn from his Bank, inclusive of exchange and everything, I having taken 150 Roman scudi before going away and £70 s^t on my arrival here; in order that I may know how much, consequently, of the said £400 s^t remains in the hands of Mr. Coutts, to guide me in drawing from here the drafts upon the same."

The good health of the Cardinal, mentioned in the foregoing letters, was not of long duration, and the ill effects of his compulsory journey from Rome to Paris, and that too when he was sick and ought to have remained in his bed, soon began to appear, and the Cardinal was obliged to call in physicians. Dr. Portal was one of the first doctors of the time in Paris, and had known Erskine in former days. He could find no great disease in Erskine, and prescribed Tisane or some other decoction of herbs, and recommended rest and country air, as soon as the season would permit, which meant about the end of April. When questioned more particularly, Dr. Portal confessed that he took a very sinister view of the case, and that Erskine was a worn out machine without any recuperative energy. Care and repose contributed to cause an apparent improvement in the Cardinal's condition, but he had relapses which compelled him to keep to his bed. He was able occasionally to take drives in his carriage, and to make visits. But his ill health retarded his presentation to the Emperor which took place, as usual, on a Sunday, after Mass, and by means of Cardinal Fesch. The presentation was very brief. Erskine's name was pronounced by the Grand Almoner, and the Emperor, in tone of interrogation, said :—" English ?" and Erskine answered " Scotch." With these two words the interview began and ended. Yet Napoleon must have recollected the Monsignor Erskine whom he had, as First Consul, received with so much distinction in 1801. But circumstances—and manners of Reception—had changed.

The miserable condition of Cardinal Erskine's health forbade his acceptance of invitations to Court and excused his absence, on the 2nd of April, from the ceremony of the ill-fated marriage of Napoleon with Marie Louise, archduchess of Austria. Those Cardinals who attended that ceremony were styled *Red Cardinals*. Those who refused to attend it were styled Black Cardinals, and were not permitted to use in public the insignia proper to their rank, and were reckoned the Emperor's enemies. Erskine, whose infirmities were known, Despuig, who was liable to semi-apoplectic fits, and Dugnani, who suffered from no slight malady, were exempted from censure, and although not present at the marriage remained in the number of those who were reputed to be " Reds."

During his illness, Erskine was visited daily, especially in the evenings, by Cardinals, Prelates, and Roman gentlemen. The Abbé Denina, Barruel, and Count Aldini, the Secretary of State for Italy, were among his guests. Many were surprised at the frequency of Count Aldini's visits, not knowing that Aldini had been the assistant of Erskine in his lawyer's studio at Rome.

In April, by advice of Dr. Portal, the Cardinal engaged a country house close to Paris, outside the Barrière du Maine, on the plain of Montrouge. It had a tolerably large garden and once belonged to some noble family, but now had fallen into the hands of an Auctioneer and Valuator named Sibilet. Erskine took it for a term ending the 1st of October, and went there to reside on the 1st of May. The Cardinal's daily routine at this country place was to hear an early Mass in the chapel on the second floor—then to walk in the garden, and then to transact business in his study. At mid-day he received visitors from Paris, such as Despuig, Dugnani, Zondadari and other Cardinals, the Prelates, De Gregorio and Valle, the Duke di Zagarola, the two Massimi and Count Alexander Baglioni. Count Baglioni introduced to Erskine a Roman family, residing not far off near the Barrière de Fourneaux, the head of which was Francesco Belloni, Director of the School of Mosaics in Paris, and this acquaintance was not only most agreeable to Erskine but exceedingly useful, because Belloni assisted the Cardinal very much in his business matters.

After dinner and the usual siesta, the horses were put to the carriage for the Cardinal and Del Medico to take their drive which almost always ended in a visit to Hôtel Taranne to see Cardinal Despuig and other friends. Before ten o'clock P.M., Erskine invariably left the *conversazione* to return to the country. These evening reunions—the Cardinal used to say—instead of cheering, saddened him. Sorrowful news were constantly announced concerning the affairs of the Church and of Rome, and worse events were threatened. Erskine was so sensitive and susceptible that he felt he never could be cured of his malady as long as he remained in Paris, where he daily experienced fresh motives of affliction. His digestion became bad and his spirits were sinking.

Yet the country did him much good: the air was pure and open, and he could walk freely in the garden and on the roads. He gave little dinners to his friends, followed by games of cards and chess. Sometimes he sent the carriage for Cavalier Guiseppe Ciccolini, a noted chess player, and had a game before dinner.

After two months of this wholesome country life, Erskine felt so much better that he resolved upon a short excursion about Paris, and fixed on Versailles. He was joined in this trip by Cardinal Dugnani, who was the last Papal Nuncio in Paris under Louis XVI. and had witnessed the excesses of the Revolution. Arrangements were made for the 10th of July, and the Cardinals met at the place appointed, Erskine with his Secretary Del Medico, and Dugnani with his Secretary and Monsignor Gaetani Marini and his nephew. They stopped at Sèvres and were courteously received at the Porcelain Factory by the Director. Then they went to Versailles and saw all the rooms in the Palace. The Cardinals had no external signs of their rank, but were recognized, and Erskine was allowed to retain his stick, a privilege not usually accorded. They admired the gardens, the theatre, the Grand and Little Trianon, etc., and ate a good dinner, which had been ordered beforehand at the Restaurant *Du Gran Reservoir*. Alquier, French Ambassador at Rome when the city was occupied by the troops of General Miollis, was, with a large party, in the room next to that in which Erskine was dining. And when the Cardinals were walking in the Orangery, Alquier pointed them out to his friends. But the Cardinals took care not to look at, or take notice of Alquier. They then drove to the Barrière of Sèvres and there separated, each to his home. Erskine felt no fatigue and enjoyed his excursion.

They made another excursion on the 29th of August to the

Church of S. Denis, with Cavalier Guiseppe Ciccolini, and remarked the *basso relievo* of the decapitation of the Saint, which the Revolutionists thought worthy to be preserved because it resembled a guillotine. The dinner at the inn was good and the Cardinal ate heartily, but the food was not sufficiently delicate for the Cardinal's stomach, and he soon felt a kind of heaviness which portended in him an attack of his usual indisposition. They hurried away; left Ciccolini at his house; and omitting the visit to Despuig, went at once to the country. In the evening the disturbance of the Cardinal's stomach increased to nausea, and for the next few days he had to remain in perfect quiet.

Autumn was approaching and it was necessary to make arrangements about returning to Paris. Erskine would come to no immediate decision, for he still indulged the hope that by means of Count Aldini he might be permitted to go elsewhere, perhaps to England. Paul MacPherson, the Rector of the Scots College in Rome, had been lately allowed to pass into England. But the public was altogether ignorant of the favour shewn to MacPherson, while the passage of a Cardinal, and of a Cardinal who had been Papal Envoy in London, would have aroused attention, for it could not be kept secret, and would have excited unpleasant comment in a thousand ways. In fact the visits of Aldini to Erskine had ceased altogether, and by a third person Erskine was given to understand that it was useless to expect Aldini to move in the matter. Erskine then resigned all thoughts of going to England.

In the beginning of October, the Cardinal told Del Medico to search for a lodging in Paris, in the suburb of S. Germain, but to avoid large hotels and hotels *garni*. He wished to rent and furnish an apartment of his own. The apartment was to be well exposed to the sun, with few stairs, and with a carriage entrance, and tranquil, in regard to the number and quality of the lodgers. Del Medico and Belloni set out to search, and found a first floor apartment in a small hotel in Rue Grenelle,

S. Germain, no. 25, not far from the *Croix Rouge*. It had a carriage entrance, a courtyard with stable and coach house, and a convenient staircase with few steps. The apartment consisted of servant's hall, dining and drawing rooms, and large bedroom with two connecting cabinets, of which one had an outer door, and was suitable for a chapel. In this suite of rooms, which were exposed to the south, and looked into the courtyard, the Cardinal was to live. Two other rooms looking into the street, and subject to the noise of carts and carriages, were destined for Del Medico. There was a spacious kitchen on the ground floor and upper rooms for servants. The second floor was occupied by a relative of the proprietor, who had a wife, but no children. The apartment, although not sumptuous, was, for a French one, convenient. The Cardinal liked it when he saw it, and immediately came to an agreement with Couragciod, the landlord. Del Medico bought some furniture which belonged to Cardinal Ruffo Scilla, archbishop of Naples, who had to leave Paris, and the rest he purchased with the help of Signor Belloni.

By the end of October all was ready, and Erskine went to live there. He was pleased with his new abode, and seemed strengthened by his country life.

But very soon the Cardinal fell again ill in Paris, in consequence of the cold which set in severely during the first days of November. Cardinal Giuseppe Doria advised him to consult Dr. Laennic, the doctor employed by Cardinal Fesch, and a man of rising reputation. Dr. Laennic, by observation and questions, endeavoured to discover the cause of the malady, but his prescriptions afforded only temporary relief. The Cardinal however delighted in his visits and in his conversation, both because he showed such evident anxiety to cure him, and because he did not hesitate to display openly his opinions, which were those of a deeply religious man.

Monsignor De Gregorio, perceiving the attendance of the French physicians to be useless, persuaded Erskine to try an

Italian, Dr. Camillo Corona, then living in Paris. Dr. Corona came and began by declaring that the symptoms mentioned by the Cardinal, did not seem to be such as not to leave hope for great alleviation and even a cure by means of the prescriptions he would give him. Erskine was naturally pleased at this encouraging view of his case, and cheerfully submitted to the treatment adopted by the new doctor which was apparently very simple. Corona, knowing Erskine's high reputation for learning, did not, when visiting the Cardinal, confine himself to medical matters, but began to show off his own literary knowledge which was very extensive, and made a great impression on the Cardinal, who, to enjoy his society invited him to supper every Wednesday along with Monsignor De Gregorio. When Corona came, his medical examination of his patient was brief, and the conversation was entirely on literature, and was protracted sometimes into the hours of the night.

Corona's treatment proved as ineffectual as that of the French doctors, and the malady, not being checked, augmented towards the end of the year to such an extent that the Cardinal had to stay in bed. Corona, who tried to buoy up the Cardinal with hopes, privately confided to Del Medico his real opinion, which was that as the malady resisted all remedies, dissolution could not be far off. He therefore suggested a consultation with the French doctors, which was, accordingly, held on the 2nd of January, 1811, by Doctors Portal, Laennec, and Corona.

The three doctors, after the French manner, first went together into the sick man's chamber, and examined him in presence of each other. They then retired by themselves for private and free discussion unrestrained by the presence of the patient. One doctor after the other, at intervals, was seen to re-enter the Cardinal's bedroom, to make additional enquiries and then to retire in silence. Finally the three doctors concurred in deciding upon the measures to be taken, and wrote their decision on a paper which they all three signed. There is an adage that when doctors differ the patient dies. In this case the doctors agreed, but the result was the same. It is needless to trouble the reader with all the details. It is sufficient to mention that they advised some mechanical appliances, which Erskine absolutely rejected, and twelve pills daily, which he consented to swallow, provided he found them beneficial. He made no objection to use seltzer or Spa waters at his meals in place of common water.

In the first days of the new year, 1811, Cardinal Erskine received a terrible shock by the arrest in Paris of Mgr. De Gregorio, Father Fontana, and Cardinals Gabrielli, Opizzoni, and Di Pietro, who subsequently were all shut up in prison in the Donjon of Vincennes. These violent measures were caused by the Brief of Pius VII., dated from Savona, in which His Holiness severely blamed Cardinal Maury for assuming—albeit merely as Vicar Capitular—the administration of the diocese of Paris, on the sole nomination by the Emperor to the archbishopric of Paris, notwithstanding that Maury was still the bishop of Monte Fiascone. The persons now arrested were charged by the Government with having taken part in the drawing up, transmission and final expedition of this Brief, and against them the French police displayed the utmost rigour.

Attempts had been made to keep all this a secret from the Cardinal, not to distress him. But even while Erskine was ignorant of the arrest of De Gregorio, Erskine sent Del Medico one morning to fetch De Gregorio, whom he wanted to consult on some business. Del Medico went and was astonished to learn that De Gregorio had been arrested and carried away by the police on the previous night. It was necessary to tell the Cardinal the reason why De Gregorio could not come to him, and eventually Erskine was made acquainted with all that had happened.

During the greater part of January and February, Erskine made some slight rally from the severe attack he had had in the month of December, but yet had constant relapses and alternations more or less injurious. He resumed his drives, when the weather permitted, and received visits from Despuig and the few Cardinals remaining in Paris, and from Monsignors Morozzo and Valle, as well as from some Italian friends, and notably from Count Alexander Baglioni. He also occasionally invited some of them to supper to distract his mind from painful thoughts. He was much pleased at the arrival in Paris of Prince and Princess Chigi, who came every now and then to visit him. He had an old intimacy with the Chigi family. The Princess was a woman of spirit and talent, and her husband had no ordinary learning. Their conversation cheered him greatly.

Hopes were now entertained by the Cardinal that as he had outlived the worst of the winter, he might expect benefit from a change of air in the spring. He was the more encouraged when he perceived towards the end of February a disappearance of a certain swelling of his legs. But this symptom was but the prelude to a fresh apoplectic seizure at the very end of that month. The three doctors now unanimously recognized the true nature of the Cardinal's malady, and adopted the necessary means to arouse him from his state of profound somnolency and stupor. They succeeded in this, but without hope of saving his life. The stroke left no exterior signs and must have acted internally as in previous attacks. In fact the difficulty of administering nourishment was extreme, and the disturbances of the stomach were more frequent. All prescriptions were useless.

From this moment the Cardinal remained in bed, but had all his senses about him, and even received a few visits. He consulted frequently, and alone, with Mgr. Valle about his will, but delayed the making of it, always saying there was yet time. He was perfectly aware of his condition, and told the Parish Priest who was exhorting him to resign himself to the will of God, that he would not say an *Ave Maria* to have his life prolonged. He occupied himself chiefly with the affairs of his soul, and on the morning of the 16th of March, received the

Viaticum in his chapel after Mass and in presence of all his household. On the next morning, Sunday the 17th, he received Extreme Unction from the Abbé Harel, the *Vicaire*, who was his Confessor, and before its administration, asked in a clear and distinct voice, the pardon of all those present for all his offences against them, and gave charge to Abbé Harel to inform his colleages, the Cardinals, that he wished to die in peace and concord with all, and therefore begged their pardon for whatever he might have said or done to their displeasure.

Having thus provided, in his full senses, for his spiritual needs, he wished to complete all his worldly dispositions by making his will, and on the same morning—Sunday, March 17th—sent for Monsignor Valle and the Notary, Mr. Denys, and proceeded to the Act in presence of Monsignors Morozzo and Valle, the Abbé Harel, and others. The Cardinal had forgotten to name a testamentary executor, and Mgr. Morozzo suggested Cardinal Latier de Bayanne, and went at once to the house of that Cardinal, who lived close by, to ask his consent to undertake the charge. But the Cardinal was not at home, and Morozzo, not wishing further delay, took his acceptation for granted, adding a clause of sub-delegation, intending Mgr. Valle to be named sub-delegate. And so the will was reduced to writing by the Notary, and was signed at about half-past 12 o'clock by the Cardinal and the witnesses, and remained secret until it was opened by the Notary after his death.

The business of the will occupied two hours and greatly fatigued the Cardinal, who was unable to take nourishment, except a spoonful of jelly, and yet seemed by repose and quiet to revive a little. His exhaustion in the afternoon was so extreme, that in the expectation of immediate death, they began the Prayers for those in Agony, but in the evening his pulse grew stronger, and Dr. Corona said that the end was not yet come. The two succeeding days passed much in the same way, with an occasional crisis. On the Tuesday one of these attacks was so violent that Dr. Corona told Del Medico to lose no time, but proceed at once to the Prayers Recommending the Soul to God. But the Cardinal, who preserved his senses all through, told Del Medico the time had not come for that, and Del Medico desisted. On Wednesday morning, after a very agitated night, the Cardinal got calmer, and while Del Medico was saying Mass in the adjoining chapel, gave signs to those about him that he heard distinctly all the parts of the Mass. Del Medico after finishing the Mass, went to the bedside, and was asked by Erskine for something to drink. Del Medico offered him a glass of tisane, and Erskine asked for his spectacles. These were given and then were changed for others of greater force. Then Erskine made Del Medico indicate with his finger the part of the glass which separated the tisane from the empty part. He drank nothing and it was thus evident that the Cardinal, being conscious that his sight had become enfeebled, wished to make experiment to ascertain the fact. His sense of hearing was also enfeebled. On the night before, a child was born to the Emperor. The event was to be announced by the cannon of the Invalides, twenty-one guns for a female, and one hundred and one for a male child. At 10 A.M. the firing began and was loudly heard in Erskine's house, which was not far off. They all counted the guns and after the twenty-first gun, knew that a son had been born. There was much noise in the street, but the Cardinal heard nothing of all this, although the day before he was sensible of the least sound. They told him nothing about the guns or the birth.

The end was now at hand. Three priests recited slowly and in a loud voice the Prayers for those in Agony, and at the end of the first, Erskine was distinctly heard to answer Amen, and to the last, articulated the letter A ; thus shewing that he heard and understood. His life was thus reduced to mere stertorous breathing, and finally passed away at six P.M. with a strong gasp. The patience and resignation displayed by Erskine during his long agony, and this slow and gradual extinction of life, without a single murmur or complaint of suffering, was a subject of wonder and admiration to those who witnessed this exemplary death scene. He died in a manner truly worthy of a prince of the Church.

The same evening (of the 20th of March) Mr. Denys, the Notary, was sent for and in the presence of Del Medico, Dr. Corona, the servants and others, read out the Cardinal's will.

From the certified copy of this will, now preserved in the Ghislieri College in Rome, it appears that the will was written in French by the Notary, and signed by the Cardinal and the witnesses. The witnesses actually present and signing were M. Marie Maximilien Harel, Vicaire of the parish of S. Germain Déprez; Dr. Corona; François Mauie; and Signor Belloni, the Director of the School of Mosaics. After directing three hundred masses to be said for the repose of his soul, and prescribing that his funeral should be decent, and such as was suitable to his circumstances, and that a certain inscription should be put on a tablet in the church of S. Maria in Campitelli at Rome, he makes the following bequests:—

"To Princess Chigi, her choice of any English work in his library.

"He begs Madame Marianna Dionigi to accept, in memory of him, all his engravings, framed or unframed, to be found among his properties at Paris or in Rome.

"He directs all his money securities, his plate, furniture, and property of every kind to be sold for payment of his debts, expenses of his illness, etc., and the residue remaining after such payments, to be divided into two equal portions. One of these portions or moieties, he gives absolutely to his Secretary, Dom. Michel Angelo Del Medico.

"The remaining portion he bequeaths to those persons who, at the time of his death, should happen to be in his service on yearly salaries, including the Secretary as one of these, but excluding the French chamber maid, the cook and coachman, who are to get only one hundred francs each."

Del Medico then gave notice of the death to the French Minister of Worship, who exhibited no surprise at the intelligence, having perhaps already heard of it from the police. Del Medico enquired how he was to act about the funeral, and the Minister replied that he must consult the Emperor, and this was no time to mention death at the Tuilleries, and that consequently Del Medico must wait. In the meanwhile, he advised Del Medico to follow as much as possible the Roman custom about embalming, etc., until the Emperor's pleasure should be known concerning the public functions. Del Medico caused to be celebrated every morning in Erskine's chapel, as many requiem masses as he could, inviting the parochial clergy and the Italian priests attached to other Cardinals, to say these masses.

Del Medico also visited Cardinal Latier de Bayanne, who was by no means overpleased at having been nominated executor testamentary without previous notification or acceptance, but consented to accept the office, to show his respect for the Sacred College. The embalming was performed by two surgeons, Cayal and Sauvage, in presence of Dr. Laennec, all three signing the *proces verbal*.

Cardinal Vincenti, in the meanwhile, fell suddenly ill, and on the second day of his illness, while in the act of dictating his will, expired. This second death of a Cardinal complicated matters.

Del Medico went every second day to the Minister of Worship to learn what was to be done about the funeral, and the Minister's reply was that they should wait for the decision of the Council of State, to which the matter had been referred. It was certain that the Cardinal's own wishes for a modest funeral would not be followed, and the Minister said that the body should be buried in the Subterranean of S. Genevieve, which was not then called the Pantheon, as the Emperor intended to restore the Church. For precaution the corpse was placed, on the eighth day after death, in a leaden coffin with a leaden tube attached to the hands, and containing the inscription dictated by the Cardinal himself.

Finally, at the end of March, the Minister of Worship informed Del Medico that the Council of State had decided to pay to Cardinals dying within the empire the same funeral honours as were paid to Senators, and that the Mass would be celebrated on the second day of April, in the Church of S. Thomas Aquinas, the parish church of the late Cardinal Vincenti. One Requiem Mass was to serve for both Cardinals. This arrangement of one mass for two Cardinals was unseemly and without precedent, but there was no remedy. The Minister gave all the orders for preparation of the church, the cortege, etc., as if it all depended upon him. He afterwards in excuse said that this course was adopted to save expense to Erskine's heirs, but it turned out in the end that the expenses were charged double, although there was but one *Messa Cantata*.

Before 10 o'clock A.M. on the 2nd of April, the courtyard of the house wherein Cardinal Erskine died, was filled with infantry and cavalry, with a band of music, and all the mourning coaches, and the hearse for the corpse. In good time came the Parish Priest of the Abbaye au Bois (Erskine's parish) with his clergy, for he wished to try whether he could succeed in preceding the funeral convoy publicly with the cross uplifted and the priests in *cotta*, as was done for Cardinal Caprara. But the moment the attempt was made, the Commissary who presides on such occasions, interposed resolutely, and forbade it, saying they had not the permission which had been granted in the case of Caprara, who was considered always as a Cardinal Legate. The funeral was almost entirely a military one, except for the Cardinal's insignia on the hearse and the body of priests who followed on foot in *sottana* and *mantello*.

The two funerals arrived almost simultaneously at the church; and the two coffins were placed beneath a catafalque raised in the middle of the nave, with a Baldacchino. The church was decorated with the cyphers of the two Cardinals instead of their family arms. The clergy of S. Thomas Aquinas, Vincenti's parish, and of the Abbaye au Bois, Erskine's parish, and all the Seminary of S. Sulpice filled the church. Near the High Altar, on the Gospel side, the Cardinals, along with the Minister of Worship, were placed; and on the Epistle side were the French bishops then in Paris. By decision of the Cardinals, the Mass was celebrated by the Parish Priest of the Church, and Cardinal Guiseppe Doria gave two absolutions, one for each Cardinal.

After this function, the bodies of the two Cardinals were carried to the subterranean of S. Genevieve with the same order of procession, save that now the two parish priests proceeded in a mourning carriage, with cotta and stola, and none of the cortege went on foot, but all rode in mourning coaches. This second procession was more imposing than the former, because there was double the number of troops and military bands, the two corteges of the two Cardinals being united. The Cardinals who assisted at the Mass went also to S. Genevieve, but privately and by a different route, and were at S. Genevieve before the corpses arrived there. The subterranean was illuminated. The archpriest of the Basilica of Nôtre Dame, with part of his clergy and with his cross raised in sign of his jurisdiction, was in the vestibule to receive the bodies. Here, in consigning the corpses, the two Parish Priests made brief eulogiums of their respective Cardinals, and the archpriest replied with laudatory notices of the defunct Eminences. The singers of Nôtre Dame then intoned the last prayers of the tumulation service, and the archpriest closed the ceremony with benedictions. The coffins were deposited in a private sepulchral cell wherein was also the body of Cardinal Caprara. Over the coffins were placed two marble slabs, and on that of Cardinal Erskine was put the inscription dictated by himself.

Thus, after an interval of fourteen days from his death,

Erskine was buried and his testamentary wishes concerning the inscription were fulfilled in Paris.

The Minister of Worship made the executors furnish all the bills for the expenses of the funeral which he himself had ordered, and these bills were all paid out of the assets of the deceased. The personal property of Erskine in Paris was valued at 3,900 francs.

Finally the executors sent notice of the death to Erskine's Scotch relatives, who, on learning the sad intelligence, withdrew the funds which they had placed at Erskine's disposal in the bank of Lafitte.

There still remains preserved in the Angelini-Rossi Collection the paper on which the Erskine epitaph was originally written, and which contained a much longer inscription of a laudatory kind. All was marked out by the Cardinal except the part prescribed by the will, and which may be seen upon a circle of whitish marble under the cupola of the Church of S. Maria in Campitelli in Rome. It is as follows :—" CAROLO. COLINI. FILIO. S. M. IN. PORT. DIAC. CARD. ERSKINE. QUI. PATERNO. GENERE. SCOTUS. ROMAE. NATUS. DIE. XIII. FEB. AN. MDCCXLIII. OBIIT. PARISSIIS. DIE. XX. MAR. MDCCCXI. NOMINI. MEMORIAE- QUE. EJUS."

APPENDIX.

CLEMENT VII. in the year 1528 had given to Cardinal Lorenzo Campeggi, to reward his services to the Holy See, the lands and rock of Doccia or Dozza, with title of Count and with *mero e misto dominio*, for the annual tribute or *canone* of one pound of red wax, on condition, however, that if such tribute were not paid to the Apostolic See for the Feast of S. Peter, and if it should remain unpaid for two consecutive years, the Campeggi family should forfeit the right to the said feudal possession. On the 3rd of May, 1530, the Pope issued a brief for investiture of the Cardinal into Dozza, and the Cardinal, as the family records testify, took formal possession in 1531. His son, Count Rodolfo, succeeded him in 1539, and retained possession until he died in 1545. On his death the Imolesi, with 300 infantry, seized Dozza, and compelled the inhabitants to submit to the dominion of Imola. This forcible possession lasted for thirteen years, the Imolesi, by means of a protracted and costly litigation, opposing the restitution of Dozza to the Campeggi. In 1558 Paul IV. compelled the Imolesi to restore Dozza, and Count Antonio Maria Campeggi became its possessor. By *motu proprio* of Pope Pius IV, dated the 22nd of August, 1562, Giovanni Campeggi, Archbishop of Bologna, was nominated Governor for life of the castle of Dozza and its territory. In 1563 the Imolesi again tried to repossess themselves of Dozza, but the Campeggi appealed to the Pope, and offering 4,000 scudi of gold obtained Pontifical Bulls in 1565 for a new grant of the lordship of Dozza, in favour of Count Vincenzo Campeggi and his brothers, Counts Annibale and Baldassare, who were all sons of Count Antonio Maria.

In 1592, Francesco Sforza, the Papal Legate of Romagna, attempted for his amusement to enter Dozza, but without the consent of the Feudal Lord, and the gates were shut in his face by Francesco Bonini, the governor of the castle. In consequence of this incident, Pope Clement VIII. transferred Dozza to Ercole II. Malvezzi; but after earnest entreaties was induced to re-concede the Lordship to Count Rodolfo, son of Count Vincenzo Campeggi. Count Rodolfo died without male issue, and his brother, Count Alessandro, died in 1593, having had a son, Count Girolamo, who died without issue, and by his death the descendants of Vincenzo became extinct in the male line. The heirs of Dozza were now the sons of Counts Annibale and Baldassare. Count Baldassare had two sons, Count Giovanni (who died in 1600, leaving one son, Lorenzo, an ecclesiastic) and Count Rodolfo, who died without male issue in 1624.

Count Annibale, who died in 1588, had children by his wife Orsina Volta, and among them was Count Antonio, successor to his cousins, Rodolfo and Giovanni, in the Lordship of Dozza, and who was created by Urban VIII., by Bulls, dated 20th of March, 1629, Marchese di Dozza. This first Marchese died in 1637, and left, *inter alios*, a son, the Marchese Tomaso, who married twice and had numerous children, but his sons all died without male issue. On the death, in 1728, of his son, Marchese Lorenzo, the last male of the family, the succession to Dozza devolved upon Lorenzo's sister, Maria Francesca Campeggi, who married the Marchese Matteo Malvezzi.

Before this date the Bolognese families of Malvezzi and Campeggi had been connected by marriage. Count Vincenzo Campeggi (nephew of Cardinal Lorenzo, and son of Antonio Maria) married Brigida Malvezzi; and Vincenzo's sister, Paola, married Giovanni Filippo Malvezzi, and built the palazzo Malvezzi de' Medici in Bologna.

Emilio Malvezzi, son of Matteo Malvezzi and Maria Francesca Campeggi, was declared entitled to the inheritance of the Lordship of Dozza by decree of Pope Benedict XIII., dated December 5th, 1729, and accordingly was styled the Marchese Emilio Malvezzi Campeggi. He married Teresa Sacchetti of Rome, and dying, July 3rd, 1767, left as co-heirs to Dozza his sons, Floriano, who had no issue, and Giacomo.

The Revolution of 1797 wrought a total change in the conditions of Italy, political and governmental, and the feudal rights of the Lords of Dozza were not spared. In the month of February in that year, the Marchesi Malvezzi Campeggi were compelled to present an inventory of all the cannons, swords, firearms and other weapons which were in the Castle of Dozza, and to consign them to the Commandant of the piazza of Imola. In the following April, however, by a decree of the Senate of Bologna, still extant, the Rock of Dozza was restored to the Marchese Giacomo Malvezzi Campeggi as his private property, proved to be such by legal evidence and documents. And thus after 267 years of possession by the Campeggi family, the feudal Lordship, with all its special rights and privileges, became extinguished.

The Marchese Giacomo, last Feudal Lord of Dozza, died in 1806, leaving a son, Antonio, who was Knight Grand Cross of the Order of S. George of Bavaria, and married Donna Giuseppina, daughter of Prince Corsini, by whom he had, besides other issue, two sons, the Marchesi Emilio and Carlo Malvezzi Campeggi, who, after the death of their father in 1827, made a division of their inheritance, when the Rock of Dozza became the property of Emilio.

The Marchese Emilio Malvezzi Campeggi married the Contessa Bianca Petrucci, and died in 1872, leaving, among other issue, an elder son, the Marchese Girolamo, who married, firstly, the Contessa Anna Angela Grisaldi del Taja, and secondly, the Marchesa Giovanna Durazzo, and has a son, Giacomo.

The Marchese Carlo Malvezzi Campeggi had also two wives, Rosa Bonaccorsi, by whom he had daughters, and the Contessa

Vittoria Ranuzzi, by whom he had daughters and a son, the Marchese Alfonso, who married the Marchesa Anna Misciattelli, and has issue three daughters and three sons, Antonio, Carlo and Luigi.

The Campeggi arms are, a black dog rampant, in a field of gold, and on the right the half of a black imperial eagle, displayed and crowned. To the coronet of a Marchese are added two silver anchors crossed.

INDEX.

Abergavenny, Earl of,	33
Adrian, *see* Hadrian.	
Alarcon, ...	57
Albano, Lake of, ...	210
Albany, Duke of, ...	63
Albert, ...	32
Albert, Chevalier, ...	253
Alberto, Count de Carpi, ...	52
Aldini, Count, ...	255, 257
Aleriensis, Cardinal Della Porta,	13, 15
Alexander VI., 10-15, 25. His sickness and death, ...	13, 14
Alquier, ...	256
Ameland. Lady Augusta de, ...	126
Amiens, Treaty of,	155, 159, 182, 192
Ammonius, Andreas,	17-18, 20, 22
Angelini, Archbishop,	121, 215, 252
Angiolini, Cavalier, ...	139, 162, 163
Antiquarian Society of London,	137
Antiquarian Society of Scotland,	200, 201
Antonelli, Cardinal, ...	218
Arcangeli, Francesco, ...	216
Armanni, Vincenzo, 95, 96, 105, 110,	117
Artois, Count d', ...	151
Assemani, Stephen, ...	203
Astalli, Marchese Tiberio, ...	82
Atanasio, Mgr., ...	234
Aubigny (or Juvigny), 109, Footnote.	
Aubigny, Duke of, ...	94
Audley, Bishop, ...	44, 47
Augerau, General, ...	186
Augsburg, Diet of, ...	75
Austria, Archduke of, ...	46
Austria, Archduchess of, ...	254
Azara, Cavalier Nicola De,	161-163, 165
Baglioni, Count Alexander,	255, 261
Bainbridge, Christopher, ...	29, 45
Balbo, Girolamo, Cardinal of Gurk,	28
Baliol, John, ...	202
Baptista, ...	62
Barras, Member of Directory,	169
Barthélemy, Director, ...	178
Barruel, ...	255
Bassville, Hugo De (Nicola Hugou)	83, 84
Bath, Bishop of, *see* Clerk.	
Battista, Giovanni, ...	22
Bayanne, Cardinal De, *see* Latier de Bayanne.	
Bayonne, Bishop of, ...	72
Beauharnois, Mademoiselle, ...	167
Belknapp, Sir Edward, ...	41
Bellay, Du, ...	70
Belloni, Francesco, ...	255, 257, 264
Belloy, Jean Baptiste de, Archbishop of Paris, ...	185, 194
Benet, Dr. Thomas, ...	49, 76, 77
Benimbene, ...	15
Bentinck, Lord William, ...	171
Bentivoglio, Annibale, ...	30
Bentivoglio, Count Antonio,	226, 227
Berington, Bishop Charles, ...	143
Bernadotte, General, ...	186
Bernier, Bishop of Orleans,	164, 165, 175, 185, 188
Berthier, General, ...	164, 166
Bethune, Mademoiselle de, ...	182
Bigot de Priameneu, Count, ...	224
Blois, Bishop of, ...	152
Boero, Father, S. J., ...	94, 117
Boisgelin, Cardinal De,	163, 194, 195
Boisgelin, M. de, ...	163
Boleyn, Anne, ...	59
Boleyn, ...	42
Bombarderio, Francis, ...	50
Bonaparte, Joseph,	159, 164, 183, 191, 207
Bonaparte, Louis, ...	176, 181
Bonaparte, Lucien, ...	183, 191
Bonaparte, Madame,	169, 171, 176, 181, 182, 185, 248
Bonaparte, Napoleon, His personal appearance, habits, character, etc., 168-170. His Military Reviews, 175, 180. Marriages in his family, 176. Made President of Cisalpine Republic, 176, 177. His bad temper,	

163, 188. Birth of his son, 263. Mentioned, 163, 174, 178-182, 184, 185, 187, 216, 217, 225
Boner or Bonner, ... 76
Borghese, Prince Camillo, ... 241
Borghese, Giovanni Battista, ... 81
Borghese, Giulio, ... 85
Borghese, Marcantonio, ... 81
Borghese, Orazio, ... 190
Borghese, Scipione, ... 81
Borgia, *see* Alexander VI.
Borgia, Cardinal, ... 144, 161
Borgia, Cesar, ... 13
Boschi, Marchese, ... 240
Bouligni, Signor, ... 162
Bourbon, Cardinal of, ... 42, 63
Bourbon, Duke of, ... 53
Bouterlin, Count, ... 196, 197
Bovio, ... 13
Bramante, ... 9,
Brancadoro, Guiseppe, ... 208
Braschi, Cardinal, ... 83, 218, 239
Braschi, Duke, ... 239-241
Brian, Sir Francis, ... 63-65, 69
Bristol, Earl of, Bishop of Derry, 163, 197
Bristol, Fifth Earl of, 198, 199
Bruce, Sir Henry Hervey, ... 204
Brueys, Admiral, ... 177
Brunot, Madame, ... 164
Buchan, Earl of, ... 200, 204, 211
Buckingham, Duke of, ... 38
Burdett, Sir Francis, ... 195
Burgoin, General, ... 169
Burk, Mr. De, ... 178
Bute, Marchioness of, ... 213
Bute, Marquess of, ... 214, 215
Buzi, Bali, ... 208

Cacault, ... 153
Caetani, *see* Sermoneta.
Cambacérès, Jean Jacques, Duke of Parma, ... 177
Cambacérès, Cardinal Stephen, 185, 194
Cameron, Alexander, ... 209
Campbell, Monsignore, ... 123
Campeggi, Cardinal Lorenzo. His birth, parentage, marriage and issue, 28-30. Made a bishop and Nuncio to Vienna, 30-31. Second embassy to the Emperor at Vienna, 31. Created a Cardinal, 32. Legate to Henry VIII., who gives him the English Palace in Rome, 32-40. Visits the King of France and refuses a pension, 42. Returns to Rome, 43. Sent to the Diet of Nuremberg as Legate to the Emperor, 46. Is made Bishop of Salisbury, 47. Returns to Rome, 50. His palace rifled by the troops of the Bourbon, 55. Governor of Rome after the sack, 60. Second Legation to Henry VII., 62. Adjourns the Divorce Case, 70. Leaves England and protests against the breaking open his trunks at Dover, 73. Attends the Diet of Augsburg, 75. Deprived of Salisbury, 77. Makes his will and dies, 79. His issue and relations, 80. His brother's descendants, *see* Appendix.
Campeggi, Marchese Antonio, 81
Campeggi, Marchese Tommaso, 81
Campeggi, Marco Antonio, ... 78
Campeggi, Maria Francesca, ... 270
Campeggi, *see* Malvezzi-Campeggi.
Canus, Armand Gaston, ... 187
Canning, Mr., ... 139
Canterbury, Archbishop of, Henry Dean, 12. William Warham, 33, 34, 64, 65, 68.
Capalti, Marchese, ... 217
Caprara, Cardinal, 153, 159-163, 168, 171, 180, 183, 185, 187, 267
Carafa di Traietto, Cardinal Francesco, 236
Cardelli, Count Alexander, ... 230
Carmine, Church of the, ... 175
Carnot, Director, ... 169
Casale, Sir Gregory, 44, 50, 51, 56, 59, 60, 61, 75
Caselli, Padre, ... 161, 165
Casoni, Cardinal, ... 139
Cassini, Count, ... 197
Castiglione, Cardinal, ... 194
Castiglion, ... 211
Cavalcanti, John, ... 44
Cayal, Surgeon, ... 205
Cayer, Lady, ... 177
Celestini, Orazio, ... 197, 226, 230
Cellini, Benvenuto, ... 53, 59
Cento Preti, Hospital of the, ... 82
Chapuys, Ambassador of Charles V., 72
Charles I., ... 96
Charles II., 95, 96. Letters of, 97, 99-103. Mistresses of, 93-94.
Charles V., ... 46, 59, 72
Charles VI., ... 111
Chateaubriand, ... 243
Chiaramonti, Cardinal. Elected Pope as Pius VIII., ... 146
Chiaramonti, Don Gregorio, ... 189

Index. 275

Chiaveri, Luigi, Giuseppe, Carolina and Agostino, ... 230, 250, 251
Chichester, Bishop of, ... 33
Chigi, Prince Sigismond, ... 124
Chigi, Prince and Princess, 261, 264
Chisholm, Æneas, ... 209
Chisholm, John, ... 209
Cibo, Cardinal, ... 51
Ciccolini, Cav. Giuseppe, 256, 257
Cingoli, ... 210
Circelli, Marchese de, ... 139
Clement VII., ... 46, 47, 60, 75
Clement XI., ... 111
Clerk, John, Bishop of Bath, 45, 47, 48, 50, 62-66
Cloche, De la, 95, 97-100, 105, 116
Clossé, Mr. William, ... 195
Cobentzel, Count de, Austrian Ambassador, ... 160
Cobham, Lord, ... 33
Colerain, Lord, ... 171
Colonna, ... 51, 52
Colonna, The Conestabile, ... 208
Colonna, Antonio, ... 81
Colonna, Filippo, ... 82
Colonna, Giovanni, Prince, ... 102
Colonna, Girolamo, Cardinal, ... 81
Colonna, Lorenzo Onofrio, ... 81
Concordat, The, 149, 150, 152, 153, 156, 163, 165, 183, 186, 187
Conestabile, Signor, ... 173
Consalvi, Cardinal, 146, 149, 163, 165, 171, 189, 190, 192, 249
Cooper, Lady, ... 190
Cornwallis, Lord, ... 159, 165, 183
Corona, Dr. Camillo, 259, 262, 264
Corona, Francesco and Teresa, etc., 105, 106, 108
Corsini, Prince, ... 271
Corsini, Princess and her son, Neri, 190
Coutts, Thomas, 160, 161, 195, 204, 223, 231, 233, 250-253
Cretet, Emmanuel, ... 164
Crivelli, ... 252
Cruzolle, Duchess de la, ... 160
Croce, Santa, Princess, 162, 164
Cunic, Raimondo, ... 215

D'Arcy, Lord, ... 34
Dauphin, The, ... 38
Dean, Henry, see Canterbury.
De Gregorio, Mgr., ... 234, 258, 260
Della Porta, see Aleriensis.
Della Porta, Cardinal, 228, 230, 236
Del Medico, Michel Angelo, 121, 226, 227, 229, 230, 262, 263

De Medici, Julius, see Clement VIII. and Worcester.
Denham, Joseph, ... 127, 128
Denina, Abbé, ... 255
Denis, or Denys, Notary, 262, 264
Denon, Baron, ... 178
Despuig, Cardinal, 218, 221, 222, 254
Dionigi, Marianna and Enrichetta, 214, 215, 226, 239, 264
Di Pietro, Cardinal, ... 260
Doccia or Dozza, 40 *footnote*, 75, 269-272
Doria, Andrea, ... 62
Doria, Giorgio, afterwards Cardinal, 219
Doria, Cardinal Giuseppe, 130, 217, 248, 249, 267
Douglas, Bishop, ... 143
Ducci, Abbé, ... 185
Dugnani, Cardinal, ...254-256
Dunmore, Earl of, ... 126
Dunmowe, John, Bishop of Limerick, 10
Duphot, General, ... 142
Durham, Bishops of, Christopher Bainbridge, 29, 45, Thomas Ruthall, 34
Duroc, General, ... 175, 184

Edward I., ... 202
Edward IV., ... 10
Elia, S., ... 206
Ely, Bishop of, ... 34, 37
English College, ... 122
Erasmus, ... 42
Erskine, Sir Alexander of Cambo and Lady Anne, ... 122
Erskine, Cardinal Charles. Materials for his life, 121. His birth, parentage and ancestry; and education, 122, 123. His first preferments, 124. Sent as Envoy to George III., 129. Visits Lord Kellie, 130. His residence in London, 131. His services to the Propaganda, 144. Loss of his Roman revenues; and aid from George III., 145. Celebrates Funeral of Pius VI., 145, 146. Created Cardinal *in petto*, 149. Deals with the French bishops in England, 150. Leaves London for Paris, 156-159. His visits to Bonaparte, 168, 180, 185, 189. Leaves Paris for Rome, 189, 191. His views on a Roman Land Question, 192-3. Published as Cardinal, 194. Protects the Earl of Bristol's property, 197-199. Defends the property of the Scots College, 205-209. Loses his Roman revenues, 217. Is made Pro-Secre-

tary of Briefs, 218. His account of the seizure of the Pope in the Quirinal palace, 220-222. Retires to Castel Rubello, 223. Is summoned to Paris, 224. Returns to Rome and falls into sickness, 225. Is forced to leave Rome, 226-234. His journey from Rome to Paris, 235-248. His presentation to the Emperor, 254. His lingering sickness, death and burial, 249-268.
Erskine, Clementina, ... 225
Erskine, Colin, ... 122, 123
Erskine, David, Henry, and Thomas, 203

Fabbrica di S. Pietro, ... 83
Falconieri, Cav., ... 240, 241
Farnese, Cardinal, ... 56, 76
Fegan, Mr., ... 163
Fergusson, Lt.-Col., ... 200, 204
Ferrari, Pio, 123, 225, 230, 234
Fesch, Cardinal Joseph, 160, 194, 216, 249
Fleury, Bartholomew, 11
Floriano, *see* Montinus.
Follet, Mr., ... 250
Fontana, Father, ... 260
Fonseca, Marchese, ... 164
Fox, Mr., the Statesman, ... 232
Fox, Richard, Bishop of Winchester, 23
France, King of, ... 26, 42, 62, 101
France, Queen Dowager of, ... 37
French bishops in England, ... 150
Furlo Pass, ... 238

Gabrielli, Cardinal, ... 218, 248, 260
Galimberti, Monsignor, ... 122
Galli, Cardinal Tolomeo, ... 80
Gardiner, Stephen, ... 60, 61, 66
Garret, Mr., ... 158
Gavotti, Monsignor, ... 191
Geddes, John, ... 204
Genga, Della, Monsignor, ... 139
George III., ... 132, 133, 149
Gerdil, Cardinal, ... 147, 161
Ghinucci, Jerome, *see* Worcester.
Ghislieri College, ... 121, 122
Giacomo, ... 48, 49, 66
Gilberti, Marchese, ... 237
Gigli, Agatha, ... 123
Gigliis, De, *see* Worcester.
Giles, Monsignor, ... 122
Girandin, President of the Tribunate, 183
Giraud, Cardinal Bernardino, 82, 83
Giraud, Giovanni, and his family, 82, 83

Giraud, Counts Pietro, Giovanni, Giuseppe and Francesco, ... 83, 211
Giustiniani, ... 14
Giustiniani, Sebastiano, 23-26, 36-38
Gloucester, Duke of, ... 125
Gobelin Tapestry, ... 166, 167
Gonzaga, Luigi, ... 59
Gordon, Principal, ... 165
Grammont, Madame de, ... 163
Grand, Madame, ... 162, 170
Gregorio, *see* De Gregorio.
Grenville, Lord, ... 146, 214
Grimain, Cardinal, ... 22
Guiana (French), ... 178
Guillaumot, M., ... 166
Gurk, Bishop of, Matthew Lange, 31
Gurk, Cardinal of, ... 28

Hadrian VI., ... 29, 45
Hadrian de Castello or Corneto. His birth and preferments, 11-13. His Biblical and classical learning, 13. His Supper to Pope Alexander, 13-14. Gives his palace to Henry VII, 14-15. His first flight from Rome, 16. Unjustly accused of conspiring against Leo X., 21. His second flight from Rome, 22. Mention of him, 11-29, 32, 33, 39.
Haeffeler, Monsignor, ... 253
Haller, Commissary. ... 178
Halsey, Thomas, Bishop of Leighlin, 34
Hamilton, Gavin, ... 203
Hammond, Captain, ... 156
Hannibal, Mr. Thomas, ... 45
Harel, Abbate, ... 262, 264
Hattecliff, William, ... 34
Hawkins, Nicholas, ... 76
Hay, Bishop George, 148, 209
Henry VII., ... 10-15
Henry VIII., 9, 10, 17-29, 46, 53, 59, 66-78
Hereford, Bishop of, ... 4
Heywood, J. C. His library and MSS., 88-91
Hughes, Victor, ... 179
Hugou, Nicola, alias De Bassville, 83-84
Hungary, King of, ... 31, 48, 51, 52
Hussey, Monsignor, ... 143

Innes, Abbé, ... 165
Innocent VIII., ... 10, 12

Jackson, Mr., English Minister, 161, 163, 165, 171, 175
James III. of Scotland, ... 12

Index.

Jardine, Mademoiselle, ... 196
Jarry, M., ... 185
Jenkins, Mr., English Agent in Rome, 126
Jocourt, M. Deputy, ... 183
Jourdan, General, ... 189
Julius II., ... 12, 14, 16, 29-31
Juvigny, *see* Aubigny.

Katherine, Queen, ... 59, 67, 68-70
Kellie, Earl of, ... 223, 232, 233
Krathoffer, Mr., ... 160

Laborde, Madame, ... 175
Lacchini, Monsignor, 149, 190, 198, 211
Lachene, Signor, ... 174
Laennic, Dr., ... 258, 259, 265
Lafitte, ... 268
Lama, The Grand, ... 174
Lange, Matthew, *see* Bishop of Gurk.
Lante, ... 210
Lastreto, ... 217
Latier de Bayanne, Cardinal, 262, 265
Latimer, Hugh, ... 77
Laurenzi, Cardinal, ... 88
Lauriston, ... 168
Lautrec, ... 58, 60
Lavalle, Duke de, ... 182
Law, Minister of Finance, ... 168
Le Brun, Duke of Placentia, 177, 179
Lecotte, M., ... 185
Lemarrois, General, ... 217
Lennox, Duke of, ... 96, 109
Leo X., 17-20, 27, 29, 31, 32, 40, 45
Leo XIII., ... 127
Le Surre, M., ... 185
Lepri, Marchese, ... 238
Lessine, ... 162
Lincoln, Bishop of, ... 34, 35
Locatelli, Cardinal, ... 194
London, Bishop of, ... 35, 37, 68
Lorenzo, ... 224
Loricato, ... 217
Louis XII., ... 12, 31
Louis XVIII., ... 152
Lucchesini, Marchese, ... 160, 165
Luther, ... 46-48, 53, 75
Lyons, ... 189
Lyons, Congress of, ... 161, 176, 179

Macrae, Mr., ... 158
MacDonald, General, ... 186
MacPherson, Sir John, ... 174
MacPherson, Paul, ... 206, 257
Malvezzi, Marchese Matteo, ... 270
Malvezzi-Campeggi, Marchesi Emilio and Carlo, Alfonzo and Girolamo and Giacomo, 40, *footnote*.
Mangaud, M., ... 157, 159
Marbois, Marbè, ... 178, 181
March, Earl of, ... 96
Marcorelle, President, ... 183
Marcost, Count, ... 162, 182
Marescalchi, Count, ... 177
Maret, M., ... 180
Marini, Mgr. Gaetani, ... 202
Marino, ... 208
Mariscotti, Count, ... 85
Marmont, General, ... 178
Martiniana, Cardinal, ... 153
Mary, Princess, ... 38
Massacre of Bishops and Priests, 175
Massena, General, ... 169, 170
Masseria, Signor, ... 157, 160
Massimi, ... 255
Massimo, Camillo, ... 84
Maury, Cardinal, ... 260
Maximilian, Emperor, ... 16, 31
Maynooth College, ... 205
Mazio, Canonist, ... 185
Melzi, Count, ... 177
Mennato, S., ... 206
Menou, General, ... 171
Merry, Mr., ... 159
Michou, M., ... 158
Milan, Duke of, ... 31
Milling, Thomas, Bishop of Hereford, 10
Minio, Marco, ... 21
Minto, Lord, ... 146
Miollis, General, 83, 217, 226, 227, 228, 229, 230, 234, 235, 240, 243
Misciatelli, Marchesa Anna, ... 272
Moire, Mr., ... 173
Moncada, Don Hugo de, ... 51
Mont Cenis, ... 189
Monte, Cardinal de, ... 76
Monte Luce, ... 211
Montesson, Madame de, 169, 182
Montinus, Florianus, ... 33, 66
Montmorency, Eugene, ... 182
Moor, Baptism of a, ... 44
Morcelli, Stefano Antonio, ... 216
Moreau, General, ... 170
Moroni's Dictionary, quoted, ... 189
Morozzo, Guiseppe, afterwards Cardinal, 261, 262
Morte, Confraternità della, ... 81
Mosaics, Factory of, ... 83
Moscardini, Monsignor, ... 237
Mountcashel, Earl and Countess of, 174, 177
Murat, General, 176, 181, 243

Murphy, Mr.,	164
Mutle or Mout [misprinted "Hutte,"] Stephen,	84
Narbonne, Archbishop of,	155
Narbonne, Count of, ...	162
Naro, Monsignor,	219
Nassau, Prince of,	162
Necker, Madame,	178
Nelson, Lord,	159
Noaille, Madame de,	175
Norfolk, Duke of,	32, 34, 38, 75, 78
Nuremberg, Diet of, ...	46
O'Callaghan, Archbishop Henry,	122
O'Connor, Abbé,	164
Odescalchi, Monsignor,	144
O'Leary, Rev. Dr.,	146, 158
Oliva, Gian Paolo, S.J.,	95, 99-105
Oppizoni, Cardinal,	260
Orange, Prince of,	55
Orfei, The Contessa,	216
Orleans, Duke of, Egalité,	169
Orleans, Duchess of,	101
Osmond, Madame,	159
Otto, Count de Mosroy,	157
Pacca, Cardinal,	218, 219, 220
Pacca, Nephews of,	219
Pace,	37, 39
Palace, The English, OWNERS, see Cardinal Hadrian, Henry VII., Henry VIII.. Cardinal Campeggi and his family, Cardinal Borghese, Marchese Antonio Campeggi, Cardinal Girolamo Colonna and his heirs, Pope Innocent XII., Clement XI., Fabrica di S. Pietro. Prince Torlonia, Prince Borghese Torlonia.	
Palace, The English, OCCUPIERS, see Cardinal Galli, John Baptist Borghese, the Arciconfraternità della Morte, Don Antonio Colonna, the Queen of Sweden, Cardinal Radziejowski, the Cento Preti, the Mosaic manufactory, the Duke di Saldanha, Pius IX. for use of bishops attending the Vatican Council, Mr. J. C. Heywood, Cardinal Parocchi, Cardinal Laurenzi.	
Palmoni, Livio,	248
Palombi, Cav.,	240
Pancemont. Bishop of Vannes,	185
Pardo, General,	165
Paris, Archbishop of,	37, 38
Parish, Mr.,	164
Paul I., Emperor of Russia,	142, 143, 159, 162
Pelham, Lord,	156
Perregueaux, Mr.,	160, 162, 250, 251
Petrucci, Cardinal,	21, 22
Phiffer or Phipher, Captain,	220
Pianciani, Count,	237
Pietro, Di, Cardinal,	260
Pisa, Cardinal of,	59
Pitt, Mr.,	155, 232
Pius III.,	11, 12, 14
Pius VI., 123, 124, 125, 126, 129, 134, 135, 137, 138, 139. Letters of, 140-143. Death of, 145, 155, 161	
Pius VII., 146. Brief of, 147, 149, 150, 153	
Pius IX.,	88
Poniatowski, Prince Stanislaus,	210
Porta, Della, Cardinal, see Della Porta.	
Portal, Dr.,	171, 253, 255, 259
Portalis, M., 160, 164, 166, 168, 169, 177, 183, 184, 187	
Portland, Duke of,	149, 171
Portlock, Captain,	158
Proceno,	211
Propaganda Accounts and Missions,	147, 148
Propaganda, Suppression of,	144
Radet, General,	224, 225, 230, 235
Radziejowski, Cardinal,	82
Rangoni, Count Guido,	59
Reaumont, Baron de,	94, 95
Renzo da Ceri, or Rans,	53, 54
Reveillere-Lepaux,	169
Ricci, Marchese, 98, footnote.	
Rich, Bishop,	187
Ridolfis, Card. de,	51
Rochefoucauld, Cardinal de la,	239
Rochester, Bishop of,	33
Rodolfo, Cardinal,	57
Rohan, Henry de,	95, 103, 104
Rohan, De, Cardinal,	239
Rossi. Cavaliere Giancarlo, Collector of Autographs,	122, 252
Rotondo, Pio,	139
Rubbi, Abbé,	185
Ruffo, Cardinal Fabrizio,	230
Ruffo-Scilla, Cardinal,	258
Ruspoli, Bali,	149
Sabatier. Abbé,	165
Sack of Rome,	52-58
Sala, Cardinal Giuseppe Antonio,	123, 185, 188

Index.

Salisbury, Bishopric of, 87. Bishop of, 44, 47
Saldanha, Duke di, ... 88
Saluzzo, Deodata, ... 241
Salvatori, Domenico, 123, 223, 224
Salviati, Giacomo, 55, 63, 67, 69, 71
Salviati, Giovanni, Cardinal, ... 62
Salviati, Duke, ... 122
Sanga, ... 68
Sanuto, Marin, ... 22
Sarum, Register, ... 77
Sauli, Cardinal de, ... 21
Sauvage, Surgeon, ... 265
Savary, Duke di Rovigo, ... 163
Scarpelli, Monsignor Antonio, 209, 240
Schimelpenning, Mr., ... 159
Scipio, Master, ... 14
Scots College, ... 206-209
Scultheis, Anna Maria, ... 84
S. Croce, Princess, ... 162, 164
S. Crucis, Cardinal, ... 22
S. George, Cardinal, ... 21
Sermoneta, Don Francesco Caetani, Duke of, ... 211
Serristori, Marchese, ... 162
Seyes, Director, ... 169
Sherborne, Robert, ... 11
Shirwood, John, Bishop of Durham, 10, 11
Siena, Cardinal of (Petrucci), ... 21, 22
Simeon, M. Deputy, ... 183
Sloane, Alexander, Francis and William, 172, 173, 174
Smith, Mr., ... 177
Soderini, Francesco, ... 13, 15, 40
Soderini, Count Tiberio, ... 211
Somaglia, Cardinal, ... 217
Souvarow, General. ... 143
Spada, Prince, ... 238, 239, 240
Spalding, Hugh, ... 10
Spina, Monsignor, ... 159, 161, 165
Spinelli, Cardinal, ... 207
Stael, Madame de, ... 177
Stapleton, Mr., ... 165
Starhemberg, Count, ... 160
Stephens, Dr., ... 62
Strocchi, Cavalier Dionigi, ... 239
Strozzi, Duke, ... 197
Stuart, Prince James, 95, 97, 98, 106-108
Stuart, Prince James the younger, 111-114, 119
Stuart, David, ... 213
Stuart Papers, ... 165, 166
Stuart, Maria, ... 96, 108
Suffolk, Duke of, ... 38, 65, 78

Surrey, Earl of, ... 34, 36, 38
Sussex, Duke of, ... 126
Suwarow, General, ... 171
Sweden, Queen of, 81, 82, 98, 100, 101
Talleyrand, M., 162, 164, 175, 179
Tayler, Dr., ... 52, 63
Terni, Bishop of, ... 236
Torlonia, Alexander and Giovanni, 9, 223, 230, 231
Torlonia Family, ... 83-85, 87
Torlonia Balls, ... 85-87
Tor Mellina, ... 32
Trani, Cardinal of, ... 76
Trappists, ... 138
Tremouille, Duchless de la, ... 159
Trent, Council of, ... 80
Triulzi, Cardinal, ... 58, 59
Tunstall, Cuthbert, afterwards Bishop of London, ... 38
Valdorini, Abbé, ... 185
Valle, Mgr. Agostino, 149, 261, 262
Vannes, Peter, ... 69
Vatican Council. Bishops lodged in English Palace, ... 88
Ventimiglia, General, ... 174
Vergani, Monsignor, ... 269
Vergil, Polydore, ... 17, 18, 78
Vernègues, M., ... 197
Vincenti, Cardinal, 228, 229, 230, 240, 265, 266
Visconti, Archbishop of Milan, ... 175
Visconti, G. B. A., ... 210
Visconti, Madame, ... 182
Volterra, Cardinal of, ... 21

Warham, Dr., see Canterbury.
Welch, Canon, ... 165, 175, 185
Westfalen, Count de, ... 162
Weston, John, ... 10
Williams, Helen Maria, ... 179
Winchester, Bishop of, (Wolsey), 17
Winchester, Dr. Fox, Bishop of, 23
Winkleman, ... 210
Windesore, Sir Andrew, ... 66
Wolsey, Cardinal, 9, 17-28, 32, 35-52, 56, 59-61, 63-74, 77
Worcester, Bishops of. Jerome Ghinucci, 50-52. John de Gigliis, 10, 11, 29. Sylvester de Gigliis, 16, 17, 19-23, 26-29, 40, 43-45, 52, 77.
Worcester, Cardinal Julius de Medici, afterwards Clement VII., ... 45
Woronzow, Colonel, ... 171

Woronzow, Prince, ... 195, 196	Zagarolo, Duke of, ...	255
	Zalt, Mayor of Paris, ...	170
York, Cardinal, Duke of (Stuart), 123,	Zauli, Monsignor, ...	239
194, 204	Zelada, Cardinal De, 127, 136, 161,	225
York, *see* Wolsey.	Zondadari, Cardinal, ...	255

www.ingramcontent.com/pod-product-compliance
Lightning Source LLC
Chambersburg PA
CBHW032113230426
43672CB00009B/1727